THE DIARY OF A BUDGET BACKPACKER

Little Backpack Big Dreams

CALLY TRANDELL

Our Journey across Europe

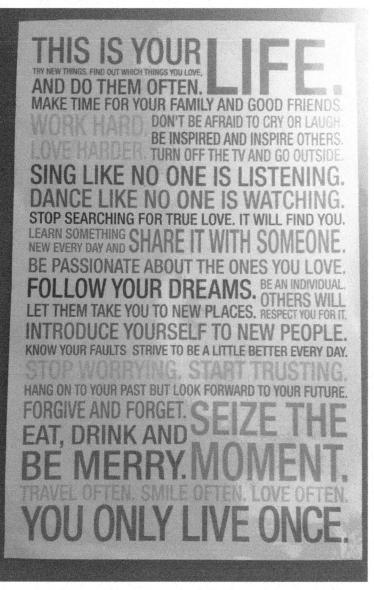

This was a poster on the wall of our first hostel in Dublin and it was the perfect message to start our journey.

Dedication

This book is dedicated to all those who have always wanted to take off and explore the world but don't think it's possible because of fear, life obstacles, kids, money, whatever it may be. Know that it is always possible and never stop dreaming and working to make those travel dreams come true.

Table of Contents

Acknowledgements

When I first entertained the idea of turning my simple diary entries from traveling Europe into a tangible book, it was just a dream—an exciting thought of accomplishing a life-long goal: publishing my own book. Gradually, I began copying my handwritten journal onto a computer, which took much longer than I thought. But over the years my simple hand-written diary has blossomed into my first published book.

First and foremost, I want to express my heartfelt gratitude to my husband, Ron. Right from the beginning, Ron cheered me on and shared in the excitement of my journey towards becoming a published author. Throughout the years, as I painstakingly read my journal over and over again, tirelessly editing its contents, Ron stood by me. He was there every time I broke down in tears, doubting whether my work would ever be worthy of public release. Ron supported me each time I wanted to read to him what I thought was a groundbreaking sentence that filled me with immense pride. He was also there for me during moments of self-doubt, comforting me when I questioned my abilities as a writer. His unwavering support carried me through the stressful eight-year writing process, turning my dream into a reality.

Secondly, I would like to extend my gratitude to Brittany, my trusted partner in crime during our travels. Brittany was always the voice of reason, mediating any disagreements between Ron and me, or helping me journal at the end of a long day, filling in the gaps of lost memories while traveling.

Thirdly, I am immensely thankful to both my parents. My mom, for diligently reading each new version of my book and providing invaluable feedback. Just days before we submitted the book for publishing, I was on the phone late at night with her giving me a few more editing mistakes that I needed to correct. And my dad, from the moment I first mentioned my desire to publish a book, he sprang into action, utilizing his connections in the printing industry and urging me to "Just get it out there and publish already!" Without my dad's help in the process of publishing, it may have taken me another 8 years to get my book on the shelves. I wholeheartedly thank both of them for always supporting my dreams, even when they may not have fully agreed with them. Whether it was quitting various jobs to travel the world or publishing a book, some of my life choices undoubtedly raised their blood pressure more than others, yet they continued to stand beside me in their support for whatever path I chose.

Fourth, I want to express my gratitude to my faithful furry companion, Meeka, my fluff ball of an emotional support animal. There were countless times when I simply needed a nonjudgmental listening partner or soothing cuddle to calm my stressful demeanor while writing.

Lastly, I want to thank everyone that made our backpacking journey across Europe so unforgettable. The gate attendant in New York that let us through to our flight at the very last minute even though Brittany technically didn't have a ticket. The stranger that shared an old subway sandwich with us when we were starving. The locals that offered a kind smile and directions when we were lost. Our friends Cat and Andy that hosted us in their home outside of London and treated us to a proper meal of British fish and chips. Sheri in Greece for quite possibly saving my life and pulling me out of the ocean before I crashed into the rocks. Wilhelm and Daniel for meeting us in Berlin and showing us the time of our lives out on the town. Tommy and Adrian for sharing your Polish beers with us on the train ride to Germany which began our friendship. And then taking a train to come visit us in Dublin one last time before we flew back home.

We experienced so many acts of kindness and met so many wonderful people in our travels, that it reminded us of how good people can be. Thank you all for being part of this incredible journey. Your support, encouragement, understanding, and kindness have made this dream come alive.

Little Backpack Big Dreams

CALLY TRANDELL

Prologue

Ever since I was young, I have dreamed of traveling the world. Meeting strangers and connecting over stories while staying up until 2 am laughing and talking. Tasting exotic and new cuisines that would shock my taste buds. Exploring new cultures, beliefs, and ways of life. Discovering myself while changing and growing as a person as I learn about the world around me.

In the last few years, the world has changed in unspeakable ways. I know I'm not the only one who has halted their travel plans and lifestyle because of the pandemic. I have only stepped foot on a plane twice in the last three years, and my heart is aching to board a plane again. To traverse the lawlessness of an airport where you can drink at 7 am and nap wherever you feel like it. I now know what freedom tastes like. I know that my soul was made to travel and learn from the world and explore the globe's diversity. I had traveled a handful of places outside of the US growing up, but it was that first crazy backpacking trip to Europe in my 20's that truly set my soul on fire with wanderlust.

In the Summer of 2014, my boyfriend Ron, one of our friends, Brittany, and I, all decided to quit our jobs, give up our apartment and take off to Europe for three months. Ron and I started planning to travel to Europe just two weeks after meeting each other for the first time. Call it fate or the stars aligning perfectly, but I never imagined meeting someone that not only had the same values as me but who was also just as crazy. But a good crazy. Crazy as in having an insatiable thirst for life and adventure and stopping at nothing to quench that thirst.

When I first met Ron, he was very handsome and quite a gentleman, if not a bit awkward with words and expressing himself. But that matched perfectly with me as I had always been quite the odd duckling looking to find my other quacker. When we met, Ron worked as a car porter and lived in an old huge Victorian house that originally belonged to his aunt, and I was in my second year of graduate school. To be completely transparent, Ron and I met online, and the first time we met for a date, that date turned into me spending the rest of the weekend at his house. There were instant sparks and some invisible force field that connected us. After that first weekend, I think I spent every weekend with him for the next month until we spent New Year's Eve together, and I proceeded to meet his entire family. Later that night, he turned to me and timidly said, "So what is this? What are we?" And we made our relationship official.

After a month and a half of dating, I gave Ron a hand-decorated "Travel Savings Jar" for Valentine's Day. I remember having the conversation only a few days after meeting one another that both of us had wanted to travel the world, and I thought Valentine's Day was the perfect time to symbolize that promise with a Travel Jar where we would start saving our money. As we got to know each other, my time at graduate school was ending, and I had to decide on a career and where I wanted to live. After a few applications, I got my first real-world job in a town near where Ron lived. We had both discussed moving in together, and although we knew it was pretty soon to be shacking up, we figured we should probably live with one another and get the kinks worked out before we travel the world together.

Now rewind a bit and let me tell you about Brittany. I had known Brittany since our Sophomore year at college when we were put together as roommates. Brittany seemed like the shy nice girl at first, but once I got to know her, she became bold, daring, and one of the strongest women I know who always spoke her mind. Brittany and I shared a lifetime of good memories in college, and on graduation day, as we shared good-bye shots in Marty's Bar, we sobbed our eyes out, not knowing when we would see each other again or what our lives would look like after college.

Flash forward two years when I finished graduate school, and I decided to move to Metro Detroit. Brittany and Ron both lived in the same general area, and I had a great idea that Ron and Brittany, and I should all move in together. Especially since we were all looking for roommates and splitting a rental with three people is cheaper than with two. But, Ron and Brittany had only met once before this point. Apparently, I was a good negotiator because they both agreed, and we began our search for rentals.

Thankfully it ended up being a pretty good living situation. We all got along for the most part, even though Ron and I were quite a bit messier than Brittany, and they had both adopted the nickname for me "Hurricane Klimczak," my last name. Somewhere between when we all moved in together and when we left for Europe, Ron and I were able to talk Brittany into traveling with us. Because let's face it, we were young, free, all had money saved, and this would be the adventure of a lifetime.

For that first year that we all rented the apartment together, Ron and I gave up many things to be able to save to travel. We ate a ton of ramen noodles for dinner. We saved by not going out to eat or drinking too often. We worked hard and put away savings, and by the time our year lease came to an end, we were both able to save up $5000, which would be just enough for us to travel around Europe for three months if we budgeted around $50-$60 per day. In no way, shape, or form would we be able to travel luxuriously, but we felt that the experience of traveling without an abundance of cash would just add more to the adventure. I wholeheartedly believe that money should never be the reason that holds you back from something you want in life, and if you want it bad enough, you can make it happen.

Saying Goodbye

Do you know that feeling? Racing heart, short breaths, spinning head? That is the feeling of reality hitting you right in your core. I could feel the tiny salty tear droplets start to well up in my eyes, and my throat only got tighter as I struggled to hold back the tears from rolling down my face as I walked out of my dad's house this morning.

Last night, I said goodbye to my mother and this morning to my father. Although I have been saying good-bye to them my whole life for different moves and life transitions, somehow this was different. It was different because everything is so unknown from here on out. Although we officially have our flight booked to fly back into the U.S. on September 10th, there are still many "what ifs." What if we fall in love with a particular country or culture and somehow magically acquire the funds to stay a bit longer? What if we decide we want to live overseas for a year? What if we decide that we want to keep traveling somewhere else while we can before we go home? There are so many unknowns. Now I know most of these are very extreme "what ifs," and all have what my mom would call "a snowball's chance in hell" of happening, but still a chance. Ron has always told me that I live in my own fantasy world where everything is perfect, everyone is friendly, and absolutely anything can happen. And that is precisely the mindset I have for this trip and life in general. Anything is possible. A few years ago, I would have never thought that I could quit a job and give up a home to be able to travel to Europe for three months, but now that dream is coming true. So, although we do have a realistic plan of coming home, settling down, and getting jobs again, I still have in mind my fantasy world and am ready for anything and everything.

Completely Surreal

I was completely restless and full of weird, confusing dreams and anxious thoughts the night before the flight. Like always, before a new adventure or trip, I don't sleep very well. In fact, now that I think about it, I don't think I have ever gotten more than maybe two hours of sleep the night before a flight. And that's being generous. However, the drive to the airport was surprisingly tranquil. Once I got in that car, I just knew that was it, and whatever I had with me or whatever I had forgotten, I would just have to deal with it.

I did spend months planning and trying on outfits and laying everything out that would be stuffed in my 45-liter backpack. So logically, I should have everything I need, but it is a little frightening flying to a foreign country to survive the next three months with only the things strapped to your back. I mean, I packed a bag larger than this one when Ron and I went on our first official trip together to Punta Cana for only 4 days. I am still amazed that I was able to narrow down all my essential items to last me three months into a backpack this small. Good for me.

As I sit in the airport waiting for our first flight to board, I feel the excitement slowly building and washing away all the nerves and anxiety. I am excited to arrive in Ireland and excited for a great trip, but it is still very surreal that we will be gone for three months. So for now, I am just waiting for the surreal to become real.

Speed Bumps

Multiple hours later and the excitement has turned into pure adrenalin. We went from boarding our first flight, sitting on the runway, and then going back to the gate and de-boarding, only to learn that our flight had been canceled and we had to re-book. About an hour or so later and a few long lines, we finally had our flights rescheduled, and now instead of flying from Michigan to Chicago to Dublin, we will be flying out of New York and on a different airline. Speed Bumps. Not everything always goes according to plan, but things will always work out one way or another. Once we land in New York, we will also have to transfer to a different airport to fly out. Our changed itinerary includes taking a taxi, picking up our checked bags, and making our way through security again. So here is hoping that the luck of the Irish is on our side.

The Unluckiest Luck

Well, I guess you could say that up to this point, the luck of the Irish has been with us because I am currently sitting on a plane on my way to Ireland. Getting to this point, however, didn't go very smoothly. When we first had our flight transferred, we had to make our way to another airport terminal, which included the three of us running like mad through the airport, thinking that we might now miss our rescheduled flight. Me, picking up the rear of the group as Brit Yells at me with a dead serious yet still jokingly tone "RUN FASTER!". But I'm no track star and my little legs just don't have the stride to keep up with everyone else.

Thankfully we made it just in time, and the flight went smoothly. Unfortunately, when we landed in New York, we had to transfer airports from LaGuardia to JFK, which officially used up all the American money we had left for the cab ride. You would think that leaving a three-hour gap would be enough time to transfer airports, but not for us. The car ride was relatively easy and quick with no typical New York traffic jams or screaming drivers, but once we got to JFK, well that's a different story.

As we checked in for our second flight, we found out that they had not yet rebooked Brittany's flight, which meant that she had no ticket. For the first few moments, we thought that this was just a mistake and they would fix it. Then the first, second, and third hour went by with us standing there helpless and time ticking closer to when our flight was due to depart—pure agony. The anxiety hits, the clock ticks, and everything is entirely out of our hands. And then, at the last possible second, we heard the man behind the counter say to the other, "just give her a ticket, and we will figure it out later."

With that, we all just stared blankly at the man in astonishment and asked him if we even had time to make it to the flight now and his one-word answer was "run." Once we got the go-ahead from behind the counter, we started sprinting to security with less than a minute before our flight was scheduled to take off. With some luck, there was no line at security, and we were able to make it through the process with no time left for Ron to even put his shoes back on before we started sprinting down the terminal to our gate to arrive just as they were calling our flight to board. We had made it. The unluckiest of luck.

In the Air

We all settled in on the plane and met our seat neighbors. Of course, none of us were seated together but all within shouting distance. As many times I have been on an airplane, this was the largest one yet. The aircraft was humungous, and I was seated on the end in the center row next to a few very nice older ladies. Once we got in the air, the time passed quickly, and the whole "fine dining" experience aboard a plane was a welcome surprise. It was my first experience being served a complete meal on a flight, and I would have to say that I was pleasantly surprised. The options were chicken or beef, and I opted for the chicken, which was quite delicious. It was an Indian dish with a decent amount of spice, but I decided to risk it with my sensitive stomach, so we will see how that sits with me later.

The rest of the meal included a small dinner roll with butter, two crackers and a sliver of cheese, a bite-size salad, and a chocolate brownie. To tell the truth, it was too much to eat, so I stored the crackers and brownie for later. Overall, the meal was quite lovely, and everything was a positive experience except the woman sitting in front of me.

Before I finished eating, the woman began trying to violently push her chair back so that she could recline. She launched herself forward, grabbed the armrests, and then catapulted herself backward. Everything happened so quickly that my brain had just enough time to figure out what was going on and throw my hand up to brace her chair from coming down on all my food at full force. My food tray and drink all survived the earthquake but just barely.

Call me naive, but I thought she would have gotten the picture that I was still eating, so she couldn't recline yet, but apparently not, because not long after I had taken just a few more bites of food, she began again. Imagine an angry toddler having a temper tantrum and violently throwing his entire body weight against the back of the chair he was sitting on; that was pretty much the scene. That was when the nice elderly Irish woman whom I was sitting next to threw her arm against the seat back and exclaimed loudly enough for the woman in front of me to hear, "you just go ahead and eat in peace, Hunny, I've got this." I just love the kind people in this world. Unfortunately for some, they will never learn airplane etiquette or etiquette in general.

Dublin, Ireland

*Although English is the main spoken language in Ireland, Gaelic is still practiced and recognized as the official language.

Hello- Dia duit
Thank You- Buíochas
Please- le do thoil

As a reference, Dublin is a fantastic city. Since boarding the plane in New York, landing in Dublin, and then spending our first night exploring the city, this day has gone on forever. At around 9:00 a.m., we landed in Dublin with two out of our three bags. Brittany's bag did not make it to Dublin with us. But being the laid-back trooper that she is, Brit kept her spirits together, hoping that she would get her bag eventually on another incoming flight as we ventured into the city center. The hostel we are staying at is great. It has many open and community spaces, so many small stairwells that you could get lost, and is covered with character and hand paintings on the wall around every corner.

For those of you wondering if I misspelled the word "hotel," I did not. We are, in fact, staying in a hostel. If you have never heard of a hostel before, it is shared accommodations for budget travelers. Every hostel is different, but typically, you will stay in a shared room with 4- 12 people packed with bunk beds. Each hostel usually has multiple bathrooms for everyone to use and shared community space or a shared kitchen. It is an excellent opportunity to socialize with other like-minded travelers, and it seriously helps you stretch your budget. I think we paid somewhere around $18 US a night for this hostel. WAY cheaper than shelling out $100 a night for a hotel room…but back to the city!

Exploring the city today was amazing. I was so exhausted from traveling, but I feel like we walked the entire day and got to know the city better. We found the Guinness Factory, which we will be exploring tomorrow. We saw the Dublin castle, which was beautiful from the outside, and also got a look at Trinity College. As we explored the college grounds, a young student named Ania asked us to take a picture of her. Come to find out, she had just finished cycling the entire Island of Ireland in just over four weeks! Ania was very friendly, and she also invited us to tour the Trinity College Museum as her guests for free. For us, this was the first significant act of Irish hospitality from this wonderful country. This girl didn't even know us but invited us to come in as her guests; otherwise, we would have had to pay 10 euros per person to tour.

Trinity College was founded in 1592 and is not only Ireland's oldest university but also one of the top ranked universities. The Trinity College Long Room Library is what the college is most famous for because the library's old-world beauty and sheer magnitude looks like something straight out of a Harry Potter movie. The Long Room of the library was built in the 1700s and holds over 200,000 copies of the library's oldest books. Legally this Trinity library is the only library in the United Kingdom that owns the right to receive works published in the Republic of Ireland, free of charge. Just walking through this majestic room was an experience.

The rest of the college grounds weren't as majestic as the library but still deeply rooted in history. Trinity College is Ireland's highest-ranked university, and two notable people to graduate from Trinity College include Oscar Wilde and the former president of Ireland, Mary Robinson.

After the tour and a lovely goodbye with Ania, we got lost exploring Dublin and found ourselves at Temple Bar, yet another famous location in Dublin. The bar was established in 1840 and serves the most extensive collection of rare whiskeys in Ireland, over 450 different kinds. Ania had been telling us about Temple Bar and said we couldn't miss it while we were here. It wasn't hard to find with its bright red exterior, and the mouth-watering smells of food coming from inside were too much to resist. We enjoyed our first Irish beer here, which paired perfectly with bangers and mash. Our stomachs were full, and we were still exhausted from traveling, so we decided to rest up back at the hostel.

We woke up from our nap around 10:00 p.m., ready to finish exploring the pubs! The night turned into a bit of a blur, but to my knowledge, we visited the Darkey Kelly's, Turks Head, and Porter House, but who knows, there were a few beers in between each visit. The beer was good, the company was engaging, and the locals were friendly. For now, it is time to call it a night for our first day in Ireland.

Side Note #1: You cannot be a baller on a budget day one of a trip and spend all your money. Buying one drink each would have been much more frugal than going to three different bars and having three drinks at each one. Between drinks and dinner, my bill clocked in around 28 euros. Not horrible, but NOT budget friendly.

Side Note #2: The hostel we are staying at is under construction, and they start work here very early. Also, we are the only ones fazed by this because everyone else is still sound asleep.

Side Note #3: My shoes already smell a little, so this will be a very, very LONG journey.

Side Note #4: I suck at packing, everything in my bag is disorganized, and I could have packed way less.

Side Note #5: My legs better look damn good at the end of the trip with all the walking.

Side Note #6: My first full day in Ireland clocked in at $68 budget wise. Not too horrible, but overbudget on day one. Good start. (Just pretend "good start" was written in the font "sarcastica", because sarcastic tone doesn't translate well over text, and unfortunately no one has developed a specific font to relay this tone yet- someone get working on this.)

So besides learning a few key things on our first day in Ireland, sleep felt terrific. We started the day with a free breakfast provided by the hostel. It was just cereal and toast, but you can't beat free when you are on a tight budget. After breakfast we started off on a guided walking tour.

I've never been much of a history buff, but this was by far the best tour I have ever been on. Our tour guide was very energetic and highly knowledgeable about Ireland. It was also a fantastic experience to hear the stories behind everything we had seen yesterday. A few interesting points we learned included the explanation behind the Irish flag. Each color on the Irish flag has a specific representation. The green represents the Irish natives, the orange represents the British supporters, and the white represents the peace between these two groups of people. Also, before traveling to Ireland, I never knew that this Island was split between the Republic of Ireland and Northern Ireland. Officially, Ireland is an independent country, but Northern Ireland is still under the Queen's rule and is technically still a part of the UK and established as an independent country.

I will spare you all the details of the walking tour, but one other point of information that especially most American's don't know about is St. Patrick. St. Patrick is the Patron saint of Ireland and is known for bringing Christianity to various parts of Ireland. St. Patrick's Day dates back to the 17th century and was initially celebrated to commemorate St. Patrick on March 17th, which was thought to be the day of his death. Now, St. Patrick's Day is celebrated across the US as one of the deadliest holidays for drunk driving, and drunken debauchery as American's roam the streets with their green-stained mouths from consuming beer saturated with what

I can only believe is completely unhealthy levels of green food dye. Cheers, St. Patrick...

After the walking tour of the city, we headed to Saint James Gate Guinness Factory, because a tour of the factory for only 13 euros was a steal. The factory was a huge building where each level had a different theme. The tour was self-guided, so we were able to walk along at our own pace and read about the making of Guinness and the history and take part in interactive learning experiences.

The first floor was dedicated to the beer-making process, including ingredients, techniques, and storage. The tour started with the wow factor of a massive waterfall inside the building. This water circulating was of the highest quality and would later be turned into the famous Guinness beer.

The second floor, one of my favorites, was the tasting experience, fully equipped with Guinness samples and smoking columns of Guinness to enhance your sense of smell. Here we learned how to drink a Guinness properly.

Step one, you need to hold your arm out so that your elbow is horizontal with the Guinness glass.

Step two, as you tilt the glass toward your mouth, you need to take a big enough sip to get a mixture of the foam and the beer. Leaving the foam on top of the beer keeps the Guinness fresh but combining each sip with foam and beer helps with the velvety smooth texture.

Now you can use this fun fact next time you drink a Guinness with your friends!

The third story was decorated with multiple Guinness advertisements over the years. We skipped the fourth-floor exhibit because it would have cost extra, but for those that wanted to learn, this is where wanna-be bartenders could learn how to pour a pint perfectly. Now onto the top floor, a 360-degree gravity bar with full views of the city. Here, the three of us enjoyed our free pint of Guinness and truly took in the city's beauty. You could see all of Dublin and the mountains beyond it. It was one of those views that really brings things into perspective. Like the realization that we were actually in Dublin, and for the first time, it was all right in front of me.

After finishing at the Guinness Factory, cooking dinner that night was also an interesting experience. Since our budget is low, we decided to explore a local market where we found some frozen pizza items to heat up (typical Americans). The kitchen at the hostel proved to be confusing for first-time backpackers. You would figure that an oven would be self-explanatory, but that was not the case. After waiting for about ten minutes for it to pre-heat, we discovered that it was not hot, so thankfully, someone decided to help us.

The ONE place where I always felt comfortable and at home, whipping up magnificent food creations, I now felt like a foreigner. Everyone else moved around with ease, preparing their meals, while we just sat there waiting for our already prepared food to heat up. While we were waiting, one man in the kitchen was preparing fancy pasta with all the fresh ingredients. Bottom line, next time, we will just make pasta. Overall, I am not sure if everyone at the hostel has been here longer or is just used to the environment, but everyone seems right at home as I feel a little more out of place. I think that as time goes on, I will feel more comfortable and just relax. But for now, I will just wander aimlessly until I find my groove.

Gassy and Uncomfortable

Let me get real personal here for a minute. I have traveled and shared accommodations with different people before but it's just now hitting me that for the next three months, I will pretty much never be alone. Not to mention that I am currently sharing a room with 23 other people which equals zero privacy.

Also sharing a room with this many people kind of reminds me how I felt when I first started dating Ron- gassy and uncomfortable. Let me explain…

When we first started dating like any new relationship, you can't just let your bodily functions go in front of one another. You are still trying to keep that "mystery", or at least be polite, which sometimes results in you being gassy and uncomfortable. Especially as someone who has had tummy troubles her whole life, this has been a bigger challenge than most.

I specifically remember when Ron and I use to cuddle on the couch and watch a movie, one special night there was a war waging in my intestines. All throughout the movie I was squirming around and would turn around to face on the couch instead of the tv every time I needed to clench my cheeks to prevent a toot from escaping. I did this so that he wouldn't feel my ass constantly contracting and wonder what in the hell was wrong with me-true story. He just thought I was a very squirmy person and thought nothing of it.

Well, I felt just as uncomfortable sharing a room with over 20 strangers. God forbid I let out a little toot as I'm trying to fall sleep at night. So instead, I just hold it in and squirm around uncomfortably, because let's be honest, if any of these random people I meet in Europe remember me, being the night tooter is not something that I want to be remembered for. Therefore, cheers to my new nightly ab and buttock workout of trying to keep my toots to myself.

Laundry on the Road

For those who detest doing laundry, I dare you to try hand-washing your clothes, or for that matter, cleaning them in a hostel shower. It is interesting, to say the least. For me, the best process that worked included filling up a plastic zip-lock bag with water and just a tad of soap and then just kind of jumbling the clothes around in there for a bit. (Just small things like underwear and socks) Then you rinse and wring and realize that you now have nowhere to put your wet clean clothes. It just includes a bit of juggling. After that, you get to use a hostel bed to hang up all your "unmentionables" to dry. No privacy. At least I brought cute underwear! Also, as a travel hack, the bathroom hand dryer works quite nicely as a blow-dryer for your hair if you can get it to stay on.

But I should feel lucky that I even got to wear clean clothes the last few days as Brit was stuck in the same airport outfit. However, her bag finally arrived today at the hostel! We all celebrated dancing in a circle around Brit as she held her precious cargo above her head. Now she gets to share in the privilege of also washing her clothes in a hostel sink!

Diving into Ireland

Yesterday's trip around Ireland was incredible. We left Dublin around 7:30 a.m. and began our journey to Galway. We had booked a tour earlier to take us to the Burren area and the Cliffs of Moher for around 35 euros. The tour day was anything but boring. When we arrived in Galway, our tour bus just dropped us off on the side of the road and told us that another bus would be along shortly. For a minute there, everyone was very confused, and we weren't all quite sure if there was another bus coming for us, but sure enough, it pulled up not too long after with another very lovely and enthusiastic tour guide. From there, we made our way to the Burren area.

The Burren is a geological park and only one of two in all of Ireland. It is known for having little soil and an abundance of exposed limestone along with unique flora and fauna. Once there, we went to a small family farm where a guide took us up on a hike through the mountain. He called it a prosperous rock area because even the hills looked like all rock (limestone, to be exact), but as you climbed up higher, you realized that vegetation and greenery is growing up the entire hill. It was beautiful. He explained to us that the cows would graze down in the valley during the summer, and in the winter, they would move the cows up the mountain to graze because it doesn't really snow in Ireland, and winters are very mild.

While climbing, our guide showed us the fairy tree that had multiple random objects like hair ties hanging off it. He said that according to legend, the tree was supposed to be a cross between this world and the spiritual world. People would leave a piece of themselves behind on this tree, and this would be the representation of essentially leaving your problems and worries in the past. Brit and I tied a hair tie to the tree in good adventurous fashion to leave all of our worries behind us.

All in all, the Burren was gorgeous, and you could see forever across the landscape once we were higher up. We also made a friend, Nicole, who was from Portland and who was also backpacking. She was even kind enough to share some chocolate with us that she had purchased at the small Burren store. With our new friend by our side, we then departed for the Cliffs of Moher.

The Cliffs of Moher, run for about 9 miles on the Southwest side of Ireland, rising from 400-700 feet above the ocean. They are one of the biggest tourist attractions in Ireland and have been featured in multiple movies such as the Princess Bride and even Harry Potter.

It took about two hours to get to the cliffs and it was beautiful along the way, but everything changed when you reached the edge of those cliffs. The natural beauty that the cliffs offer is something that could never be recreated by mere pictures or written words but something that must be experienced first-hand. When you first walk up to the edge of the cliffs and see the jagged rocks that plummet down to the crashing ocean, you feel like you have reached the edge of the earth. The adrenaline rush you get from sitting on the edge, swinging your feet over and the wind blowing in your face with a slight salty mist, the distant crash of the waves below on the ocean is something that I will never forget.

We all took this opportunity to take many pictures together as we could to try to capture the true beauty of the cliffs and the beginning of our journey. I think each of us experienced the cliffs a different way, either sitting in solitude and marveling at what nature had created, walking along the cliffs and exploring, or like Ron, testing the boundaries and seeing how far over the edge he could hang himself to see the bottom.

I could probably write an entire small book just on the Cliffs of Moher themselves, but instead, I think you should experience them for yourself. It was hard walking away and leaving the cliffs behind, but I knew that many more adventures were awaiting.

Now to get back to the present, we returned to Dublin on the bus, and now I am currently sitting on a train waiting for it to leave so we can make our way across Ireland to Belfast. After a few more rough bus rides, I would have to say that I have never been more excited to be on a train. The seats are comfortable, and we have lots of room that includes a good-sized table to sprawl all our stuff across. Not to mention, we could have made it on the train without even purchasing a ticket. We walked through a door, passed the turn station, and walked on the train without anyone even checking our tickets, so we will have to see how this goes. Also, free Wi-Fi on the train!

We're not in Kansas Anymore

The train ride was short and sweet, and the conductor eventually came around to stamp our ticket. However, when we arrived in Belfast, stress hit like a freight train. We quickly learned that since it is Northern Ireland, they use the British pound and not the Euro, so the exchange rate was working against us. The exchange rate was close to 2 American dollars for every 1 British pound, which is not something we had budgeted for.

When we got into Belfast, we began walking to the city to find some accommodations. We stopped at the visitor's center, and after searching for a while, it looked like our options were shelling out 20 pounds a night for a hostel or sleeping in the train station. For reference, our budget was 50-60 American dollars a day. So just to pay for a bed in Belfast would have put us right at the top of our budget. Luckily, we came across a campground about 5 miles out of the city for only 14 pounds a night, which we could all split- so we booked it, and what a little adventure that turned out to be.

Since travel days ate up most of our budget, we didn't want to spend money on a bus to get to the campground in a different city. We figured we would have no problem walking the 5 miles to the campground with our backpacks on. We were prepped and ready for this hike, map in hand. The only problem was that Belfast has no street names or signs, so when you have a map, it really doesn't help unless you know which street you are on. Okay, they may have had signs, but if they did, they were only visible to the Irish because out of the three of us, no one could locate a sign.

To make a long story short, a lovely gentleman ended up helping us out and letting us know that there was a train we could hop on, which would be much quicker. That is, and just cross our fingers that we didn't have to pay. So we decided to make our way to Jordanstown by train.

When we got off in Jordanstown, we had no clue where we were going and had to rely on strangers again to help us. As out of place as I felt in Dublin, this was ten times worse. Dublin was a security blanket compared to this place. The train had dropped us off in a nice little suburban area with no tourists and barely anyone else walking around.

We somehow magically found our way to the campground where things got worse. I have camped in different places my whole life, and I have never seen anything like this before. The entire campground is about maybe an acre of land with small parking spaces for campervans, and the whole lot is gated. Not to mention there was almost no grassy area to be found. We did NOT fit in as tent campers. But, nevertheless, we pitched our little tent in a lot full of campervans and spent the rest of the night collecting beach glass along the shore and playing card games in the tent.

Although our first few days in Dublin were over budget, it will be days like these that help balance things out. The day's total spending came in at only $18.02 between money on a few food items and the campground cost.

Well, that first night in the tent was God awful. We really did try to make the best of it. It got freezing cold by the time night fell, and my tiny sleeping bag wasn't enough to keep me warm. The first time I got up and out of the tent to use the bathroom, I used the hand dryers to blow warm air on my hands to warm me up. No shame and no one there to judge. I probably stayed in the bathroom for about a half-hour doing this. It was absolutely freezing cold, and we all barely got any sleep. As bad as the night was, this morning's warm shower somehow washed away the sleepless night and gave me a fresh start. We are currently sitting on a bus waiting to go up the coast of Northern Ireland to see the sights.

Carrick-a-Rede

Driving along the coast of Northern Ireland was breathtaking. Our first stop was the Carrick-a-Rede rope bridge. The bridge is suspended 100 feet above the Atlantic Ocean and was first built in 1755 by salmon fishermen so that they would no longer need to rely on a boat to get to Carrick-a-Rede Island. Although salmon fishing was once a flourishing industry near the island, due to pollution, the last fish said to be caught at the island was in 2002. Not only was the bridge draped in culture and history, but the ocean-side cliff views once again took our breath away. However, crossing the bridge with a slight fear of heights was a little more terrifying.

The first time I walked across, I felt like my heart was pounding out of my chest, and I could feel the beads of sweat run down my palms as they tightly gripped the rope rails. The bridge would sway side to side with the wind and had a little bounce to it with every step you took. All I could picture was the news headline that read "American tourists falls to her death on Carrick-a-Rede." But Ron was behind me the whole time cheering me on and trying to calm my nerves.

Once you crossed the bridge, you were on this little piece of land that looked back on all the cliffs and out into the ocean. One of those views makes you happy to be alive and wants to make you strive for more in life.

More adventures, more views, more everything. Sometimes, I think people get too caught up in life and don't take enough time to really step back and appreciate it. This whole adventure so far has been so exhilarating. I just feel so alive and like a different person. Although not everything is smiles and rainbows, I love this crazy adventure and can't wait for more.

Gourmet Dinner on a Laundry Room Floor

So here it is, the end of another successful day, as we end it sitting on a laundry room floor eating cold beans, spaghettiO's, and chips for dinner. As odd as it sounds, I know that the moments like this will be the most memorable. When we returned to the campsite, we decided to hide out in the laundry room because it was freezing outside, and we needed to charge all of our electronics. Apparently, Northern Ireland is not the best place to go camping in a tent. But even if it is another cold night tonight, the day was worth it.

Now back to the events of the day. After the Carrick- a- Rede Bridge, we headed to Giant's Causeway. Unfortunately, to catch the last bus back to the train station to continue onto Jordanstown, we didn't have much time to spend at the Causeway, so we ran around taking pictures and trying to take in as much as possible in the little time we had. If you have never heard of the Giant's Causeway, it is an area of basalt columns in Northern Ireland that all perfectly form together in hexagon-like shapes. The scenery was so picture-perfect that you would have thought someone hand drew a picture and placed it right in front of your eyes.

There are many different stories about how the Causeway came to be. If you are one to believe in ancient legend, then you would appreciate the story of the two fighting giants that inadvertently formed the Causeway. However, if you are more of a scientific person, you might more realistically believe that the Causeway was formed from the aftermath of a volcano. Whichever story you choose to believe, when you come face-to-face with the Causeway, the intricate yet perfect puzzle pieces of rock that fit magically together will still awe and intrigue you.

While at the Causeway, we also decided to scale up a small mountain, which was incredibly exhilarating. Although this was no expert rock climbing mission, the few feet that we climbed, trying to scramble up the side, and finding small handholds to keep from falling was enough of an adrenaline rush for me. When we get back to the states, I think I would love to invest more into rock climbing and adventure sports, some hobbies that I could really love!

Once we hit the top, you could see the gorgeous ocean hues and the water splashing and glistening off the Causeway rocks. However, after our spurt of energy, we had to rush back to jump on several trains and busses, which brought us back home where we are now, eating cold dinners on the floor of a laundry room. Another successful night for the books.

Even after spending $29.50 for the tour, I was able to keep under budget for the day with a total of $42.93

Today we say farewell to Ireland and head off on what can only be categorized as a cruise ship to Scotland. As we leave Ireland, I just wanted to jot down a few notes to remember about the country.

First, Ireland and Northern Ireland are drop-dead gorgeous. The natural scenery, luscious green lands, and cliffside views are all stunning. Second, the locals of Ireland are so unbelievably friendly. Never have I experienced this kind of hospitality while traveling, especially from strangers. Random strangers would just walk up and help us almost everywhere we went when we got lost. Third, there is a huge difference between the Republic of Ireland and Northern Ireland. The Republic is independent as Northern Ireland is still under British rule. The Euro is still used in Ireland, and everything is reasonably priced. In Northern Ireland, the British pound is used, and the British take you for every pound you are worth, overcharging you for each attraction you go to. You can clearly see the difference between these two parts of the country.

Actually, strike that. We didn't even learn until we came home that Northern Ireland is an entirely different country than Ireland. It should have been obvious, but we didn't really connect the dots at the time. Technically, Northern Ireland is a part of the U.K., like Whales, England, and Scotland. Although Whales, England, and Scotland are all a part of Great Britain. At the time, my brain just thought that Northern Ireland was still technically considered a part of the country of Ireland, but just maybe a section that the queen ruled? Who knows how my brain works because I don't. But now you know just in case a question like this ever comes up on Jeopardy.

But overall, Ireland as a whole was beautiful with breathtaking countryside and courteous people. Without a doubt, I would love to come back to Ireland again and explore this incredible culture even more.

Scotland

**English, Scottish Gaelic, and Scots are the recognized languages
of Scotland. Although most locals speak English, the Scottish accent
is so thick sometimes, you might mistake it for another language.*

Hello- Halò
Thank you- tapadh leibh
Please- gabhaibh

After a very long day of travel, my first impression of Edinburgh, Scotland is that the city is beautiful. It has this esoteric, old-world feel with enchanting architecture that makes you feel like you have gone back in time. To step back for a minute, though, we didn't arrive in Edinburgh until around 6:00 p.m. today after a long day of busses and a ferry.

The Scottish people are very friendly, just like the Irish, but their accents are thicker, and the jargon is hard to understand. I would compare the Irish accents to a small child trying to talk to you to make a new friend. With the Scottish accents, it's more like a 6 ½ foot tall drunken bearded man with a mouth full of bread trying to point you in the right direction on your way home from the bar; Still extremely friendly but just harder to understand.

When we arrived at the bus station, one Scottish man began helping us with directions and telling us what to see around the city. However, the only thing I could understand from the conversation was that we had to go see a dog statue and kiss its nose for good luck. I find that it just works to nod and smile in these situations. After the "help" from the local man, we somehow found our hostel and settled in to grab a bite to eat at the pub downstairs. I think this will be a routine where we sample the local cuisine every time we arrive in a new country. It's not really in the budget for us, but after a few days of only eating bread, peanut butter, nuts, and dried fruit, a delicious meal sounds so good.

We all had a bit of comfort food tonight. I chose the chicken sandwich, Ron finished off a traditional American burger, and Brit went with the black bean burger. The meal was so simple but so damn good, especially after a few days of just snacking on food and not eating authentic meals. It's only the beginning of our long journey, and I have already developed a deeper appreciation for food. It's times like these that make you think about how picky you are back at home with your food choices, and now when I'm hungry while traveling, I will pretty much eat anything or just survive off sunflower seeds for the day. But anyway, appreciation is one lesson that I have soaked up reasonably quickly on this trip.

After the food, we ventured up Calton Hill, an old dormant volcano location, now a beautiful site overlooking the city. Calton Hill is home to a contemporary art gallery and an unfinished national monument, and it is the headquarters of the Scottish government. Once you get to the top, you can see the entire city below you. And even though the sky is scattered with gray clouds, the glow from the setting sun is just bright enough to peak out through the clouds and illuminate specific parts of the city. A view well worth the walk.

Today is actually the first day that my legs and feet are starting to get sore from all the walking. With every step that I take, I can now feel the burn of each calf muscle aching to stop. But I push on because it is way too early in the trip for sore muscles. Here's to hoping that a good night's rest and some TLC will take care of my aching muscles so that they are ready to start the day tomorrow.

Don't Drink the Scotch in Scotland

Lesson of the day: *Do not order Scotch in Scotland just for the "experience" when you know you don't like whiskey.*

Besides the scotch, the day in Edinburgh was "lovely," as they say here. We began the morning with another walking tour to learn all about this new city. The most famous site of the day was of course, Edinburgh Castle. This fortress sits above the city on Castle Rock, which was originally formed from a volcano. Archeologists have dated the castle back to 2nd century A.D., and it served as a royal residency until 1633. It is even rumored to be one of the most attacked strongholds in the world. This stronghold looks like something straight out of Games of Thrones. You can just imagine all the wars and battles fought on the grounds and the rich history draped around the castle. It just gives you goosebumps thinking about everything that happened in the place where your feet are today.

After the tour, we took an adventure that was 100% free! We climbed to the top of Arthur's Seat right in the heart of the city. Arthur's Seat is an extinct volcano that sits above the city at 822 feet high. The climb was exhausting, especially with sore legs, but the adrenaline rush was enough to push me to the top, and the view was worth it. Again, another experience at the top of the mountain that is hard to put into words. If I lived in the city, I would love to make this climb a few times a week just for the exercise and to appreciate the city from a different viewpoint.

Once we had our fill of city views, we headed back down and grabbed a simple subway sandwich for dinner because it was quick and cheap. That, and unfortunately our hostel did not have a kitchen so we couldn't prepare food. After dinner, we had the chance for some downtime at the hostel to plan our next move.

Planning our next move was, for the best word, stressful. First, Great Britain is incredibly expensive. Second, our Eurail pass does not cover transportation here, making it even more costly. Third, planning as you go instead of ahead of time is double stressful. After a few hours of trying to plot our next move, we had a few successes followed by a few failures.

Win-We successfully booked a bus to London tomorrow night.

Fail- The money for the bus took a big chunk out of our budget. Like 91 Pounds worth.

On the positive side, we will save money on accommodations for the night with it being an overnight bus. But, we still have no clue how much money London will cost us or how much it will cost us after that to get into Paris. Stress was high today, but I really do believe that times like this will prove how well we work as a travel team and how to overcome obstacles. I think that we will not only learn about the places we visit but also about ourselves. But for now, just to cut the stress, we went to a Scottish bar for a drink.

This was my personal downfall; ordering something that I knew I wouldn't like just for the experience. We found a cute little hole-in-the-wall pub with some live music. We could barely hear each other over the music, but the atmosphere was fitting. As I skimmed the menu for a scotch, I might as well have been reading Chinese. I had no idea what I was looking for. With the bartender's recommendation we all choose a 10-year-old scotch with a quirky name that was supposed to be the new "up and coming drink of choice". Instead, it tasted like straight-up gasoline. I literally felt like I was poisoning my body trying to gag down this glass of scotch. But in exchange for drinking gasoline, I marked off an item on my bucket list- Drinking Scotch in Scotland. Was it worth it? Absolutely not. Will I learn from this experience? Maybe, but I'm sure I will make the same mistake again, because when in Rome, right? Or in Scotland for this matter.

Ron loved his choice because he is a whiskey drinker at heart. You could see Brittany's face pucker up every time she took a sip, but she was determined not to waste a drop. So there we were, halfway across the world, in a dive bar, drinking scotch and listening to live guitar music that sounded like it came straight out of Mississippi. But we enjoyed the hell out of that night. Hopefully tomorrow will be a low-budget day, and I know for sure that there will be no more whiskey drinking for this girl.

Fun fact- Scotch is the exact same thing as whiskey, except that Scotch is only made in Scotland, whereas whiskey can be made anywhere- and now you know!

June 16th

I have realized that it is really hard to keep track of the day of the week, let alone the calendar date when you are not working, because frankly, it's not relevant. Even most of the time here, the time of day escapes me. So, it is kind of nice not having to worry about the time or the days. Something freeing that I'm sure I will miss.

We started the day by packing up our things at the hostel, St. Christopher's Inn, and then we headed out on the town with no plans. Along the way, we ran into a small circus where there were a ton of reporters and photographers. Probably just to advertise and to take pictures for the upcoming big event, but we were able to sneak in.

We enjoyed a free sneak preview of events, including strength acrobatics, juggling, and hula hooping. One of the best random finds yet. That is the cool thing about not having any plans and just being able to wander the city. Sometimes you come across the most spectacular things. After wandering around, we enjoyed a nice picnic lunch in the park and a small snooze in the grass. Right now, we are just killing time, exploring the city aimlessly until our bus leaves for London tonight at 10:00 p.m. On a side note, I am super excited to be staying with friends tomorrow night.

We are staying with our friends Cat and Andy in Luton, right outside of London. Ron and I met these friends on a company vacation just a few months before leaving for Europe. We had told them that we were planning on traveling Europe that Summer and we would be coming through London. They (probably jokingly) offered for us to stay with them while we were coming through town, not ever thinking that we would take them up on the offer. Joke is on them!

To this day, we are still great friends and see each other every few years.

It just shows you that you can make friends and connections anywhere! I'm so excited to see them, but I have also run out of fresh underwear, and my shoes are pretty smelly, so a friendly environment and a chance to catch up on my personal hygiene is most welcome. Not to mention that I caught a glimpse of my face in a well-lit mirror today, and my skin and eyebrows are in desperate need of some TLC.

Other than that, all is well. My muscles are a bit sore from walking and climbing, but I think they are getting accustomed to it. Everyone was coughing and sneezing in the hostel this morning. Ron and I hope none of us have caught anything, but our throats are feeling a bit off this afternoon so let's hope that goes away. I will be sad tonight to leave Edinburgh and its beautiful architecture, but I am excited about London.

Privacy is a Privilege of Home

Today I really learned how much I like the privacy of my own home. The bathroom privacy, bedroom privacy, just privacy in general, especially when you want to have a personal conversation with someone. This is a high value on my list that I guess I never appreciated before. To be 100% honest, the rest of the afternoon in Edinburgh kind of sucked. After hanging out and napping on the grass, we went out to find Brit a belt, and my stomach kicked in with pains at the worst time ever.

Instantly I had to drop everything and rush back to the hostel because that was the only restroom nearby. Thank God it was close. I knew that coming to Europe would be a problem for me as someone with many stomach issues, but I was hoping to just deal with it. But in the moment when you need a bathroom NOW, it can get a bit complicated.

Everywhere I go, I have to be conscious of absolutely everything I eat and where the closest restroom is at all times. If there isn't a restroom nearby, I get very nervous and stressed, which in turn makes the problem worse. It's a vicious and shitty cycle... pun intended.

It's incredibly embarrassing, especially when traveling with others because I have to be so open and honest with them about it instead of discretely being able to hide my problem. It just sucks. But in the big picture, I guess it's just one of the sucky things in life that I have to deal with, just as everyone else has their own "sucky things" that I might not know of. So it's just another obstacle that I will have to overcome and deal with. Then again, maybe traveling will teach me how to better deal with this issue.

England- London Bridge is Falling Down

English is obviously the recognized language of England. However, if you don't want to look dim, and want to have a chinwag with a mate, you might want to pick up on a few posh words and phrases before you visit so you sound bloody brilliant and can feel truly chuffed.

I was doing well writing in my journal and keeping up every day, but I've started to fall behind. To catch up, our transportation from Edinburgh to London was a horrible experience. No one slept, and it was incredibly uncomfortable. Not to mention, I felt like I was going to puke for about the first hour in. To say the least, we arrived in London a little cranky, which did not make for the best first day.

We wandered around London and saw three big tourist attractions that we wanted to see within the first 15 minutes. Also, our first impression of London was not the best because the people were not very friendly or helpful and the area we were in just did not seem safe. I'm sure a lot of our negative attitude was because we were all exhausted from the overnight bus ride. We tried to pull ourselves out of our slump to just enjoy the day and soak it all in.

Thankfully, it was an amazingly warm welcome when our friends Cat and Andy picked us up from the bus station at the end of the day. A few friendly faces and a lot of warm hospitality lightened my spirits. When we got to their house in Luton, they took us out to one of their local watering holes, where they treated us to drinks and dinner. The beer was cold and much needed, as well as the hot meal. Brit got a burger while Ron and I indulged in the traditional fish and chips. The fish was battered to perfection with a crispy beer batter, and the salty fries just melted in your mouth.

Which I should mention that when you order "chips" here what you get are french fries. If you want actual "chips" you have to order "crisps"

We were also washing everything down with a pint of Stella, which made for the perfect English meal. It was great to see our friends, and for a moment, we felt like we were back at home just enjoying a few drinks in a pub. It was a taste of home comfort that we desperately needed. That night we got a much-needed full night's rest and were ready to start a new day exploring London.

This was also a great budget day to make up for the cost of our ticket to get to London, coming in at just $13.60 spent for the day. So thankful for Cat and Andy's hospitality treating us to dinner and free accommodations!

I was so happy and comfortable to get a good night's sleep in a warm and comfy bed surrounded by a household of friends. However, when I woke up in the morning, that happiness turned to dread. My throat was dry and scratchy, I had the sniffles, I was hot and sticky, and I was popping cough drops like tic-tacs. Of course, I knew this was coming on the day before, but my optimistic side was hoping that just maybe, I was losing my voice, or I was just tired. But sure enough, when I woke up, it had hit me full-on, and I just wanted to curl up in bed with some chicken soup and a Netflix marathon. But unfortunately, you don't always have this luxury when you are traveling, and I knew this was our only full day in London, so I had to make the best of it.

On that note, we headed out to London again for the day. Thanks to some advice from Cat and Andy, today in London was a much better experience than the first day. We invested in an underground rail pass, which took us to all the different parts of London, which meant we could explore quicker. And explore we did. I am pretty sure that we saw every monument or important attraction that there is to see in London.

While wandering around, one of the best things we stumbled upon was the changing of the guards at Buckingham Palace. Of course, we knew we wanted to see the palace, but we arrived at the perfect time! The changing of the guards at Buckingham Palace is basically a ceremony where the guards protecting the palace are relieved by new guards. We bobbed and weaved our way through the crowd until we found a spot near the fountain to witness everything taking place. There was a military band in the background playing traditional march songs as the guards marched in militaristic perfection to exchange duties for the day. It was such a treat to witness this traditional and historic event. Once the ceremony was complete, the crowds dispersed, and we marveled at the beauty of Buckingham Palace without everyone standing in the way.

Although London is known for quite a few landmarks, the one I was most excited to see was the London Bridge. Much to my surprise, what I had thought was called the "London Bridge" was realistically the "Tower Bridge." Most people get these two bridges confused. The Tower Bridge is the most well-known symbol of London. This beautiful medieval-style drawbridge suspension bridge hybrid spans across the river Thames. The Tower Bridge is an icon worldwide and is depicted in multiple movies but is sometimes mistaken as the London bridge. The actual "London Bridge" is much less glamourous crossing over the Thames River. Although less glamourous, The London Bridge was made famous from the song "London Bridge is falling down."

This popular children's rhyme has some truth to it because the real London Bridge crumbled many times, and countless resources were used for reconstruction. Hence the confusion between the well-known song depicting the London Bridge and the beautiful pictures of Tower Bridge.

Most people assume the two bridges are one and the same but, in all reality, very different! It took a while for me to find this out myself.

The iconic Big Ben Clock and the London Eye were not too far from Tower Bridge. We would have loved to catch a ride on the stunning London Eye to see the gorgeous city views, but one time around on the Eye would have cost us more than our entire day's budget. So, we sadly had to remove that experience from our bucket list.

It really is a catch 22 traveling on a budget. Traveling cheaply has allowed for some interesting experiences that we wouldn't have had staying in lavish hotels or traveling first class. But at the same time, simply viewing the world on a budget means we can't fulfill all our bucket list items. Maybe another time, in another world...

At one point in the day, we got lost and stumbled upon a gay pride festival happening in one of the squares. We tried to get closer to the festivities and the huge crowd, but it was too packed. However, there were so many people celebrating that we found ourselves smack dab in the middle of the celebration while we wandered around. It was the best atmosphere ever. Everyone was so kind and happy and just freely themselves.

If you are ever looking for a cultural experience, a gay pride festival is the place to be. People were singing and dancing and just enjoying life. We saw outfits that ranged anywhere from almost entirely naked to fully covered in leather. You couldn't help being happy being among everyone celebrating and enjoying life. If everyone in this world were just more accepting of one another and all shared the same goal of pure life enjoyment, I think it would be a much happier planet.

We also ran into a few street performers, including dancers, real-life statues, hula hoop dancers, and singers. At least my second impression of London was much better than my first. Today the city was much more exciting, fun, and full of culture. Overall, I would come back to London again, but I will have deeper pockets next time.

After our full day exploring the city, the journey back to Cat and Andy's was no walk in the park. I had sent Cat a message when we were leaving to hop on the tube (train), but I didn't realize that I had no internet, so none of my messages were going through. We thought we would be stuck at the train station forever, not having any way to get ahold of our friends. When we arrived in Luton conveniently enough, we found an old-school payphone nearby right outside the station; what are the chances!

I can't tell you the last time I saw a payphone let alone try to use one, and this payphone was in a foreign country. Each of us took a turn trying to figure out how to use this ancient machine. It was grueling. Any bystanders probably looked at us like we were trying to fit a square block into a round hole, but we didn't care. We just wanted to be with our friends again.

After what seemed like forever, Ron spotted a car in the parking lot that looked like Cat's car, and I couldn't believe it! Cat had just assumed that we wouldn't be able to contact her, so she drove up to the train stop. Bless her heart. I have absolutely no idea how things magically worked out for us like this, but they always do. We ended the night watching football with Cat and Andy and saying our goodbyes to Andy that night and Cat in the morning.

That's a Big Boulder

Lesson of the day: Most Europeans we have met so far are terrible at explaining things to "tourists." We are currently making our way out of London and into Paris, but we have been given ZERO information on what to expect. In our minds, we thought we would get the chance on a semi comfy bus to get some sleep while smoothly traveling into France. Instead, we started our bus journey and then boarded a ferry where we were woken up twice during the night to show our passports; Once as we were leaving the port and once when we arrived in France. This left us exhausted and with another sleepless night in the books. At one point, the bus driver came over the loudspeaker and announced something but the only audible words we could make out were "25 minutes". We have no clue what that was about, and we may never know. Moving on.

To recap our England experience, our last day was "just lovely," as the locals would say. We boarded a tour bus to Stonehenge in the afternoon but ran into traffic delays. Instead of taking an hour and a half to get to our destination, it took three and a half hours. At this point, none of us thought that we would make it back in time to catch our bus to Paris, but with a little luck, we caught our ticket out of England because I am currently sitting on our connecting bus. Once we did get to Stonehenge, since it took us so long to get there, we only had an hour and a half to take it all in. It gave us just enough time to rush through the audio guide and learn more about this ancient mystery.

In 1986, Stonehenge was added as a UNESCO World Heritage Site. The prehistoric stone columns are perhaps one of the world's most widely recognized tourist attractions. However, these giant monuments have carried so many secrets buried deep inside for centuries that we may never know the real truth behind these beauties. There are numerous theories as to who could have possibly erected something so massive and the reasons behind its construction. Theories about Stonehenge range anywhere from a burial site, a coronation location, an astronomical tracking system, a temple, or a place of worship to a home for healing and supernatural powers. Enough cremations have been found at the site for Stonehenge to be named as one of the largest cremation cemeteries in Neolithic Britain.

Stonehenge is believed to be over 5,000 years old, but the construction process was thought to take around 1,000 years to complete the entire site that we see today. Scientists have even discovered that several of the massive stones are not native to the area but were transported to their final destination from more than 150 miles away.

Can you imagine?! Most people have difficulty hauling the laundry basket up from the basement to their bedrooms, let alone hauling massive stone structures more than 150 miles without using a semi-truck and crane machinery. But while I'm on a roll, just a few more tidbits of information! Stonehenge is comprised of two types of stone, the larger Sarsen stones that make up the outer circle and the smaller Bluestones that make up the inner horseshoe. Initially, 30 Sarsen stones made up the outer circle of Stonehenge, but only 17 stones remain standing today. Additionally, the Heel stone is a large Sarsen stone that stands outside the main monument and aligns perfectly with the summer and winter solstices.

Each year thousands of tourists flock to the site for the summer and winter solstice, where the sun perfectly rises and sets over the heel stone and magnificently illuminates the center of the stone circle. Whether these visitors are seeking enlightenment from this ancient site or simply want to witness the beauty during this time of year, it is impossible to ignore the connection of the sun's movement and the placement of the stones.

These two times a year are also the only times that the stones are open to the public for foot traffic to enter the circle and lay their hands directly on these wonders. All other times of the year, the stones are roped off from about 10 meters away to prevent the massive foot traffic from ruining the grounds and to keep the integrity of the stones.

While walking around the grounds, you could almost feel the mystical powers, invoking so many questions about its existence that we may never know the truth. It's crazy to think what or who was at this site thousands of years ago, or even the background stories about whose remains will forever be scattered amongst this burial site. Our time at the ruins was short and sweet, but it will forever leave a hint of mystery in the backs of our minds.

However, the mystery of Stonehenge rapidly faded in our minds as we were directed like cattle back into our bus accommodations, and we quickly realized how hungry we were. As travelers on a budget, we were trying to stretch our money as far as we could get it, and since we spent a few days' worth of our budget on the trip to Stonehenge, we had only eaten breakfast for the day and a few sunflower seeds that we had packed in our bags.

Not being able to ignore the loud grumbles coming from my stomach, I was talking to Ron about the extent of my hunger. A woman was sitting a row over from us overheard our conversation. A few minutes later, she leaned over and offered us the other half of her old sandwich, which had been baking in the heat of the bus all day. She said that she had eaten the other half earlier and had stashed this half on the bus for later but was just going to throw it out.

We politely and gratefully accepted the sandwich and then proceeded to eat a soggy old sandwich that had been sitting under a bus seat all day. But let me tell you, that was one of the best damn sandwiches I have ever had. (Ron and I still talk about that simple sandwich to this day.) Be it the fact that the sandwich was free, the sentiment behind the offer, or the fact that we hadn't eaten all day, that was one of the best meals I have ever had. So with a full stomach and happy heart, we find ourselves sitting on a bus that is on a boat, a little past midnight, on our way to France.

We might have splurged a little on the tickets to tour Stonehenge at 44 pounds a person as well as our train and boat tickets to Paris, but thankfully we were able to be frugal the next few days to balance out the budget.

Foreigner in France

Hello- Bonjour
Thank You-Merci.
Please- Si'vous plaît.

Yes- Oui.
Sorry- Excusez-moi.
Do you speak English- Parlez-vous anglais

Have you ever walked into a room and felt like everyone abruptly stops what they are doing and instantly locks eyes with you like you have just infiltrated a secret spy meeting? That's what it felt like to arrive in Paris. As we wandered around the metro station with our big backpacks, not knowing where we were going, I could feel the glaring eyes of judgment staring down at me. Travelers in the station seemed to move quickly and with purpose, while we were just in the way. Everyone around us was speaking French, and all the signs and information were French, so we were completely lost.

The tsunami wave of anxiety hit me hard. I felt the most out of place I have felt thus far on our adventure. Not knowing where we were staying for the night in Paris, we are currently huddled together on the floor of a Starbucks, frantically charging our dying phones, and trying to find a stable enough internet connection to hunt down accommodations for the night.

The good news is that we found somewhere to stay for the night. We will be staying in a small hotel in a little town called Bussy-Saint-Georges, just outside of Paris. The bad news is that finding the hotel was more than my already emotionally and mentally unstable mind could handle for the day. Before we ventured off to find our hotel, we explored Paris while in the city center and found the Arc de Triomphe and the Louvre, which were both checks off my bucket list to see for the first time.

While we walked around the Arc de Triomphe and took pictures, I suddenly felt a sharp jab of pain in my toe that I couldn't ignore. I hobbled my way over to the nearest bench and took my shoe off to investigate. Sure enough, one of my toenails had partially ripped off and caught on my sock. Obviously, if this is ever a problem, you simply take care of it and move on with your day. But there we were, tourist central, in the middle of rush hour with hundreds of cars and people trying to marvel at this Parisian landmark. And there I was, digging toenail clippers and a nail file out of my bag. I slung my foot up on my lap and took care of my problem while Brit practically peed herself laughing that I was doing this right in the middle of a Paris Landmark. What a proud moment. I just hope that no one recognizes me once we ditch our big backpacks and can shower and come back into the city later. At least, that's what I tell myself to make the moment bearable.

So, we trotted around the city with our heavy backpacks on, the fresh smell of baguettes baking in the oven, and our skin baking in the sun. Although it was a great accomplishment to try to take in the city attractions as soon as we arrived, we merely wandered the streets for a few hours taking the obligatory touristy pictures before we decided to start searching for our hotel.

To start, we took the metro tram to the town that we believed our hotel to be in and then proceeded to walk for what seemed like hours before we found our hotel. Just imagine wandering around a strange city where you can't speak the language and where the small road directions on your phone don't make much sense. It was awful. To me, during this long walk with my pack on, wondering if we were ever going to find our hotel was one of my lowest moments so far.

Morale and energy were extremely low from our long day and night of travel, but sure enough, we eventually found our hotel. Unfortunately, since we were technically outside of the city of Paris, the front desk staff at the hotel didn't speak a word of English. This was when the language books we brought came in handy. I read through quickly and found enough information to communicate that we were checking in and needed to get to our room. Thankfully, my broken French was just enough for the woman at the front desk to understand me. Thank you, high school French class. At this point, I was so happy to have a nice place to relax for the night, but that wasn't exactly the case.

I could have handled staying in the small, cramped room if the ceiling hadn't been covered in spiders and their intricately well-established homes made from the finest silk. I have a crazy phobia of spiders, which was the absolute last thing I wanted to see at the end of a long and trying day. Fortunately, Ron meticulously went around killing each one of them for the sake of Brit and me. After that was taken care of, Brit and I enjoyed a random meal of chips, hummus, and avocado, while Ron had his usual ham sandwich and a cookie. We played some music to boost our spirits for the night as we replayed the events of the day. Already the night was looking up, and I had forgotten my worst moment from earlier.

Although we had already had a long day, the night was still young, so we caught the metro back into town and headed for the Eiffel Tower. I can't tell you what a relief it was not to be carrying around my big backpack through the city. Once we got to the Eiffel Tower, it was everything I had dreamed, and the experience turned around the entire day. We ended up buying a bottle of wine from a man walking around the area just toting an arm full of wine, up charging the bottles to sell to only the most touristy of tourists. We talked him down from 35 euros to 7 euros- still paying too much for the wine, but we paid for the convenience. Before we even had a chance to open our bottle of wine, we asked two men to take a picture of us, and then they asked for a unique favor in return.

The two men explained to us that their friend was planning on getting engaged in front of the Eiffel Tower, and they wanted OUR HELP with the proposal! So they handed us each a rose, and when it was time, we were supposed to bring the rose up to the woman and ask her to marry the man. Now in my mind, I had this grandiose romantic scenery played out where one by one, each person would come up and hand the woman a rose and, in a gentle, sweet, and romantic voice, say the phrase, "will you marry him"?

When the time came, in typical drunken fashion, everyone who was supposed to present the woman with a rose ran up simultaneously and started chanting "marry him, marry him", like a rowdy group of sports fans chanting after a big win. Less than enthused about how things were unfolding, we also ended up running up with our roses and just standing in the back of the crowd. I'm sure the man had a more romantic version of this in his head as well, but things don't always go as planned. As far as we could tell, the proposal worked, and the woman said yes (even though she didn't seem that enthused, but who can blame her with a drunken crowd all chanting around her).

After the proposal charade, we enjoyed our time in front of the Eiffel Tower, drinking wine and admiring its beauty. Fun fact- Did you know that when the Eiffel Tower lights up at night, not only does it just light up, but it sparkles!? I'm sure by now most people know this because they have seen it on tv or in the movies before, but for some reason I have been living under a rock and had absolutely no idea this was going to happen. Which just made the experience that much better.

Technically, the lights "blink," but the results are pure magic. At random times, the lights start to alternate and shimmer, creating a sparkling effect that takes your breath away. No joke, I bawled my eyes out when the Eiffel Tower began sparkling. My entire life, I had dreamed of coming to Paris and getting to see the Eiffel Tower and IT SPARKLING? Well, that was just too overtop for my childhood dreams to handle. There I was, sitting on a lawn in Paris, drinking wine, and marveling at the Eiffel Tower under the moon's glow.

The view and the experience were a dream come true for little Cally. The Eiffel Tower was everything and more than I had ever dreamed it to be. Out of all the natural wonders and breathtaking sites we have seen so far, this weird man-made structure surprisingly lived up to the beauty and amazement I had always dreamed of.

A Day in Paris

After our full day of travel and just a trickle of the Paris city nightlife, a full night's sleep felt terrific. We had planned to wake up early to spend the whole day in Paris, but we accidentally slept until 10:30 a.m. Even with a later start to the day, we were able to climb the Eiffel Tower, walk along the river, cross the love bridge, and visit Notre Dame, along with one more unexpected stop. One place that I didn't even know about until now or thought I would ever find myself visiting is the Paris Catacombs.

The Paris Catacombs are an extensive network of underground tunnels over 65 feet below the bustling city. The limestone within these tunnels is the very limestone that built the city's infrastructure long ago. Unfortunately, by the 18th century, Paris' rapid population growth had started to cause an overflow of dead bodies in the cemeteries. To say the least, this caused unsanitary living conditions for those in the city.

To solve this problem, nearly 6 million human remains were dug up and relocated throughout the 200 miles of winding tunnels under the city. The human remains through the catacombs were arranged in an ornate fashion as a kind of ritual during reburial and to attract tourists. And for just 8 euros we knew this was something we couldn't miss.

Stepping down into the Catacombs for the first time was like stepping into your own real-life horror movie. (Which again, I still can't believe I agreed to this because I detest horror movies and being scared). So I slowly climbed down the latter, 65 feet below the city's surface, and suddenly I was face-to-face with human skulls and millions of bones that once belonged to people who walked the city streets above me years ago.

Just the first glance at the Catacomb's entrance is enough to make the strongest person's blood run cold. As the rest of our tour group all arrived at the base of the ladder, everyone became silent. We all just stood there trying to soak up the sheer magnitude of what was right in front of our eyes. Death was all around us. I will never forget the eerie feeling as we navigated the extensive labyrinth of bones that lay beneath the street of Paris. The only way to describe the tunnels was hauntingly beautiful. The amazing art structures formed using human remains were just that, a work of art. But then you would snap back into the realization that these were REAL human remains. Most of the walk through the tunnels was silent, as I'm sure everyone had their own experience and thoughts walking through.

For me, I walked the tunnels just observing and internally questioning everything I saw. Who were these people? What was their life story? Were their souls not at rest because their bodies had been violently dug up and moved to another location? By just stepping foot down here, was I inadvertently pissing off an old spirit? There were so many questions in my mind. When we finally climbed back up to the warm sunlight of the city, I felt like I could breathe again. We were among the living, but now I knew what deep secrets lay deep beneath the streets I was walking on. Even with the creepy tour, the rest of the day was filled with remarkable sights, smells, food, and sounds.

Another checkmark off my bucket list was to climb the Eiffel Tower. What many people don't know is that the top of the Eiffel Tower is not open to the public, but we did get our exercise by climbing the staircase to the second level. Once we reached the top, the panoramic views were more than worth the physical exhaustion of climbing 674 steps. The sweeping views of the city were incredible. Even from almost 400 feet above the ground, I swear you could still smell fresh baked French bread. It was like a dream looking over all of Paris. Seeing Notre Dame, The Louvre, Grand Palais, the Seine, all in one glance. The only downside was it was packed with tourists, so we soaked up every bit that we could before heading back down.

Although the restaurants serving food in the Eiffel Tower were too expensive for our backpacker budget, I had to visit a bathroom in the Eiffel Tower before heading back down to the ground- just for the sheer fact of being able to say I used a bathroom in the Eiffel Tower- weird I know. Funny enough, the bathroom in this steel structure was one of the nicest bathrooms I had been in for a while. The bathroom walls were painted red, and the decor was all golden metal structures that resembled the design of the Eiffel Tower itself. Clearly, the design expert thought of every single detail that went into this bathroom.

Looking from the outside, you would never know there were museums, exhibitions, souvenir shops, and three restaurants inside the Eiffel Tower. This little city inside the steel walls is strategically hidden from the public. On the third floor, there is even a hidden apartment inside. While Gustave Eiffel was designing this iconic tower, he created his own secret apartment. Although Gustave didn't truly live in the apartment, he used it for work, quiet reflection, and to entertain the occasional prestigious guest such as Thomas Edison. Unfortunately, the apartment was not open to the public when we visited, but that has since changed.

I could have spent the entire day just marveling at the Eiffel Tower, but there was much more of Paris for us to see! We spent the rest of the afternoon walking along the Riverwalk, which was filled with vendors and artists galore. There were handmade crafts and paintings, flowers, factory-made trinkets, and antiques alike. Each vendor with a hope and a dream of becoming famous in Paris. Walking along the river was so romantic and peaceful. I can see why this is the city of love.

Speaking of love, one of our visits included a stop at the famous Love Lock Bridge. Of course, we had to share in the tradition of putting a lock on the love bridge, formally known as Pont Des Arts. We all purchased a lock, signed our names on a padlock, attached it to the bridge, and threw the key into the Seine River below. At the time, we thought our locks would forever be attached to the bridge, and we would be a part of the rich history. Come to find out, about a year after our visit, the city of Paris began taking down every single lock on the bridge because the sheer weight of the locks was too heavy for the structure. The metal panels with all the locks attached have since been replaced with street art by local artists. Even now, knowing our locks were removed, I still loved the experience while we were there. The remaining evening included aimlessly wandering around Paris and taking in every little bit that we could.

After taking the train back to our hotel, we found a little restaurant where we all ordered Greek kebab sandwiches to go. It was so nice being able to eat a hot meal. Most of the time for food, we just bought a fresh loaf of French bread to munch on throughout the day, which I wasn't angry about.

That night in Paris, I should also mention that we made a core memory that I know I will keep with me no matter how old and gray I get. After wandering the streets for hours and taking in maybe one too many glasses of wine, we had our own little adventure on the way back to the train station. As we were crossing one of the many bridges that spanned across the Seine, Brit and I could no longer hold in the happiness and elation bursting from every corner of our souls. I'm not sure who started it, but suddenly, we were both running and skipping across this bridge under the stars, loudly humming the tune to Indiana Jones. You know the song... dum dum dum dum.... dum dum dum.....

If you grew up anywhere around my generation, this sound was the introduction to any good adventure. Just hearing those first few beats would make your heart skip a beat with anticipation. I think there is even a very short video clip that Ron recorded of this moment floating around one of our computers somewhere. But there we were, on the dark streets of Paris, under the stars, running and skipping to the tune of our own adventure. Something I will never forget.

Changing Plans

Well, we are currently on the wrong metro headed outside of the zones covered on our train passes as two men entertain us by singing Spanish songs but in a French Dialect. What a morning. We woke up this morning planning to stay one more night in our hotel, only to find out that the hotel is now fully booked, and we are being kicked out. So much for our plans. So instead, we hopped on a train that we thought was headed into the city, but instead, it is going in the opposite direction, and we are just hoping that it turns around eventually. However, during our busy morning, we were able to find a campground around the Paris area to stay at for the night. So at least we know we have a place to stay. More updates to come!

Thankfully, we got the train situation figured out, and eventually, we checked into our campsite. Funny enough, the campground is still technically inside Paris, but it's on the outskirts and quite a walk from where the train dropped us off. The walk to the campground was yet again very long, tiring, and hot, carrying our heavy packs.

I would have to say that out of the few campsites we have stayed at so far, European "camping" is nothing like American camping. As a child, the fond memories I have of camping include being nestled in between a group of pine trees with a wooden picnic table and stone firepit. What we have experienced so far in Europe, is setting our tents up on a bare gravel lot, no fire pit or tables and barely any trees in sight. Not to mention we haven't seen one other tent camper yet. Sleeping on top of gravel isn't nearly as comfortable as a nice patch of grass, but what can you do?

By the time we made it to our campsite, we had bought a few beers at the camp store to revive our spirits and decided to stay two nights instead of one so that we could have time to plan out our next travel moves. We had planned to have a nice relaxing night at the campground and get some good sleep, but the universe had other plans for us. While we were in the game room playing Uno, a man from New Zealand came in and invited us back outside for a drink with his friends. And so began the wild night of drinking in Paris.

Catching Up

Currently, we are sitting on a train headed to what will eventually be Pamplona, Spain. But before I get started today, I have the previous day's events to catch up on. Last time I left off, it was the night of the 14th day of our travels, and we had just met new friends from New Zealand and England. What a night.

We started the night just sitting and drinking and talking, which turned into meeting more people and playing a game of "grab the box". One of our new friends from New Zealand taught us this game where a beer box is placed on the ground in front of you, and you have to pick it up with your mouth without using your hands. You are also not allowed to let any other body part other than your feet touch the ground to help you balance. Every time someone picks up the box, they have to rip off a piece of the box, large or small. Over time, the box gets smaller and closer to the ground making it much harder to pick up unless you are incredibly flexible. Add copious amounts of alcohol, and you call that a good night.

As the night went on, more people joined in on our drinking shenanigans, none of whom I can remember their names. The only names I can remember were Simon, Andrew, and Rachel, the original three that we met who got the night started. We drank more beers than I can even remember, made new friends, and played drinking games throughout the night. The night was filled with loads of laughs and great times. Unfortunately, the lack of sleep and absurd amounts of alcohol took a toll on us the next day.

Even so, we woke up early the following day to head into town and figure out our train reservations to Pamplona. We arrived at the station and were directed to about six different lines until we finally found the correct one to get our tickets. The line looked innocent enough to start, and we thought we would be out of there in no time, but not one person moved during the first hour.

Then one hour turned into two, two turned into three, and I believe three turned into four. We spent this time quietly sitting on the floor, brushing up on some Spanish, running back and forth to the bathroom, and meeting fellow travelers in line. Finally, after waiting forever, we arrived at the front of the line to purchase our tickets. Brittney said it best, "That was the longest-short line I have ever been in." And that it was.

We told the woman at the booth that we needed to get to Pamplona for as cheap as possible. Come to find out, there were no more seats available on the train besides first-class seats. However, since that was our only option, we obliged because we needed to make it to Pamplona by a certain date. In all reality though, the tickets only cost us 48 Euros, which isn't too bad for first class. Once that ordeal was through, we went back to the campsite for the night to do more travel research.

Well, Ron and Brit did more research while I napped for about three hours. I'm not sure if it was because I was hungover or still sick, but I just had no energy left. Once I woke up, I met them in the game room and we all hung out with Rachel, who we had met the day before until it was time for bed. I loved talking to Rachel because even though she was younger than us, she was extremely cultured and had such a knowledge of world politics and policies and even American history. With all the people we have met so far, I am amazed at how much knowledge they have of their own governments and the American government. From my personal perspective, it seems like the European school system is much more comprehensive and more in-depth than what I learned in the American school system. But then again, school doesn't teach you everything you need to know, and you will never grow unless you take the initiative to push yourself beyond the primary education you received. To be honest, at times, I felt like an uneducated American in comparison to Rachel. But that just gives me more motivation to learn and grow!

Anyways, that night we headed to bed early, around ten or eleven, because our alarms were going off at three, to get ready in time for our train to Pamplona. The train's departure was scheduled for 7:15 a.m., but we had to get up so early to walk to the train station because buses don't go out that early in the morning. The long walk wasn't bad at all compared to the same hike to the campground we had made the other day when checking in. Which leads me to where I am now, sitting on a train in first class, on my way to Pamplona, Spain. First-class on a train was a completely different experience than the cramped spaces we had been used to. There was a ton of space, and the seats were most definitely superior on the comfort level. I could get used to this.

Overall, I absolutely loved Paris. I am sad that we didn't have much time in this romantic city, and we did not have the budget to experience the city the way we wanted to. This is definitely a place I would love to visit one day when I have saved up enough money to treat myself-true Parisian style. I would splurge on French food and wine with all my meals instead of relying on a fresh loaf of French bread every day for food. (Even though the bread is fantastic). I would also take the time and visit inside the Louvre or Musée D'Orsay along with a few others. I do understand, however that being able to do this trip is all about trade-offs. Yes, we are seeing an incredible number of places all in one summer, yet we do not get to indulge like we would like to. But that's okay. It just gives me more ideas for where we would like to return to visit in the future.

Back to Paris. The people are semi-friendly (although Ireland still wins the friendly card), and the language barrier was not as bad as I thought. I would have to admit that Ron's language phrasebook was extremely helpful. Although most people in Paris understood and spoke enough English for us to get by, it was still fascinating learning more of the language and at least attempting to converse in French with other people before we switched over to English. I just hope that Spain will be just as simple, but I'm not sure at this point. We are currently on the train headed into Spain, and the conductor is talking so fast in Spanish that we don't have the slightest clue what he is trying to say. If you have ever seen the movie Billy Madison when he is learning Spanish, and with a blank stare he tells the Spanish-speaking man to slow down: That is my life right now. I just hope that all Spaniards do not speak this fast.

We were all able to stay either on or under budget each day in Paris by surviving on croissants, French bread, and fresh baked patisseries. Although we never got to enjoy a full French cuisine meal, the tradeoff of spending each night in front of the Eiffel Tower was worth it.

Two Weeks In

Seeing as how we have gone past the two weeks mark in the trip, I figured I would just do a general checkup on everything. Since I got sick in London, I've come a long way and am much better but still dealing with some residual coughing and sneezing. By now, I've just gotten used to carrying around extra toilet paper and tissue and stocking up on it every time I use the bathroom. It's a pain, but at least it is more tolerable now, and I just try to ignore it.

Morale is high at the moment with everyone, and I am excited to explore another country. So far, I have had some very high and some very low moments during the trip, but that was to be expected. I knew that by no stretch of the imagination was this trip going to be a vacation. Traveling this way has already pushed my wits farther than I had imagined. I know the whole idea of backpacking Europe and seeing the sights is wildly romanticized by the people who have done it before, but they don't tell you about the "in-between" time.

The travel time, the walk time, the exhaustion. The countless hours spent searching to make sure you have a roof over your head the next night. I think that I should start adding up all the hours we have spent on planes, trains, buses, metros, etc., let alone planning our next move, and it would equal up to more time than working a full-time job every day. With as much free time as we have had while traveling, it also includes a lot of waiting in endless lines, travel time from one destination to the next, and a ton of research. Don't get me wrong, of course, it takes time to get to the places you are going. I guess I just never realized how much time.

This makes me incredibly thankful that while we are staying in Pamplona, we are staying at one hotel for three nights. It will be a breath of fresh air to be able to settle in one place for a few days. Actually, it seems like a mini vacation in the middle of the trip because for those three days, we know where we will be sleeping, know our things are safe, and won't have to lug around our big bags.

Which is another thing, the days that we arrive in a new city and have to walk around all day with our big bags absolutely sucks. I think that when morale gets the lowest is on those days because my feet are sore, my back is sore, my bag is heavy, and to be honest, to carry that big bag around while doing all the tourist attractions just kind of sucks. But that is part of the adventure and just something that I am getting used to. If anything, I should have the legs of a track star by the time we get home. We're still at the beginning of this trip and it's been such an amazing journey so far that I can't wait to see what will come next.

Fiestas and Siestas in Spain

Hello- Hola
Thank You-Gracias.
Please- Por favor
Yes- Sí.
Sorry- Lo siento
Do you speak English- Hablas inglés

Before I get into our time spent in Pamplona, I should mention the whole reason we are in this city: the Fiesta De San Fermin!

*Also known as the San Fermin Festival and more popularly the Running of the Bulls.

Fiesta De San Fermin is a festival held every year to honor San Fermin, who was the patron saint of Pamplona. Some speculate that this festival dates back to the 11th century. Traditionally, the festival runs from July 6th to July 14th. Although multiple events with religious meaning take place during the festival, it is mainly known worldwide for the running of the bulls event.

The origin of the running of the bulls is a long time-honored tradition of transporting the bulls from the fields to the bullfighting ring. Before this tradition evolved into a worldwide known event, local kids would run alongside the bulls to herd them into the fighting ring. Bullfighting in Spain is a time-honored cultural event. The fights are regarded as a gladiator-type sporting event with deep cultural roots. Although bullfighting has taken place in Spain as far back as anyone can remember, some speculate that Spain adopted the bullfighting tradition from Ancient Greek and Rome, where they would fight or "sacrifice" the sacred bull. Personally, this tradition is a little too gruesome for my fragile heart, but I am still interested in learning more and experiencing the customs of another culture.

We arrived in Pamplona safely yesterday to discover that although some people know bits and pieces of English here, others do not at all. So far it has been mostly us trying to navigate the Spanish language to get anything done. Thankfully when we arrived at the train station, I was able to form a coherent enough sentence in Spanish to get us a cab to our hotel. Once we arrived at the hotel, we had to play "sneak Cally past the front desk" because we booked a room for two people instead of three because the third person was an extra charge. Because of the festival, all accommodations were pretty pricey and just for two people, the hotel clocked in around 25 euros per person per night. We did NOT want to pay the extra 25 euros a night for a third person, so I just hung around outside and wandered into the hotel with confidence afterward like I was already a guest there and knew where I was going.

Even though the hotel was busy with guests, I'm sure they noticed me sneaking inside. Either way, the room is worth the risk. We have plenty of space in our private bathroom, the beds are soft and warm, we have a TV for some in-room entertainment and even a nice skylight to let the summer sun in. This is by far, the cleanest room we have stayed in for a while. That is, besides the few baby spiders running around. Other than that, we are living in style now!

After checking in, we explored the little town that we were staying in, which is just outside of Pamplona, and we decided to have dinner at our hotel restaurant. We all indulged in some comfort food and ordered burgers. Oddly enough, the burgers tasted nothing like an American hamburger but were still mouthwatering. I couldn't even begin to describe what seasonings were on the burger, but it was delicious. Maybe it was because all of us were really hungry, or maybe they were just really good hamburgers, who knows. After dinner, we decided to settle in early to rest for the next day.

The next morning, we caught a bus and headed into the heart of Pamplona. We then navigated toward the train station to buy tickets for Madrid a few days from now. I was pleasantly surprised with the ticket buying experience. We only waited in line for about 10 minutes versus the four hours we had to wait in Paris. Although the man in the booth did not speak English, we managed to get tickets to Madrid reserved for only six euros each. Good start to the day.

From there, we explored Pamplona and bought our San Fermin festival outfits, which included white pants, a white t-shirt, a red bandana, and a red scarf. At only 11.50 Euros, it was worth the money to get the official festival outfit. However, I was not impressed with the all-white outfit. It was anything but flattering on me, but even so, we had to look the part!

We also visited the local grocery for lunch and stocked up on alcohol for the festival. A few friendly locals that we talked to let us know that it is legal to have alcohol on the street in Pamplona. Furthermore, it is much cheaper to buy your own alcohol for the festival, rather than going into the bars all day and spending money. We took that advice and ran with it.

In the fashion of being truly gluttonous, we stocked up on three massive containers of sangria and multiple cases of beer. We may have gone a bit overboard, but the alcohol was cheap, and we were in Pamplona to party! Overall, today was a good day. So far, people in Pamplona are very kind and friendly, and we are extremely excited for the festivities to start. Cheers to the beginning of a great festival!

Pamplona

Here we are, on our way out of Pamplona, and I find myself trying to remember all the events that have occurred over the past few very drunken and hazy days. To start, I will just sum up the festivities. The last few days have been filled with bulls, drinking, partying, new friends, money spending, and lots and lots of public urination (Thankfully we only had to partake in this once- story to follow). Overall, the San Fermin Festival is truly hard to put into words and unlike anything I have ever experienced before. I have heard rumors of all the craziness that happens at the festival but experiencing it firsthand was completely different.

The festival's opening ceremony was far beyond crazy, with more people than you can imagine from every corner of the globe coming together, singing, dancing, and partying in different languages, all hugging one another and just enjoying life. I'm not sure what was louder, the music being played, or all the people screaming. As the countdown to noon began, which is the official start of the festival, things got even crazier. Almost everyone we saw had either a box of sangria in their hand or a cerveza and was wildly dancing around flinging liquid into the air and onto everyone in the nearby vicinity. Our new white Pamplona outfits only lasted about five minutes once we got to the city square.

But of course, we followed suit with the craziness because we wanted to be a part of this "tradition" as well. The seasoned veterans who had clearly done this before had squirt guns loaded full of sangria in one hand and a bag of flour in the other as if being covered in wine and beer wasn't enough.

Just when I thought we had reached the height of craziness, a firework shot into the sky at exactly noon, officially signaling the beginning of the festival. The crowd erupted into the loudest screams I have ever heard, and standing at just 5'1, I was overwhelmed in the crowd of people and felt like I was drowning in a mosh pit.

Trying to move or walk around once you are among the people and the party? – Forget about it. At one point, while we were attempting to walk through the crowd, I honestly thought that I was going to get squashed to death. Since I am so short, most people's shoulders were right at my face level, so I was constantly getting hit in the face with random shoulders and hearing apologies in different languages.

At one point, my body moved about 15 feet without my feet ever touching the ground. Everyone was so squished together, and the crowd was moving. So where the crowd went, I went also. I was so squished against the people around me that my feet lifted off the ground and the crowd's movement was just literally carrying me. Even being lifted off the ground, I was still a solid foot shorter than everyone else, and most of my view consisted of other people's body parts.

Thankfully, that chaos only lasted until the crowd slowly moved outside the city square. From there, the crowd dispersed onto all the side city streets, and half of the population started funneling into the bars. The rest of our first day at the festival was filled with copious amounts of drinking, a small nap in the park, and a few very interesting bathroom experiences.

Our first bad bathroom experience at the festival was when Brit and I waited in line for about half an hour for a one-person bathroom that I had used earlier and was very spacious inside. While waiting, there was a van to the left of us situated about a few feet from a fenced-off area. I think I witnessed more episodes of public urination between that van and fence than I will see combined for the rest of my life. It didn't matter, man, woman, or child, everyone was dropping their pants and their dignity to relieve their bladders and show off their privates in public.

After waiting for an open bathroom for over an hour, I understood why. Now, I have survived bad bathroom experiences before (like the Porta-potties at Bonnaroo Music Festival on a 105-degree day) but stepping into that "public restroom" was unworldly. Using the actual toilet wasn't even an option because it had human excrement piled up higher than the toilet itself. The rest of the stall was an inch deep of urine and toilet paper strewn all over the place. Unfortunately, like the people before us, we had no option but to hoover in the corner of the room and relieve ourselves. Not one of my proudest moments, but when you have no choice, you do what you have to do. This brings me to my second unpleasant bathroom experience; Actual public urination.

As the day went on and the drinks were flowing, obviously, the need to use the restroom came again. With our previous bathroom experience in mind and no bathroom in sight, the three of us opted for a little secluded alleyway and wall, where there was a nice semi-private wall blocking two sides while the other two people blocked the rest. Yes it happened, and yes, I am writing about it because it was a life experience and good or bad, it happened. For some crazy reason, it seems like the city just gives up on hygienic restroom options during the festival and everyone there knows it and is prepared to bear it all to the world.

Come to find out the next morning, the city workers were completely unfazed by the destruction and human fluids around them and simply went about cleaning up the streets. City employees were walking all of the streets, spraying them down with hoses and rinsing away the disgust from the night before to prepare for another day of festivities.

Anyways, that first crazy night ended with going back to the hotel and attempting to shower off all the wine and flour, and beer. One aftereffect of the copious amounts of sangria in my hair was that my hair felt like

I had used an entire can of hairspray on it before going out. Between all the fluids and flour in my hair and the dirt from my afternoon nap on the ground and then baking all day my hair could have withstood gale-force winds at this point.

I'm not sure what time we got back to our hotel or what time we ended up going to sleep, but our alarms went off at 4:00 am that following day so that we could head into town for the Running of the Bulls. We hopped on a bus, and when we arrived in town, the streets were still lined with a good amount of people that had not stopped partying from the night before. That is, along with a few random people passed out on the streets and in store doorways.

We made our way through the city and said our goodbyes to Ron as he left to get ready to run with the bulls, and Brit and I tried to find a decent spot to watch. We had decided early on that we did not want to participate in the run. Something about being chased through the streets by bulls in an attempt to not get injured just didn't appeal to Brit and me.

The whole experience of watching the bulls run was so different than what I had imagined. Everything you read and see about running with the bulls romanticizes the event but experiencing it in person isn't all sunshine. First, to clear the streets of people before the bulls run, the police essentially form a human wall and begin walking and physically pushing people to the outside barriers until the roads are clear. While doing this, there is a double fenced area where people are cleared away so that police, paramedics, and photographers can occupy the space between the two gates. Once the run starts, one gunshot signals the runners at the bottom of a hill to begin running to get a head start on the bulls. The second gunshot signifies the release of the first 6 bulls, and on the third gunshot they release 6 more bulls.

My exact location for watching this event was directly under a fence post between a stranger's legs. Therefore, I couldn't see all the details of the run, but what I did witness included mass chaos, screaming, and pure fear on bystanders' and runners' faces. The first bunch of bulls came running through rather quickly, and the second round of bulls were calmer and slow-paced as the runners ran alongside the trotting bulls.

Overall, the bulls didn't seem provoked, mad, or in any way wanting to hurt the people, yet people were their own worst enemy with getting hurt trying to taunt the bulls or slap them on their asses as they ran by. After the bulls had passed, Brit and I witnessed a paramedic taking in a runner. The man was dragged from the street into the double fence barrier where the paramedics were.

We weren't sure if the man was injured by the bulls or by other people, but when the paramedics brought the man over on a stretcher, the look of shock, agony, and disbelief on his face is something that I don't think I will ever forget. We still don't know what happened to that poor gentleman, but I can only hope that his injuries were something that he could recover from.

I think most people just see the sport or fun of it but seeing the havoc and pain that this event could cause was definitely gut-wrenching. Once the chaos died down, Brit and I made our way to the location we had picked out ahead of time, where Ron would meet us. Since I couldn't see Ron during the race, my heart was pounding, waiting for him to show up, not knowing if he was injured or not. After an hour or so of waiting for Ron to show up, I was just beside myself, worrying that something terrible may have happened. Eventually, we found our way back to one another, and he informed us that the run had ended inside the actual bullfighting arena, where he got trapped with the crowd. Come to find out, when the run ends, everyone and every bull ends up in the arena, where most people continue to taunt the bulls running after them and swatting them on the back and then running away to avoid being gored. Not my idea of a fun time.

Then, Ron proceeded to tell us all about his experience Running with the Bulls, which was much different than ours. The only way I know how to truly capture Ron's experience is with his own words. Enter the Ron story…

> "*We went out at like 4 or 5 in the morning to the spot in the street, where there are several spots where you can start from. You can start from the bottom of the hill, where the bulls are right behind you, and you have to run up this extremely*

76

steep, big hill. Or you can start at the top of the hill and run straight to what they call dead man's corner, because it's a 90 degree turn, or a little more than 90 degree turn, where all of the bulls slide and pin you there. And then, you run down this alleyway where it's all buildings on the side so there's no fence to jump over worst case scenario. And you can start in the alleyway, but the alleyway is like half way through and so I didn't want to start at the bottom of the hill and waste all my energy by the time I got to the top and be too dead tired for the bulls. And I didn't want to start in the alleyway because it seemed too cheap like 'ah you start running and it's over before you start because you started halfway through, and you didn't even get to see the bulls.' So I started at the top of the hill. We got there at like 4 or 5 am and I'm jumping around trying to hype myself up and the police come, and they start pushing everyone into these little corrals where they close a gate and then they open it up and that's where you are supposed to run. And the police are pissed off because they have been dealing with drunk people all night and they don't want anything to do with more drunk people like me who is probably still drunk asking where we are going or what's going on not in their native language. And they are just pushing you, and they heard us and pack us all in and they close the gate, and I didn't make it inside that gate so they kept pushing us down and I thought 'oh ok they must be full so they are going to push us down toward the middle start point, whatever its better than nothing.' But they opened another gate and just pushed us out and shut it and that was it. The gate they opened was to kick us out because they were full. So me and this kid were looking at each other, I think he was from England or something like that, and we were like 'what do we do now, we just got kicked out' and we see some people down the alleyway sprinting off another way and without even knowing where they were going we were like 'okay' and we just sprinted down the alleyway and followed the crowd that was running. And eventually we make this big loop *around the city and then when we turned a corner there were a bunch of police just guarding this fence like this (insert Ron waving his hands back and forth like a soccer player guarding a net) like and an old video game. And people are jumping over the fence and under the fence and the cops are trying to catch them. So of course while still in sprinting motion, we decide to follow the crowd. So we jump over the fence and we both end up making it. The cops didn't get us. And we land and we turn around and once you are over, the cops don't even care about you and I thought it was so strange that oh once you are over they just don't care. And so we jump around and we are high-fiving because we are still in the race. And then we heard something snort and we turn around and the bulls are right there. We are at the bottom of the f*cking hill. They are trying to stop people from going in because it's dangerous and its stupid, and it makes sense, so at that time, I just though 'okay, I'm starting from the bottom of the hill' and decided to keep going. So now I'm jumping up and down again trying to hype myself up and the first rocket goes off, so I start sprinting up the hill desperately trying to make it before the bulls come. And then a second rocket goes off which means the bulls have been released, because I think it's like 30 seconds to a minute or something before the bulls get released and I make it to the top of the hill and I start making the turn and I'm about half way to dead man's corner and I get slammed to the wall by people trying to jump and get out of the way and it's me and one other person that watch all of the bulls go rushing past us as we are pinned up against the fence. And once the bulls go running by, people start trailing off and sprinting towards the bulls and me and this kid from England are doing this like half ass sprint and joking and laughing and high fiving and every one there and all of the people in Spain who live there are yelling 'GO, GO, GO, RUN, RUN' and we are like why? The bulls ran, and we aren't in a hurry to get to the stadium - it will be there. So we are just shooting the shit and doing this half* *ass walk/ jog and then uh we start I don't know, maybe 10-20 steps into the alleyway where there is no fence to jump over and we hear a third rocket. And everyone is still screaming 'RUN, RUN, RUN' and both of us look at each other and said, 'what's the third rocket for?' Because we knew the first rocket meant run and the second rocket meant the bulls were coming and then we kind of bursted off and just thought maybe that signaled the end. So we are maybe halfway down the alleyway and then you start hearing sounds and the ground vibrate and we turned around and see all of the bulls sliding into dead man's corner and hit the wall. And we were like F*CK" and we start sprinting as fast as we can to get to the arena where it finishes and we make it to the arena and we get in, and its breathtaking. You know big arena, and people are everywhere, and they are all just kind of standing around talking. And as I get into the arena I stopped running and just more of a slow walk just walking around kind of dumb founded and amazed and then I don't know how long I was doing that before I felt the ground shake again, turn around and all the bulls are sliding around the corner again. !@*$@! !#$*&!@*

And now I'm the one sprinting to the corner pushing people out of the way. And now I'm the one who is at the outer edge as I watch all of the bulls run across right in front of me and that was super scary and exciting. So we get done with that and I climb the fence at the end and I sit in the bleachers for the stadium and I'm looking for Cally and Brittany and you know I don't see anything but we agreed to meet at the end and I still don't see anything. So I'm sitting there waiting and they bring out like a little baby bull and the horns are all taped off like this (Ron making a wide gesture with his arms above his head like a "Y") and people are going and trying to touch the bull and the bull would move its head and just grab people's legs and like do a back flip and try to run the people over and the whole time there is a guy over the speaker phone saying 'don't touch the bull, don't touch the bull'. So of course, I jumped back over the fence and had to run and slap the ass of the bull and sprint the other way before it got me because you know I'm young and not thinking and clearly had been drinking. And so I sprint back and hop over the fence and I'm back in the bleachers and I thought 'oh maybe Cal and Brit are outside so I wait outside the arena for a while and they are still not there, so I'm walking back and forth all the way down the path and I finally see them. And we did the same thing. They were at the end but couldn't find me and we were both just going back and forth missing one another. But eventually we found each other- and that was running with the bulls"

Clearly a very different experience from Brit and me. At the time I didn't know what the third rocket was for either and I had no idea they released two sets of bulls, but I didn't even think of Ron running and not knowing he was going to have to dodge bulls not once but twice! I'm glad I decided to just watch.

Once Ron rejoined our group, we headed inside the arena to take our seats for the bull fight. Now, for most experiences in life, I tend to look through rose-colored glasses, but for this experience, I will not be sugar-coating anything. When we first got into the arena, I was so excited because we had great seats on the second level, and we could see everything. But once the fights started, it was nothing I could have ever prepared myself for. Call me an uneducated American, but I always saw bullfights as a fun-filled event where a matador simply whisks a red cape back and forth, trying not to get gored by the bull.

What I never realized was not only was the bull killed at the end of the fight, but it's not even a fight at all. This was a public execution of an animal. The "fight" starts off with one Matador taunting the bull. Then another Matador steps in with two spears, and as the bull runs past him, he tries to avoid being hit at the same time, aims to plunge his spears into the bull's back. This takes place over and over again until eventually, a Matador comes out with an even longer and sharper spear to take the bull down for the last time. If that wasn't bad enough, the bull was injured before entering the arena. When it first came in, you could see the blood dripping down its back. This was no fight and nothing I would ever consider entertainment.

Sitting there silently in the arena watching these fights, all I could do was sip my beer in shock and look away while trying to justify or even understand why in the world would they ever let a thing as inhumane as this happen? This was one of the hardest things I have ever witnessed, and I just sat there with tears streaming down my face from shock and disbelief. I was not the only one who felt this way. During the fights, I could hear multiple conversations from those around us, also confused and disgusted by this "cultural event" display.

Interesting Fact: To this day, multiple animal welfare organizations are still struggling to end bullfighting due to its violent and cruel nature.

After staying in the area for a few "fights," we decided to take off early and drown our heartaches in beer and sangria. Thankfully, so much alcohol was consumed that night that we were able to forget the terrible images from inside the arena. The rest of the night, we spent dancing and partying the night away and meeting people from all over the world. Overall, Pamplona was a great place to meet people and party but ended up being a very humbling cultural experience as well.

Madrid

Another few days have passed, and I have been picking up my pen and notebook less and less to record every significant aspect of the day. Either that or I have been napping during my free time, trying to detox from all the alcohol I consumed in Pamplona.

Either way, currently, I am sitting on a train ready to leave the city of Madrid, Spain. I hate saying this, but I wasn't at all impressed with Madrid. Of course, when we first arrived, I was excited as always to be in a new location, but in reality, I didn't have a big list of things I wanted to see in the city.

Our first priority when we reached Madrid was to find our hostel, which was pretty easy to find. Our room was tiny but cozy, with 4 beds, a small balcony, and a bathroom. The three days we spent in Madrid were filled with a walking tour of the city, a visit to an Egyptian temple, and spending time at an indoor tropical paradise located inside a train station.

I will start with the walking tour. If you haven't caught on yet, most cities we have been to in Europe offer free walking tours where trained guides will take you on a walk throughout the city and explain the city's history, cultural significance of buildings, major attractions, and all that jazz. Although the tours are "free," the guides do ask for tips at the end of the tours, but it is well worth the money, and all the guides we have had are well deserving of the tips!

However, our walking guide for Madrid was a bit more special. First off, our guide was a striking resemblance to one of my friends from back home. Second, her wittiness, charisma, and deep-rooted knowledge of the city's history made for an unforgettable city tour.

One of my favorite pieces of information from the tour was the explanation of the city's unique coat of arms. If you have ever seen the coat of arms for Madrid, you would know that it is a unique picture of a bear reaching up into a strawberry or madroño tree, surrounded by seven stars and topped with a crown.

Legend has it that Madrid's original name was something between "Ursaria" and "Ursa Major." This name translates from Latin to mean "land of the bears" or "The great bear." The name suited the city long ago because, at the time, its many forests were filled with bears, along with strawberry trees. Ironically, today neither bears nor madroño trees are found in Madrid as the city grew over the years.

If the words "Ursa Major" sound familiar to you, that's because it is part of the constellation name, more commonly known as the big dipper. To this day, I still think of Madrid every time I look up at the stars and see the big dipper. Walking tours have honestly been some of my favorite parts of each city. Just getting to explore and walk around while learning all about the cultural significance of a place.

Speaking of cultural significance, Madrid did have two of the most unique tourist attractions that I have seen so far.

1. An Egyptian Temple in the middle of a city.

2. A botanical garden in the middle of a train station.

Both attractions are entirely out of place but nonetheless spectacular. We decided to visit the temple one night right at sunset because we had heard rumors of how spectacular the views were from the light cast during golden hour. The temple was named Temple of Debod, and it was located near the Plaza de España. From what I remember of the story, Madrid volunteered to take the temple to preserve and save it. In 1960, a dam was being constructed near the Nile in Egypt because many archeological sites were in danger of being ruined. Spain provided help to Egypt to keep many of the archeological UNESCO heritage sites from perishing, and in 1968 as a sign of gratitude, Egypt donated the Temple of Debod to Spain. The temple was disassembled in Egypt and then reconstructed in Madrid in 1972. Visiting Egypt has always been high on my travel bucket list but being able to see an authentic Egyptian Temple right in the heart of Spain made my heart incredibly happy.

The temple seemed to be a popular spot as well, where a lot of people were hanging out on the grass, having picnics, just enjoying the ambiance. The strong stone pieces and reflection of the temple in the pool were quite mesmerizing. To top it off, we were there at the perfect time of day while the sun was setting on the horizon and casting a gorgeous glow over the temple. We may not have been in Egypt, but we did get to witness a sunset over the historic stones of an Egyptian temple. Check.

On the other side of unique experiences, the tropical paradise inside the train station was also a first-time experience. In 1892, a part of the Atocha train station in Madrid was destroyed by a fire. As reconstruction took place, the original part of the train station was taken out of commission and turned into a spot for cafes, shops, and a botanical garden. The magnificent skylights that sprawled across the top of the train station were the perfect excuse to use the space for a greenhouse. Not only are there over 700 plants and 250 species in the garden, but this train station is also home to various species of fish and turtles.

This was a little slice of outdoor heaven, right inside a train station. The massive palm trees, lush vegetation, and turtles splashing around in the ponds made you feel like you were in the middle of an outside garden. Out of all the train stations we have been to so far, this one takes the cake.

Speaking of cake, as far as the food went in Madrid, we did get to eat out at a restaurant once, but other than that, it was just grocery store food. The second night in town, we found a quaint little spot outside to get some food where Ron and I ordered some kind of pork burrito, and Brit ordered a "tortilla." Brit was less than enthused at the egg omelet presented on her plate when our food arrived. Apparently, when you order a tortilla in Spain, it is far different from the Mexican tortilla. In Spain, tortilla translates to "small cake," otherwise known in Spain as a Spanish Omelet. Lesson learned.

The food was good, but the portions were far too small. At least too small compared to the massive portions that we, unfortunately, are used to in the states. I know that many people love the city of Madrid, but honestly, besides the Egyptian temple, I wasn't impressed. Maybe again, it was because we didn't have the money to experience it like we wanted to, but to me, it was just another city.

The last night we spent in Madrid, we got a new roommate who was from Japan. There was a significant language barrier, but from what we understood, he had already been traveling for six months now and was tired and hungry. He mentioned that he was headed to LA and New York after he was done with Europe. It was crazy that he'd been traveling for six months now, and just before we met him, Ron and I talked about being tired after 21 days of travel. As Ron said, the most challenging part is not having any alone time or any time to decompress. I mean, honestly, the things that we have seen and done in the last month are more than some people get to experience in a lifetime, and I don't think my brain has fully processed that yet. Not to mention that we all have zero alone time between traveling together, staying in hostels, and constantly being surrounded by other people. At this point, I feel like I need a day just locked in a quiet room by myself where I can binge-watch Netflix movies and let my brain just rest. But instead, we are always on the go or constantly researching and planning for our next stop. We'll see how these feelings develop as the trip goes on.

One last note about Madrid is the city must not have any noise ordinances because, on our last night, people were partying outside so loud that they could have competed with the parties during Running of the Bulls. Every night we were there, the streets were lined with people celebrating and drinking all night long. Usually, this went on until about 4:00 am when people finally calmed down. That is for except the last night. No joke, in the wee hours of the morning, there was a full-on marching band that had come down the street right outside of our hostel window. I am assuming the marching bands were in celebration of the football game victory, but it is beyond my wildest imagination why the marching band needed to parade in the streets at 3:00 am. There was the drumline, trumpets, trombones, and screaming fans all acting like it was the middle of the day. If we hadn't just been country hoping for the last month nonstop, we probably would have crawled out of bed and joined in the celebration, but every bone in my body was tired, and my brain was exhausted beyond repair. But we shall push on- Onto Barcelona!

Madrid was a welcomed relief to our budget. The hostel was only 13.65 Euros a night, and between that, the food, and the walking tour, I was able to make up for the money I spent on Booze and food in Pamplona!

Day 25

I think it is becoming more of a theme for me to write about each city experience as we are on our way out of the city instead of sitting down every night to write. Although I know I am losing precious specific memories from my days, I feel like I can better absorb everything that has happened and really get a chance to process the magnitude of our travels and experiences. With that, I am about 3 days behind on writing, and we are currently on our third train to our final destination in Switzerland, which gives me the perfect excuse for some writing time!

To start off, the train ride from Madrid to Barcelona was quite an experience. The train was fairly nice, but right behind us was a family with 4 small boys who were loud and obnoxious the entire ride and kicked the back of my seat constantly. Personally, I don't understand bringing 4 young boys all the way to Spain for a vacation. Especially after listening to the boy's conversations, it was clear that all they wanted to do was swim and play soccer, which you can easily do at a campground. But I don't have any kids, so maybe that is outside my realm to judge.

When we arrived in Barcelona, we had to first find the address of the Air BnB that we had booked for our stay. Then, we met our host Virka outside of the apartment, and she escorted us up a tiny case of metal stairs. She was gorgeous with perfect skin and flowing long brown hair. She was wearing a beautiful light white dress that turned out to be quite see-through because while climbing the stairs, we could see all of her um… assets and her choice of minimal coverage undergarments. That is one thing we have found with a decent number of Europeans that everyone is much more comfortable with their bodies and wearing more revealing clothing than what we are used to. Or at least what I was used to growing up in a small conservative town.

But anyway, the apartment was 4 floors above the city of Barcelona, right on the main road. You could actually see the La Sagrada Familia right from our bedroom window!

After settling in, we decided to explore and set out to find the man-made park, Parc Güell. Antoni Gaudi designed Parc Güell to initially be a housing complex before the plan was scrapped and it was made into a park. Most of the structures and shapes of the park were inspired by nature, and Gaudi wanted the park to flow with the natural movements all around it. With this concept in mind, there are no straight lines throughout the park's design because "there are no straight lines in nature." Instead, Gaudi's mosaic tiles, shapes, and curves that fit the natural landscape make the park a true wonder. The park really was a work of art.

Walking through the park, you were taken aback by all the beauty of the colorful tiles and naturally imperfect lines. The stonewall, mosaic patterns, and even the handmade railings were perfection. We explored around taking in all the beauty before we made it to the top of the park, where the view overlooked the entire city of Barcelona, all the way out to the ocean.

To be honest, views like this have been some of my favorite parts of this trip so far. A view so amazing that you could sit there all day, either in complete solitude or just contemplating the world. We grabbed a seat and hung out at what felt like the top of the world for a while. There were a ton of dogs running around us at the top of the park, and one man having the time of his life playing catch with all of them. It was adorable to watch and just made me crave owning a dog even more.

Once we had our fill of gorgeous views, we started our climb back down and ran into a violin player, but not any ordinary violin player. This man had a foot pedal which allowed him to record certain stanzas of his playing and play it back underneath what he was playing live. The result? Absolutely spectacular. I have always loved music, and some melodies just resonate more feelings than others. For some particular reason, this music hit me hard. Whether it was the fact that we were in a different country, away from our habitual lives, or it was the summer air and beautiful scenery, I just closed my eyes and let the music take me away.

I could feel the cool wind against my skin, smell the fresh summer flowers, and hear the beautiful melody coming from the violin. It was the kind of music that is so beautiful it makes you feel empowered and strong like you could do anything. Which is precisely what I needed at this stage of our journey. We tipped the amazing violinist and complimented him on his work.

So with a lifted spirit and heightened awareness, we continued exploring and found an even better viewpoint. In the middle of the park was a big hill with a taller monument on it with a cross at the top. Once you climbed the little rock formation leading up to the monument, there was only room for about a handful of people, but the view was so gorgeous that people were struggling to squeeze together as close as possible so that everyone could see. I thought the first view we had was terrific, but this one topped it beyond words.

This view was a 360-degree view of the city, the mountains, and the ocean, with absolutely nothing blocking our sightlines; Magnificent yet again. Even from this first day, my love for Barcelona beat out Madrid by miles. Of course, it was still a big city, but it seemed like it had so much more to offer, and the park won me over. The first night in Barcelona was already a win in my book, but the next morning made it that much better.

On the second day in Barcelona, as we were getting ready in the morning, Virka asked us what time we would like breakfast, which we were not expecting. About 30 minutes later, we sat down at the table to discover she had made a full breakfast for us. It included coffee, tea, water, scrambled eggs with peppers, cut-up French bread with an egg salad mixture on top, and a crepe filled with Nutella and bananas. A-M-A-Z-I-N-G! This was our first home-cooked meal since we started this journey, and I was overwhelmed with happiness. Everything tasted wonderful, and we were pretty sure that she freshly squeezed the orange juice right in her kitchen because it was that good.

Virka joined us for breakfast, and we had the pleasure of getting to know her better. We found out she is from Slovakia and has only lived in Barcelona for a few months now. She doesn't have a steady job, but she moves to a new country or city every few months or so whenever she gets bored. Also, we are pretty sure that she has a maid living with her, so we have no idea how she affords all of this. But either way, good for her, and I admire her lifestyle and the courage to just get up and go whenever she wants to. Her story also explains that although her apartment was beautiful, it was very empty and minimalistic, with nothing on the walls. But then again, why bother if she is only there for a few months.

Finally, the pieces of the puzzle fall in line. Let me back up for a minute. When we first arrived at Virka's, although she was incredibly kind, something just seemed off. Her apartment was completely empty. Nothing on the walls, barely any furniture and no personal items, and it just seemed peculiar. Not to mention that in the bedroom across from ours we saw a very timid woman just peak her head out for a quick second while we said hello and she seemed to get very scared and wide eyed as she slammed the door quickly and disappeared. Another strange occurrence, especially since Virka did not mention anyone else in the home.

Fast forward to us unpacking in our shared room and Ron jumping in the shower. As Ron was showering, Brit and I were just making some travel plans and talking about the odd empty apartment we were currently in but how lucky we had gotten so far with amazing hostels we had stayed in, friendly people, and warm welcoming Air BnB hosts. You always hear these crazy stories about people being taken or trafficked in other countries as well as the US, which unfortunately is still a sad reality that you do need to be cautious of, but something we were not really worried about as we always traveled in a group.

We were simply poking fun at the fact that maybe our luck had run out and this whole Air BnB was a front and that's why there was no furniture or personal items or pictures and maybe the woman in the other room was being held captive. Bad jokes and bad timing, because just as we were joking around about this, we heard a huge crash in the shower and then everything got silent. This wasn't a noise like someone had dropped the shampoo bottle, this was loud. Like those scenes you see in movies when someone is attacked in the shower, hitting all sides of the echoing shower walls before being taken down. Or like the man in the situation had been strategically taken out of the equation as the two woman sat helplessly in the room next door.

Brit and I looked at each other wide eyed and terrified, not moving a muscle but just listening for some sign of, well anything. After a few minutes of terrified and frozen silence, the door to our room opened and I swear my heart leapt directly out of my body. I took a sharp inhale and then saw Ron emerge from behind the door. Brit and I looked at each other and simultaneously let out a huge sigh of relief before we lost ourselves in laughter.

Ron had no idea what was going on, but we could barely breathe we were laughing so hard. We then told him that for a brief moment we thought he had been taken out and we were on the verge of being the news line story for the next day about the American tourists being taken in Barcelona. Ron also admitted to knocking over a few things in the shower, but nothing to the extent of the noise we heard, so maybe we just let our imaginations get away from us for a second. After having a good laugh, breakfast the next morning solidified that we were safe and well taken care of. As well as our curiosities about the empty house and the shy maid that lived in the other guest bedroom.

After breakfast, it was time to head down to the beach for the day. The ocean was beautiful, but a bit overcrowded with people- as we expected it to be. Just imagine one of the biggest beaches you have ever seen, and then imagine every single inch of sand covered by umbrellas, towels, half-naked bodies, and a few screaming kids. Luckily, we still found a little space of our own and set up camp for the day.

As we made base camp in the sand, we noticed that it wasn't like the beach sand we were used to back home. Rather than the sand being a fine powdery substance that stuck to every inch of your body, the sand was made up of tiny rough pebbles that were more distinct than small grains. It was small enough that it was still comfortable to lay on but big enough to make a difference for me to be mesmerized by it for at least a few hours. I felt like a little kid again, just mesmerized by the simplicity of sand. Running it through my fingers and feeling the different textures on my palms. Oh, the innocence of childhood, when everything is full of magic. I absolutely love these small moments of adult life that bring you back to appreciating the smallest wonders of life.

Once the allure of the sand had worn off, I started looking around to see what was going on with the other groups on the beach around us, and not surprisingly, there were a good number of women going completely topless on the beach. Now, if you live in America, this is a HUGE cultural difference between America and Europe right away. However, it is very acceptable and even normal throughout Europe to go topless on the beaches. Also, keep in mind that these are no secluded nudist beach spaces but very large areas of family-friendly beaches.

In the states, most places you visit this is unacceptable and illegal, and you would be fined for indecent exposure. Not only that, but there is such a negative stigmatism of women "showing" themselves in public that public breastfeeding is often publicly shamed. I'm sure everyone has their own opinion on issues like these. Still, it blows my mind that an area can be so progressive that women are allowed to go topless on a beach; meanwhile, in America, most of the time, women aren't even allowed to feed their hungry babies in public without being shamed.

Yet, in Europe, women feel free to bare it all without social judgment or harassment and are completely comfortable doing so. Personally, I think American culture could benefit from more social acceptance of things like this instead of shaming, but that's an issue that would unlock the depths of Pandora's box to explore, so I will leave it alone.

Anyways, there were also a ton of vendors walking around selling mojitos and sangrias on this beach. Eventually, Brit and I splurged for a 3-euro mojito because it was so hard to say no when a person passed you every 5 seconds yelling "mojitos... fresh m-o-j-i-t-o-s-" in a very thick but bubbly accent. Come to find out, the amount of rum the man poured into the mojitos was only worth about 5 cent euro. But you live, learn, and the cooling mint spiced rum was still refreshing. Once we each had a drink and all felt like the sun had baked our skin to its core, we decided to take turns jumping in the water. I wish we could have all gone swimming at the same time, but because the beach was so crowded, and we had heard of a lot of thefts at this beach, and we wanted to make sure at least one person always stayed with our belongings.

The water was freezing at first, but it was the perfect playground to splash around once you got used to it. I have always felt completely at peace and in my element in the water. I grew up on a river, and I was constantly splashing around, testing the boundaries of how far I could go and how good of a swimmer I was. Oddly the water has always been both calming and invigorating for me at the same time. There is just something about being in the water and swimming that makes me feel free and that nothing else in the world matters. That was until I realized how crispy my shoulders were getting from baking in the sun.

Either way, it was completely worth it and another welcomed break from our hectic travel schedule. Overall, the beach day was terrific, and we spent the rest of the time transitioning from lying on the beach and soaking up the sun to jumping in the ocean. Once we got back home, it was a relaxing night, and we all just settled in to watch the movie Grown-Ups 2.

The following day there was another grand breakfast waiting for us that included bread, eggs and peppers again, as well as cereal. We took our time getting ready and slowly headed down to the beach area again. We walked this time instead of taking the subway to preserve some of our money. It was a lovely walk, and we got a chance to explore the main strip of stores, shops, and tourist set-ups. There was also a fantastic open-air market on the way filled with fresh meat and seafood, an array of different spices, fresh vegetables and fruit, delicatessen and baked goods, and enough good smells to last a lifetime. It was a complete sensory overload as far as food goes.

Along with the cultural arrangement of food, there was an abundance of people walking around the market, both locals and tourists. Brit and I went into the market about 3-4 different times throughout the day, and in the final walk-through, we broke down and bought some fruit and juice. I purchased a banana and coconut juice drink which tasted amazing since both of those are my favorite fruits. Brit had some actual coconut pieces, strawberries, and pineapple.

Although back home, we have farmer market stands every Saturday, I would kill for a permanent market like this where I lived. I would be here every single day. There is just something so much more authentic about non-pre-packaged food and specialty vendor booths. Knowing you support small family farms and individuals, rather than just walking into a superstore and grabbing something off the shelf. In Barcelona, going to the market is a full-on cultural experience versus just a humdrum obligation to feed your family in the states.

Later in the afternoon, we all met up with Brit's brother-in-law Tommy, whose cruise ship was in port, and he had received a few hours for a break away from the ship. So we stopped at an outdoor restaurant and ordered a massive sangria for Brit and me to split, and Ron ordered a pizza. It was so captivating to hear about Tommy's job as a sous chef on a cruise ship. Although he worked about 80 hours a week, he told us that he made good money and could save up quickly.

After everything Tommy told us about his work, I think cruise ship work is definitely an option for employment that I would consider after the trip. He was telling us about one job description called crew staff which is all about interacting with the guests and enhancing the experience that the guests have on the cruise ship. Which just sounds like the perfect job for me. At least for a little while, but we will see. For the rest of the day in

Barcelona, we walked along the beach, collecting beach glass and along the streets exploring before starting the long walk home.

13.60 euros per night for the Air BnB, less than 7 euros a day in food, Barcelona was also very budget friendly!

Unexpected Stops

The following day, it was time to leave Barcelona behind and begin our journey to Switzerland. Since we were unable to make a train reservation for the 11-hour overnight train, all we could do was take the first leg of the train ride to Cerbére, France, and hope there would still be openings on the next train by the time we got there.

So we took the 8:30 am train into Cerbére, and once we got to the train station, it was the most effortless reservation that we had made so far. The woman at the booth spoke English, and for only 7 euros more, we were able to get a sleeper compartment on the train! The only thing was that now we had 8 hours to kill in a city that we knew nothing about. Let the adventure begin!

We took off from the train station, not knowing where we were going, and eventually, we stumbled upon another beach! It was a rock beach, so there was no sand in sight, but still a beach with a water source. By the way, if you have never seen or been to a rock beach before, it is not the most appealing or comfortable thing in the world. Instead of fine or even coarse sand, the whole beach is made of good size rocks varying from the size of a grape to a grapefruit. But that didn't deter people away because the beach was filled with a few families who had sprawled out and were sunbathing on the rocks. We tried laying down our towels and getting comfortable on the rocks, but it was way too painful, and we ended up reverting to laying our towels down on the concrete steps leading down to the beach.

Once we were settled, Ron and I decided that we would get our suits on and test out the waters since we had some time to kill. Between traversing the rocks to get in and the frigid, icy sting of the water, it wasn't the most pleasant swim. I'm sure the families watching us were dying inside with laughter, watching us scream and shout and dance around, trying to get our bodies used to the cold waters before diving under.

I will have to admit that even growing up on Michigan Lakes and plunging into the lakes while there were still ice chunks floating, this was one of the coldest waters I had ever been in. But eventually, your body gets used to the cold, and you just adjust. There was even a little platform a ways out in the water to jump off, which was an added bonus. Ron and I played on the platform and swam until our lips were blue. At that point, we figured we should swim back in, and we sprawled out on the beach steps to dry off and take a nap in the sun.

After our nap, it was impossible to ignore obnoxious sounds coming from our stomachs, and we figured we should find somewhere to get a bite to eat. Not too far from the beach, there was a small beachside vendor that offered an assortment of sandwiches. I ordered a ham and cheese Panini, Brit got a Panini, and Ron a hamburger; Bad food choice # 2 for me on this trip so far.

My sandwich tasted so bad that I couldn't even stomach a second bite. I think it was a combination of the ingredients not being fresh and one of the cheeses on the sandwich being so strong and bitter that my taste buds revolted immediately. But I mean, I should have seen it coming. We were in the land of Fromage. (Meaning cheese in French) But what can you do? Of course, I didn't want to spend even more money to get another sandwich, even though this one was only around 5-6 euros, a budget is a budget, so I just had a few handfuls of nuts and seeds from my bag. After lunch, we still had a little more time to bask in the sun and enjoy some beachside reading.

Eventually, it was time to venture back to the train station, and we were able to board the train early and find our sleeping compartment; I loved it right away. It was a tiny space with 6 bunk beds, three on each side with a few feet of space in between each one. Even in the small area, I was overwhelmingly happy to be able to lie down in a bed and get some good sleep for the 11-hour journey. So much better than those overnight buses that we had been taking and well worth the money! We chatted and snacked on munchies in our bags until our eyes got tired, and we each made ourselves comfortable in a bunk bed of our choice. I slept on and off the whole ride but was still so happy that I wasn't stuck upright in a chair.

The next morning, we woke up and got off the train in Switzerland in a little town called Basel. Here, we had to board one more train to take us to Interlaken. It was instantly overwhelming arriving at the train station. This time, not a single person spoke French or Spanish or English, yet they were speaking German (as far as we could tell), and I had no clue what anyone was saying. At least in France and Spain, I knew enough of the language to get by, but this was completely foreign to me; Another adventure. It seemed like in the train station, at least, everything was much more expensive even though it was in Swiss francs (CHF). Ron had to pay 2 CHF just to use the restroom, which was a little more than $2 US.

But before we could even relieve ourselves, I had to get change first from the larger bills that the ATM had given me, which included me order- ing what looked like a cinnamon roll with meat on it to break our bills for change. Come to find out, once I bit into it, it wasn't meat but yet crys- talized sugar. It was actually pretty good. It tasted nothing like a cinna- mon roll, but I loved the flavors which I couldn't even guess to be able to describe. After the short train station experience, we hopped on the next train that would take us into Interlaken, which is where I am sitting now, catching up on all my writing. So, as they say here, alveterzane (German goodbye) for now, and we will see what Switzerland has to offer us!

Switzerland-
Swiss Everything

I would put the various phrases we learned before entering Switzerland here if there was one official language of Switzerland. However, depending on the region, the Swiss speak a mixture of Romansh, German, French, and Italian. Not only that, but most dialects are a mixture of all these various languages. So, if you ever travel here, good luck with the language barrier.

We finally made it into Interlaken, Switzerland, and it is absolutely stunning! Even the mountain view from the train car coming into the town is enough to take your breath away. Once we arrived in the heart of the city, it was clear to see that there were mountains surrounding all sides of this small town. Not only that, but between two of the highest mountains, you can just barely catch a glimpse of the snow-covered peaks in the distance-the coveted Swiss Alps. Also, the water here is the most eye-piercing blue that you could ever imagine. The lakes are a bright teal blue like I have never seen before, not even in the oceans. The houses are just as you would imagine them; adorable Swiss-style architecture with flowers blooming and perfectly pruned vegetation surrounding all the homes. This town seems like something straight out of a fairy tale with the intensely colored lakes, the mountains that reach toward the heavens, and the storybook homes.

Since we were blown away by the beautiful scenery from just the train ride alone, we started exploring the rest of the town as soon as we stepped foot off the train. Unfortunately, we also found out that everything in the town of Interlaken is amazingly expensive. Even so, I would still say the beauty is worth the extra expense. We walked around the town and just took it all in before we put in the directions to our campsite. The campsite was just a few streets outside of the main downtown area. While we began navigating our way through the windy roads, we quickly realized that although it was not too far of a walk from town, maybe only a mile, but trekking back and forth every day was going to tire us out. But it would be worth it for the low price of 18.47 CHF per person per night, which was an absolute steal in Interlaken!

The campground was a quaint little area with not many trees but just tiny grass plots. Enough for tents or campers. We were greeted by the very nice owners at the campground, who explained the activities we had available and the campground rules.

Fun fact- Interlaken is the adventure capital of Switzerland, so we had all the adrenaline-rushing sports right at our fingertips. Bungee Jumping. Canyoning. Whitewater River Rafting. High Ropes Course. Paragliding. Skydiving. Just name it and you could probably do it in Interlaken.

It was refreshing to speak with someone who spoke fluent English with a bit of an accent for a change, instead of having to translate every-thing! After we settled in, we went for a walk around the river and down to the lake. All of it was beautiful; the water, the scenery, the air, paragliders descending down from the mountain tops, everything. Pinch me please, I think I have reached paradise. Once we finished following the river to where it met the lake, we found this beautiful small gravel lot right on the edge of the water overlooking the whole lake and the mountains in the backdrop. I could have sat there forever just staring at the scenery; again, something straight out of a fairy tale.

As we explored, we attempted to take a different path back to the campsite and found an old, abandoned castle in the woods. So, of course, we had to go exploring. At first, going in through the front entrance was a bit creepy because the whole inside of the building was pitch dark, and we weren't sure if anyone would be living there or what might be hiding in the shadows. But we quickly got over our fear and raced up the stairs to the top. Once at the top, it overlooked the whole courtyard with old ruins where I could see Ron running around and jumping from one piece of debris to the next. The view of the lake was stunning from the top, and all I could do was look down in amazement at what we stumbled upon by simply taking an alternate route.

That is one thing that this trip has taught me so far, is that at times, some of the most precious moments in life are unplanned. Some of your greatest adventures happen when you least expect them. And if you just open your eyes and your mind to new experiences, the world is full of surprises. For example, we would later find out that although there wasn't much known about this castle, the ruins date all the way back to the 1200s. There were also rumors around the town of a "white lady" that haunts the castle. But isn't there always some kind of haunted story attached to all ancient sites?

Once we had our fill of exploring, it was time to find our way back to the campsite. Our first day in Switzerland was a success. It was more than a success. It was like I had left my body and transported to a land so gorgeous that I had only ever read about it in fairy tales. Just from one day here, I knew that Interlaken would always have a place in my heart, and one day I will return.

It's been about a week now since we first arrived in Interlaken. We were originally only planning on spending a few days here, but the country's beauty captured our hearts, and we kept extending our stay. I feel like every single day here has been full of adventure, and I have finally been taking the time needed to take in each and every precious second of it. That, and I've been so exhausted at the end of each day that I have had zero energy to journal. But once again, we are headed to our next destination on a train, which has provided me with the perfect opportunity to reminisce on our wonderful time in Switzerland.

The first night we spent in Interlaken camped in a tent was a little chilly but still like a dream. Once the sun had set, the night sky lit up the mountain tops with the most beautiful twilight glow. Since Interlaken is a fairly small town, there is not a lot of light pollution, so our view of all the night stars was uninterrupted. The next morning, we got up early and took a bus over to Iseltwald, just a few miles away, and began a hike that started in the small village, went up through the mountains, and ended back in Interlaken. The hike was pretty easy but absolutely stunning. The first waterfall (or wasserfall as they are referred to in Switzerland) was gorgeous, cascading down from the mountains. I decided to be a little adventurous and take off my shoes to cross the stream to the other side. The water was ice cold, but my toes and soul were happy.

I continued the hike a little further shoeless to give my feet time to dry. I have always admired the few hikers I run across who are barefoot traversing the wilderness. Nothing protecting their fragile feet from the elements, but then again, you get absolute freedom and no barriers between you and the earth. Every once in a while, I will take my shoes off and walk barefoot for a few minutes during a hike, and I always love the experience. But soon enough, I always end up putting my shoes back on because, let's be honest, it's not always that comfortable. And with my record of poisonous plant rashes and my luck, my feet would be covered in poison ivy oils by the time I was done with my hike.

But I did end up pushing my luck this time. I walked a little further barefoot right up to where our hiking trail looped behind the waterfall. Whoever first established this trail knew what the people would want because right there behind the waterfall in the middle of the trail was a small bench where you could sit and observe the magnitude of the water rushing down from just a few feet away. It was a good stopping point, so we decided to take a break there and enjoy our PB&J-packed lunches and share some wild strawberries. Which, by the way, were the best bleepin berries I have ever eaten in my entire life.

I would never trust myself to identify edible berries in the wild; even though these were CLEARLY strawberries, I was still hesitant to just pick a berry from a bush behind a waterfall and eat it. But I did trust Ron's judgment, and he had already shoved a few berries in his mouth first, so I figured it would be okay. Not only was this just the cherry or "strawberry" on top of having lunch behind a waterfall, but it was FREE food, which I cannot stress enough how convenient this is when you are traveling on a budget. Also, at this point in our journey, my body desperately craved more fresh fruit and vegetables. So the three of us huddled together, tucked away behind a waterfall in Switzerland, scavenging for wild strawberries and just enjoying life to its fullest.

I could have happily made my home behind that wasserfall, but we eventually had to continue onward. Further on in the hike, we came across a magnificent moss-covered road. I don't know why I was so spellbound by this mossy road, but just like the rest of the architecture and scenery in Switzerland, it looked like it was straight out of a woodland fairytale. I half expected fairies to start buzzing out of the trees or a talking deer to wander up from the trail below. But unfortunately, neither did. We did, however, get to see some goats roped off in what must have been someone's farm-land just off the path, and we did run into another spectacular waterfall.

The second waterfall may not have had a walking path behind it, but we all did get a chance to get up close and personal to the base of the falls for some pictures. It was the perfect pick-me-up after hiking; Standing right next to the waterfall and feeling the mist being splashed on your face and feeling the cool breeze against your skin with the crisp and fresh air. The rest of the walk back to Interlaken from there was long, but the day's experiences were worth it. Some much-needed rest was in order for the night and the next day was all about relaxation for the first part.

When it was time to get up the next morning, we went into town so that Brit and Ron could get some coffee and so that we could do some research for our next destination. While spending some more time in town with all the people there, a few things became very apparent to me. First, even though we were in Switzerland, at times, it felt more like we were in Asia. For the most part, everywhere we have traveled so far has been very diverse and filled with travelers from all aspects of life. But for this little town and even the towns surrounding it, it seemed like the Asian and Japanese tourists even outnumbered the locals.

At first, I thought it was just odd to me, but it became more apparent that this was a norm around here. The most peculiar thing that I noticed was the tourist booth specifically for those that spoke Japanese. Every place we have visited so far had many tourist booths dedicated to all the world's languages. They were always decorated in flags from various countries or welcome signs in multiple languages, and most of the staff were always bi-lingual. But not this booth. Right in the middle of Switzerland, where their language was some kind of mix between French, Spanish, and German, was a Japanese-specific tourist booth. Just an odd observation as far as tourist cultures goes. Maybe I will learn more about that later.

To get back to the morning coffee…After everyone had their required caffeine intake for the day, we headed back to the campsite and took a walk around the river again. The pure beauty of this place makes me feel like I could stay here doing nothing every day but sit and appreciate the scenery around me. Even the river seemed to have magical powers over me where the calm, flowing waters would just draw me in and overpower any of my thoughts or worries. But eventually, reality hit me, and we realized that we had things to do. So Ron and I headed back into town to catch a train into Grindelwald to explore the nearby town and hopefully meet up with a girl I had contacted over couch surfing who was hoping to hike in the mountains with us the next day.

Side note: *If you are an avid traveler and have never heard of couch surfing before, you HAVE to check it out! It is this fantastic online community of fellow travelers who either are looking for free accommodations, to make friends, or who have their extra spaces at home listed as accommodations for others. It has been hard trying to find someone who has enough space to take*

in three travelers, but we ended up talking to this one woman who was willing
to meet up with us and take us hiking!

On the way to Grindelwald, Ron and I were under the impression that our Eurail train passes would cover the ride, but when the woman came around to check passes, we found out that we were dead wrong. Unfortunately, the train to Grindelwald was a private train not covered by our passes, so we were forced to buy tickets on the spot. Thankfully we did not get fined for not having a ticket, but the unfortunate error ended up costing us 34 CHF for both round trips, a hit on our budget that we were not expecting. But we had no other option.

Once we arrived in Grindelwald, we were in desperate need of libations, and since we had spent more money than expected on the train, we figured why not spend more and drown our sorrows! And we also needed to find a place with internet to get ahold of the girl we were meeting up with, so it was an excellent excuse to stop somewhere for a drink.

Upon arrival in Grindelwald, it was obvious that

#1 Grindelwald was a huge tourist town and

#2 It was much smaller than Interlaken but still beautiful.

Just like Interlaken, it was an amazing town with mountains all around and little houses situated in the land below the main strip of the city with a prime view of one of the snow-covered Alps. After walking around, we found a little bar called "Avocado Bar," which looked like an adorable little establishment, which wasn't touristy, and they didn't look like their drinks would be too expensive. We took a seat at the bar and asked the bartender which local drinks he recommended.

The first beer we had was one on tap from Switzerland, which I believe was Edelweiss. It was quite good, and a house glass was only 5.5 CHF which was the cheapest beer I had seen yet! We sipped our beers and enjoyed a few minutes of live music as we got to know our bartender. I knew from his accent that he wasn't a local, so I asked. He told us he was half kiwi (from New Zealand) and half Irish but was born in Switzerland. Such a cool cultural background!

Come to find out, he had been traveling around for a while, working as a bartender in various places. I would have loved to know more about him, but the conversation was cut short by a shift change.

After some time, we were able to get a hold of Carina, our Couchsurfing friend, and she met us at the bar. She was very welcoming and came with many travel stories, including her work in hospitality at many different places and even working on a cruise ship.

We ordered another beer and kept the conversation going. The next beer was a Rugenbräu for 5.5 CHF, another local beer made in Interlaken, which was also quite good. Ron and I also realized that we were pretty hungry with the second beer, so we got some brats from a food cart outside. However, the Brat toppings were a far cry from the American toppings of ketchup and mustard.

Toppings included smooth mashed avocado with big tomato chunks, fried onion pieces, and sour cream and chives. Like any true food lover, I piled it all on, and the combination was mouth-watering. Forget ketchup. This is my new favorite topping. The brat itself, had a great taste to it, but the combination of toppings was pure mouth magic. This is one food combination that I will take home with me.

After more hours than expected at the bar, we followed Carina back to her house to plan our hiking route for the next day. Her home was only about a 5-minute walk from the town, uphill, of course, but when you got there, the front porch view of the mountains was something that people in the states would pay millions for. It desperately made me want to ask her how much she paid in rent, but I thought it might be too personal to ask.

We only took a few moments to figure out where we would start hiking from the next day because Ron and I had to catch the last bus back to Interlaken because we had already missed the last train back. Thankfully the round-trip train tickets we had purchased earlier also covered our bus ride. We arrived back in Interlaken very late and still had to walk back to the campsite. It was a very long day, and we were dead tired trying to mentally prepare for an even bigger day and bigger hike to follow in just a few short hours. But hey our total spending for the day ended up being just shy of 73 American dollars. Not bad for an unexpected expense and a splurge on some beer and brats!

We woke up very early to catch a train to a little village called Zweilutschinen. We figured that we would have to pay for the train again, but the ticket office wasn't open yet, so we figured we could just press our luck and buy our tickets on the train again. Luckily, no one came around to check tickets during this short journey, so we didn't have to pay! Check and noted; you don't always have to pay for tickets if you are lucky. Once we got to the village, we met Carina and began our hike!

To be honest, the first part of the hike was a bit intimidating. First off, it was all uphill, and the terrain was rougher than what I was used to hiking. Also, Carina started off hiking very strong and very fast, which made me feel like I had to go faster. Especially since I didn't know her very well yet, I didn't want her to feel like I was slowing her down on the hike. I have been hiking before with Ron, and he is well aware of my, shall we say, turtle crossing a tar pit pace. But with a new person in the mix, I wasn't sure how things would go. I also knew that Brit was quite a fast hiker.

At the beginning of the hike, I was working my ass off to try to keep up with everyone, and I was still behind. This was unlike any other hike I had ever done before. The beginning was not only what seemed like straight uphill, but there were absolutely no breaks or flat ground. Second, the hike was at a higher altitude, so I am not sure if it was the altitude or how much I was pushing myself, but the heavy breathing, heart racing, and sweat pouring down my back and forehead continued the entire way up the mountain. Third, I was not exactly wearing hiking shoes. The shoes that I had brought with me to Europe were a pair of Merrell Vibrams. They are more of a naturalistic shoe with not a lot of support and flat no grip bottoms.

Although they have proved to be an excellent walking around shoe, they are not the best for climbing and traversing over sharp rocks, mud, water, and steep inclines, making it a little more complicated. Still, I pushed myself about as hard as I could to make it to our first destination. The first place we took a real break was a little lookout point where we could see all of Interlaken. We sat down on a bench and shared some bread Carina had made for everyone. The view was beautiful, and the break was much needed. We also found it quite comical when Ron took out the sandwich that he had brought, and the bag had expanded so much due to the altitude gain that it was ready to burst.

After the well-needed break, we trudged on and on, going more and more uphill. The hike was beautiful, but I would have appreciated the scenery more, going at my own pace. Then again, if I had hiked at my own pace, it probably would have taken me three days to do the same hike. After the initial ascent up the mountain, Carina slowed down her hiking pace, which made me feel much better about my own pace, and that even gave us some time to talk and get to know each other.

One other lookout point that we stopped at that comes to mind was a beautiful open field where you could clearly see the Swiss Alps, including all 4 major peaks. It was breathtaking. Along the hike, we also found a few houses/cheese-making places, according to Carina, that were situated in the middle of nowhere. It was kind of neat having a small space completely secluded with such beautiful views right out your front window. At another stopping point, we found a small restaurant/shop where Carina purchased some goat cheese and other sharp cheeses. She shared a good portion of her cheeses with us, which we were extremely grateful for. The cheese was rich and creamy, and perfectly fresh. Eating Swiss cheese while climbing the Swiss mountains; Check that one off the bucket list.

The rest of the day included hiking and cheese breaks with more spectacular views of the countryside. The last view that really sticks out in my mind was an open valley on the opposite side of the mountain. After hiking in the woods for a while, we finally came to an opening, and what I saw nearly knocked me off my feet. The valley was picturesque, complete with a small stream running through the middle, greenery, and small flowers all around you, a perfect oasis right in the middle of the mountains. A part of me wanted to burst out singing "The Hills are Alive," recreating a moment from the Sound of Music, but I restrained myself.

I would have been more than happy to build a tiny home right in the middle of the valley and stay there forever, living off the fresh cheese nearby. I took so many pictures, but I don't think I could ever recreate the experience of being there. After the valley, it was time to decide if we wanted to head down the mountain or continue further up. We decided to push our luck, going up just a little further. My mind and eyes were desperately aching for more beautiful scenery and a longer hike while my body and legs were screaming no, but we pushed on. By the time we got to the next town, we had decided that it was probably a good idea to start heading back down. I didn't know it yet, but for me, that's when the real hard part of the hike would start.

At first, going down the mountain wasn't bad, but it really started to wear on my knees and ankle after a while. Although climbing up took an enormous amount of leg strength and lung capacity, going down required paying attention, balance, and a set of much stronger knees than the ones attached to my body. I didn't make it down very far before I was ready to just tuck and roll the rest of the way down - scrape me up off the pavement when I land. I could see that Carina was also struggling to get down, but Ron and Brittany seemed to have no problem. It wasn't too long before I required the help of Ron just to make it down, especially on the more significant drops. So, he held my arm and I pressed down hard on his arm with each step to relieve some of the pressure off my knees.

My knees were on fire, and I could hear their screams for help to stop, but I knew there was no other way to get back down to where we had started. With each step, I thought that I might hear a loud crunch and would see my knees buckling under me while my bones just shattered to dust, but that was, of course, my mind just being dramatic.

I honestly thought that we would never make it back to flat ground, but of course, we did. I have never been in more pain or had a more challenging hike than hiking down that mountain; Both mentally and physically. Now that the pain is over with though, and my knees are rested, I would say the climb was worth the pain, but I'm pretty sure that I thought just the opposite at the time. Without Ron helping me along with every step-down, I'm pretty sure I would have ended up just rolling down the mountain once my knees gave out. Thank God for that man.

In the end, the hike was a challenge but something that I may never be able to experience again. The scenery was breathtaking, the wasserfalls were blissful, all the wild strawberries and raspberries we ate tasted miraculous, and the feeling of accomplishment when I reached the top and admired the view is not a feeling that you can just recreate from riding a cable car up. I felt like I was on top of the world while climbing to the top of Switzerland.

After the hike, Carina invited us back to her place for a BBQ. First, she took the train back to where we started our hike and came to pick us up in her car to drive around the city of Lauterbrunnen so she could show us the valleys of wasserfalls. When we got to Lauterbrunnen, it was hard to describe the beauty of the cascading wasserfalls all along the city, but they were stunning. Carina told us that this was the city of 72 waterfalls and its beauty was unbeatable. Driving around the little town, you could see crystal clear water cascading off the mountainside and dissipating into a mist below. All around the city, there were these wasserfalls coming out of the sides of the mountains, and it was a site like I had never seen before. Especially since I am such a waterfall lover.

On the way back to her house, Carina was saying that she had salad and was making grilled cheese if we wanted to pick anything else up at the market to eat. So we stopped at the market, picked up some hot dogs, and brought back beer to complete the BBQ. Once we started up the charcoal grill, we were wondering how Carina was going to make grilled cheese on the grill, but then she brought out this small platter with a hunk of cheese on it and placed it directly on the grill and literally "grilled some cheese"; talk about culture shock. In America, "grilled cheese" is a sandwich with two slices of bread that you butter with a hunk of cheese in the middle and then pan fry. In Switzerland, grilled cheese is literally a hunk of cheese that you grill. Go figure. Carina also made two side salads for us, and I think everyone that night ate their fill and enjoyed the million-dollar view from her porch. Time went by fast, and before we knew it, it was time to say goodbye as we caught the last train back to Interlaken.

We woke up early again to travel to Zermatt to see the Matterhorn the following day. The only problem was when we got to the station the tickets were much more expensive than what we were expecting, like 54 CFS to be exact, but we did it anyway. Once we got there, we realized Zermatt was just like all the other little towns in Switzerland, filled with picturesque scenery. We walked around to a few different viewpoints of the Matterhorn and took pictures but decided that it was too much money to take a gondola up closer to the Matterhorn. It was definitely a let-down, but like I said before, this trip is all about balance, and we simply can't have everything. The whole reason that we can be gone for so long and see so many fantastic places is because we are being smart about our money. For the most part at least. Meh, life is all about choices...

Maybe it was for the best because I wasn't feeling very good that day anyway. I was just completely exhausted. I felt like I didn't even have enough energy to walk through the town. No doubt I was mentally and physically exhausted from the day before summiting the mountains of Switzerland, but sometimes you just have to push on.

We decided to take it easy and just hang out while relaxing by a small river and collecting rocks. Which yes, by the way, I am a 25-year-old who still likes to pick up and collect cool rocks that I see. (I should have been a geologist!) But the rest of the day was simply spent walking around the cute little town, exploring, and going in and out of little shops. After a full day, we headed back to Interlaken and just finished the night with some card games.

The next day was also a very big day for me. It was the day that I went paragliding! A couple of days beforehand, I was looking at going but didn't want to spend the money. I took a little time to reconsider, and I thought, "When am I ever going to get the chance to do this again, or to do this in such a beautiful place?" So I splurged and bought a ticket for 237.28 CHF to be exact. Yikes. But something worth splurging on at least. I woke up early, ready to go, and the van picked up Ron and me at about 8:30 am. (Brit decided to spend her money elsewhere). We went to a little booth to pay and then got into a van with another girl from Singapore and met our flight instructors. We started driving up the mountain, and one of the instructors explained how this would all work out. I was so nervous when we got to the top, and I saw the "hill" that we would be running down to take off.

I instantly pictured myself tumbling down the hill ass over ankles with my parachute dragging behind me as I dropped over the edge of the cliff. I think my instructor Drew, saw the look of sheer horror on my face because he gave me my harness and explained to me that the chute would fill with air and pull me back to keep me upright, and I would essentially just run off the edge as we glide into the air.

Before I knew it, Ron and the other girl from the van had already taken off, and Drew was asking me if I was ready. The next thing I know, he tells me to run as fast as I can, and we are running down the hill together, strapped into a harness with a parachute behind us. It didn't take much running until the chute gracefully picked us up off the ground and into the air just before the edge of the cliff ended. Just a few seconds later, I was instructed to sit back into the little seat attached to my harness, and just like that, we were flying over Interlaken.

The scenery was jaw-dropping. We were right over Interlaken, soaring between all the mountains. As we flew down, we came around the side of a mountain and came so close to the treetops that I swear I could have touched them. The feeling of being in the harness and in a seated position while flying was actually very secure. Between the security and the adrenaline, my fear of heights completely dissipated. Once I was in the air, I thought that I might get nervous or scared, but I was very comfortable.

The whole time we were flying, Drew took pictures of the flight and a few videos. As we came in lower to the ground, Drew asked if I wanted to do a few aerial stunts before landing. Um, Yes?!? He pulled a few strings, and we turned our bodies into the wind, and we were swept sideways into a downward spiral. Some of the maneuvers made me feel completely weightless, soaring above the ground. Others made my stomach flip like while on a roller coaster. After the maneuvers, the descent to the ground was quick and easy, with both of us landing on our feet.

The flight was amazing, but it was over way too quickly. I wanted to hold on to that fantastic experience as long as I could, so of course, I sprang for the picture and video package. I also wanted to have hard evidence to show my friends and family back home what I had done because I knew some of them would be skeptical, especially with my fear of heights.

Call it the adrenaline rush, but that one flight made me want to do more adventurous sports and more things that push me past my comfort zone. I love adrenaline, but it takes a lot for me to do something like this. But for whatever reason, when I am traveling, I am always willing to be more adventurous and try things I never would back home. Like that one time, I ate a live termite crawling on a tree in Mexico because our guide told us they were a delicacy. Of course, that's a whole different story, but that's the "Cally travel attitude" to sum it up.

The rest of the day from there was pretty relaxing compared to our paragliding experience. Ron and I stayed in town for a while and then went back to the campground for Ron to do laundry while I took a hike down to the lake. Once I got there, it was packed with people, so all I could do was find a little rock bank and situate my bag there so that I could jump into the water. When I first jumped in, I instantly felt the sharp stabs of ice-cold water grabbing onto every inch of skin. It was freezing cold but still refreshing. As I swam more toward the lake's center, it became so icy cold that it was hard to breathe. I quickly retreated back inland and decided that one jump in the lake and the quick little swim I had was enough for me. I wrapped my tiny towel around my freezing body and made the hike back to the campsite.

After warming up a bit, we headed back into town to buy our tickets to Venice and to sample some Swiss chocolate. I bought one Grand Marnier chocolate and one orange chocolate. Both were phenomenal. Ron also purchased a few alcoholic chocolates, including a rum and whisky chocolate. His chocolates were good, but the alcohol was a little too overpowering for me. Another check off our bucket list, swiss chocolate, swiss cheese, swiss mountains, and Ron had even bought a swiss army knife.

After heading back to the campsite, we had a great end to the day and made some pasta and garlic bread for dinner; it was delicious. The next day, we woke up at our own pace and hung out at the campground until about 11. Then we headed into town to wait for our train. While we were waiting, we had some time to kill, so we decided to play Yahtzee on the train station floor. So with our makeshift "rolling area" constructed by our water bottles, hanging out on the floor, we killed some time until we boarded our train to Venice.

Swiss Rainbows and Rain

In the end, I was crushed to leave Switzerland. I absolutely loved it there; the people, the land, the mountains, the water, everything. The culture was fascinating as the people spoke German for the most part but had also adopted some French words and at the same time spoke their own little language incorporated into the typical German language. In short, Switzerland is not a good place to practice your German. And even so, if you are fluent in German, sometimes you still do not understand what the Swiss are saying; Very interesting, to say the least. Without a doubt, I will come back to Switzerland again, but with more money in my pockets to really be able to treat myself.

I'm seeing a theme here- More money=more happiness? - No, no, no, - but then again, it would make traveling easier!

Also, a few side notes from Switzerland. I know I am missing a few days in my journal, and I am honestly having difficulty remembering all of it. So just assume that the days I didn't talk about were spent exploring the town, finding small hiking trails along the river, or sampling all the best Swiss chocolate and cheese. Because, more than likely, that's what happened.

Oh! Switzerland was also the location where Ron had his first haircut while traveling by yours truly. His hair really does grow at incredible speeds, and it gets so thick that it is hard to get a hat on his head, so it was about time that we put the clippers to use that we had packed in his bag taking up precious space.

We set up an impromptu barber shop right in the middle of the campground. We got a stool from the front office, and I went to town pretending to be a professional. All I remember from the experience is that there was a lot of laughter, some swearing, some yelling, and I'm sure a lot of campground guests who thought we were nuts. By the end of it all, I had given Ron more of a "high and tight" haircut instead of a very subtle shading kind of haircut that he is used to. Not bad for my first time if you asked me, but I don't think Ron was impressed. In all fairness, he knew what he was getting into.

Now, a change of pace for a minute to dive into the reality of long-term travel. To step away from the rainbows and sunshine that was Switzerland for a moment, there was, unfortunately, one bad part about Switzerland. Well, not the country in general, but an ugly part of the trip.

It took me a while going back and forth, thinking if I wanted to add this part to my journal or not and bare my relationship and soul to the world. Still, I decided that it was important for other people to know the good and the bad and realize that we are all human and we all have struggles. If you have a partner with whom you spend a significant amount of time, you know that sometimes your partner can get under your skin. Now turn that time into a month and a half of traveling together and barely ever being more than 5 feet from each other. Tensions can escalate much quicker.

Somehow, I had reached my breaking point in Switzerland, and just one minor disagreement sent me over the edge. I had wanted to take the gondola up to the top of Jungfraujoch, one of the main summits in the Bernese Alps, and Ron did not want to. Somehow from here, this slight disagreement spiraled out of control into me contemplating if I could even keep traveling with Ron or not and if we should even stay together.

That night in Switzerland was a very long, long night of both of us sitting on a bench under the stars, with the most beautiful mountain ranges in the background, contemplating our whole relationship. Most of the details are fuzzy about what was said that night; I just remember crying on a bench underneath one of the most beautiful skies I had ever seen and wondering what my next move would look like from here. It was a rough night for both of us, but somehow, I woke up to a new morning the next day. Some bits of magic from the mystical mountain air must have touched my soul that night because I woke up with a fresh perspective and the realization that this was just a speed bump.

Relationships are complex in general. But tether both partners together and put that relationship under a microscope for a month, and it gets even more intense. Not only that, but there were three people in our travel group, and we were trying to do absolutely everything together while still trying to navigate each other's needs and wants. This was a once-in-a-lifetime opportunity, and at some points, we all had different ideas about what we wanted out of this experience. Ron and I made up that morning, and I decided that I did want to continue traveling with the entire group because we had come so far already.

I will say that if you ever want to get to know someone, like truly and deeply get to know them to their core - travel together. Not to a 5-star all-inclusive resort, but budget travel. I promise you, you will get more than you bargained for. Before we even left on this trip, Ron and I had said to each other that if we made it through this together, we would probably be together for life. And if we don't, then it's probably for the best. Looking back on it now, I am so thankful for those experiences with Ron because it taught us very early on how to work through tough times together and how to compromise with one another. When they say that sometimes you have to fight through the bad in relationships to get to the good, what they mean is that you have to grow and learn from your mistakes. Of course, you should never be constantly fighting, but sometimes you have to break barriers to make progress. But enough of the life lessons, Switzerland brought us the most beautiful scenery of our trip so far but also the most tears. Onward and upward! Goodbye to Switzerland and hello to Italy!

Italia

Hello- Ciao
Thank You-grazie.
Please- Per favore

Yes- Sì.
Sorry- Mi dispiace
Do you speak English- Parli inglese
Where is a hospital- dov'è l'ospedale

Most of the train journey from Switzerland to Venice was uneventful. We had a few different train connections before we finally boarded the train that would take us right outside Venice to our campground. However, the last train connection was pure chaos. As we boarded the train, everyone was sitting in the wrong seats, and we stood in the aisle for about 10 minutes. It seemed like every person on board was arguing over seating arrangements, and when we finally found our assigned seats, they were already taken. We had to prove to the people already sitting down that these were our assigned seats on our ticket, and even after that, they were still hesitant to move.

For the rest of the journey, this is how it went. People arguing over seats and moving around-getting angry every time the train stopped. We hadn't even set foot on Italian soil yet, and the entire train ride was like an over-dramatized Italian soap opera. If this train ride is even a glimpse of what to expect in Italy, then we are in for a real ride. Finally, we made it through the chaos and arrived in Venice to discover a few new things.

#1 Venice is much dirtier than Switzerland

#2 Everyone smokes- like everyone.

#3 The "high and tight" haircut is extremely popular, which was good for us considering when I cut Ron's hair the other night in Switzerland, this is the haircut style that I accidentally gave him.

#4 Unlike Switzerland, where we didn't see a single homeless person, the streets are filled with homeless people.

Our train brought us right outside Venice, where we had to catch a bus to our campsite. While waiting for the bus, a man was just walking around and talking to himself, and then he eventually started talking to us. The man was Italian, and we had no idea what he was saying for the most part. I told him quite a few times, "We do not speak Italian," in Italian so that he would understand me, but he just kept speaking and gesturing. So that was an interesting experience. As far as I could tell, at one point, he was talking about his children, and then I heard a few food words in Italian. But I will never really know for sure.

Once at the campsite, we realized that it was probably the closest thing to a "normal" campsite that we would see in Europe. It was a pretty big campground with cabins, camper vans, and a lot of tents. There were quite a few trees scattered around the lot, which was nice but come to find out, that also meant a lot of mosquitos. Just this morning, I counted close to 40 bites on my body. For some reason, my body has always been like a walking all-you-can-eat buffet for mosquitos. Even when I use bug spray, it's like the buffet food was now covered in mold, but no one cares.

They're still going to eat it. So, to say the least, that part kind of sucked-pun intended.

But moving on, the campsite also had a little restaurant and market attached where we could get food. After the tent was up, we ordered a margarita pizza because we had just been munching on bread and bananas the whole day, and I was starving. Our first taste of Italian pizza was decent for just being from a small market. It was a simple thin crust pizza with a flavorful sauce and just a tiny sprinkle of cheese. Worlds of difference from the two pounds of cheese on every American pizza, but the flavors were on point. That night we stuck to our usual routine of meeting other travelers and playing some card games with new friends.

After a good night's sleep, for me at least, we woke up early to head into Venice. I slept very well because it was hot and humid in Venice, so this was the only time I wasn't freezing cold in the tent. While we were getting ready for the day, Ron discovered a bee's nest in his shower and promptly got attacked by the angry little creatures. He seemed surprisingly calm about it when he told us what happened. If was in the same position, it would have probably ruined the whole day. But he handled it like a trooper and only walked away with a few stings. So with that minor hiccup behind us, the day went on, and we headed into Venice on a bus. When we arrived, we weren't sure what to do, so we just started walking around and proceeded to get lost in the streets of Venice. I am sure we saw most of every significant square and statute and canal, but who knows, we didn't keep track this time. Venice is incredibly confusing. This was the first city we arrived at without any kind of plan.

While we were walking, I found a long line of people waiting to get into a church, so of course I wanted to join in to see what all the hype was about. Once we got inside, we found out that we had to leave our bags and cover up our shoulders and knees before entering. To do this, Brit and I put on our raincoats, and then I had to buy a 1-euro shall/cloth thing to wrap around our waists to cover up our legs. Now I understand this concept and even read before we left for Europe, that you had to cover up your shoulders and legs when visiting churches in Italy, but this still baffles me. First off, these people are making money off of this. Secondly, although we did have to cover up our shoulders and knees, there were quite a few other women who were very large chested and wearing the equivalent of a pastie to cover up sensitive areas.

Again, take what I am saying with a grain of salt, because I don't understand the cultural or religious significance of these rules in the churches, but if I was friends with Jesus, I feel like he might care more about covering up your ta-tas as a sign of respect, more than covering up your kneecaps. But that's just me. I am all for women being able to dress how they want and show as much or as little skin as they personally feel comfortable, but I don't understand the shoulder and knee rule. I'm sure this could potentially be a huge controversy, so I will leave it alone from here.

Moving on, the church was picturesque, filled with statues and paintings, and adornments. You did have to pay to get into certain sections of the church, so we didn't see everything. Paying more was out of the question for us, so we only saw the main section, and after that, it was back to wandering around Venice.

Thankfully we found a small market where we could fill our hungry stomachs. Brit and Ron went for a margarita pizza for 3 euros, and I got a "pizza Gondola" for 3 euros. You can probably guess what shape my pizza was in. While in Venice I couldn't resist the temptation to eat a quippy tourist pizza in the shape of a famous gondola while standing in Venice. It made my heart happy, but in all reality the regular pizzas that Ron and Brit got tasted far superior.

After the food, it was onto try to find the secret gelato shop that I had read about online! Apparently, this was supposed to be the best gelato shops of all gelato shops with a ton of unique flavors. With gelato as my motivation, I took the map for once and tried to navigate us through the winding streets. Keep in mind that I didn't have an exact location of this shop or even its name, just a street name, and the owner's name.

To make a long story short, about 2 hours later, we were still lost and still hadn't found the gelato shop. That was when Brit took over. She also struggled with the directions but not nearly as bad as me. It wasn't long before we turned a corner and finally found the hidden street with a small gelato shop in sight.

When I walked in, my heart was crushed that there was no gelato in sight. However, a gentleman came out and told me he was just getting ready to open. I then asked him if his name was Carlo, and he said yes! At long last, we had found the secret gelato shop! I have never been so happy to find anything in my life before! So we gave Carlo a few minutes to get the gelato out and finish opening up before we got into the line that was already forming outside of the shop.

When it was my turn at the front of the line, I had the daunting task of choosing which flavors I wanted! Hastily I decided on watermelon, pear, and lemon. I figured I would go with a nice fruit concoction to ease my way in. They all tasted amazing. This gelato was as smooth as butter, and each scoop was bursting with freshness and flavor.

Side note, but if you have never traveled outside of the US and tasted the fresh foods in other countries, you are truly missing out. Their flavors, textures, and freshness are something to be admired that I have yet to find a comparison for the US. Even the fresh fruit tastes better!

After round one, I was still curious about a few of the other flavors, so I had to go back for seconds. My second round included Fig, and Hazelnut with cocoa. Both were amazing yet again, and Carlo was such a nice man that it just added to the experience. Plus, both rounds of gelato were only 6 euros total which fit perfectly into my budget. We enjoyed each round of gelato perched outside on a little stoop just to the side of the street so we could continue watching the happy customers of the gelato shop.

I would have gone for a third bowl if I had no self-control, but I figured I would pace myself since this was only our first gelato shop in Italy. After the gelato break, we aimlessly wandered the streets again before heading back for the night. Oh, I almost forgot! We did get a chance to see all the Gondolas and Gondoliers while there but decided not to spend our money on the experience. I kind of felt let down because what the movies would have you believe is that taking a gondola ride in Venice is very romantic and dreamy. In reality (at least for me), it wasn't even close.

I always had this image in my mind of a romantic gondola ride complete with the "typical" Gondolier wearing the striped outfit and singing as he took us around the beautiful canals of Venice. Instead, it was a ton of tourists waiting like cattle being herded to board the boats where the gondoliers looked less than thrilled to be there, and most who were not even wearing the traditional outfits. In addition, the canals all seemed very dirty, and there was not one singing gondolier insight. If the atmosphere had been different, I would have instantly hopped in line, but the whole thing just seemed like a tourist trap designed to take people's money and get you in and out as soon as possible. Which don't get me wrong, is no different from half of the other attractions we are visiting, but I just wasn't feeling this atmosphere.

Gross fact- In the old days, the canals in Venice were used as a sewage system. That is up until the 1960s when their sewage systems were updated. Today there is a modern system that uses septic tanks to treat the water before it is released into the canals, but even now, some of the old-world systems are still intact. Just think of that if you ever get splashed by canal water while trying to get on a gondola in Venice...

Sorry to say, but Venice is much more romanticized in the movies than how it is in real life. Maybe we didn't have such a good experience in Venice because we had just come from Switzerland where the air, water, streets, and people were all held to a pristine level of cleanliness. I honestly feel like we would have had a different impression of Venice if it had been our first stop; or if we hadn't already been traveling for a month and a half, but I think at this point, we were also desensitized by certain stops. Perspective is everything. But C'est la vie, moving onto Florence!

11 euros a night for a tent, pizza, and gelato, made for a happy tummy and a happy wallet.

On the way to the train station, we met a girl from Texas who told us how to wave down a bus (after we had already been waiting for about an hour with multiple busses passing us). She told us that when our bus number drives by, we must wave them down to stop; otherwise, busses do not stop at every stop, which we didn't know. Anyways, she had also been traveling around Europe but with a ton of money apparently. She told me that while in Switzerland, she did every excursion she could because she likes adrenaline. This was on top of doing a week-long sailing trip in Croatia, visiting Australia many times, and staying up all night partying and drinking and meeting people every night. It all sounded kind of crazy and over the top. She was really nice, but I wondered where in the hell all of her money came from and was a bit jealous. I mean, just to do all the excursions alone in Switzerland would have cost thousands of dollars, and most people we have met so far while traveling are on a budget. But our meeting with our new friend was short and sweet, and before we knew it, we were on a train to Florence.

Once we arrived in Florence, I again wanted to try my hand at navigation. Probably a bad idea, but nonetheless, now I was in charge of finding our way to our campsite. At first, I got lost even getting to the bus station, and then we had a very hard time figuring out which stop to get off at until a nice woman behind me told me where to go, and after a few hiccups, we finally arrived.

This place is kind of a half campsite and half hostel in a little town outside of Florence. It took us a while (about 40-60 minutes) to get here, but it was a beautiful drive. From what I can tell, it looks like we drove through one of the many wine countryside's with rolling hills and trees all over and small vineyards scattered about. Even the roads are long and windy up and down the mountains. So much so that when our bus driver took a turn, he had to honk the horn to signal any oncoming cars to stop and give him enough space to make the turn. Talk about a butt-clencher. My heart was in my throat at every turn, wondering how many busses or cars go plummeting to their demise over the edges of this road every year due to the blind corners and tiny roadways. But with a little bit of luck, we made it safely to our destination.

Settling into our accommodations at the campground, we felt very at home. The scenery all around us was gorgeous. It is outside of a city, away from the hustle and bustle and on top of our room is the bar and patio where you can see the countryside. Overall, I would say it would be a pretty nice place if we had more money and didn't have to pay for Internet or to use the pool or little things like that add up. The price wasn't bad at 14 euros each for a clean bed and a roof over our heads, but I would rather spend the extra 5-10 euros for the pool or internet on filling up my growling stomach.

After we checked in, it was already getting late, so we took a walk over to the next town to see if we could find a market. We found a tiny little shop with only a few items on the shelf. I am pretty sure they were already closed, but when the woman saw us looking in her window, she came to the door and let us in. Since the woman was so nice, we felt obligated to buy something, so we each picked out dinner for the night and brought it to the register. While the man was ringing us up, his wife and him were having a conversation in Italian, and when he was done speaking to her, he pulled out his last 3 pastries from the display case and put them on the counter in a bag and told us "free." My face lit up like a kid at a candy shop. They must have known we were hungry and concerned about the money the way we were talking, and even though it had been a very long day with little food, that small act of kindness just made my soul happy. Kindness means everything. We scarfed down the pastries just a few steps outside the shop as we began our journey back to the campsite. That night as Ron and Brit were talking and listening to music, I decided to lay down early and close my eyes because I was so exhausted and happy to be sleeping in a bed again versus a mosquito-infested campsite. I slept great and felt well rested for the next day ahead in Florence.

That morning we woke up early to get a full day visiting Florence. All my bug bites from Venice were driving me crazy, so I took a Benadryl to stop me from scratching my legs raw, but it knocked me out the entire bus ride into town. Once we got into Florence, we took a free walking tour. Unfortunately, our guide for this tour was not as good as the other guides. First off, he wasn't very enthusiastic, and he spoke very broken English, which was completely understandable but hard to decipher. We also had a huge group for the tour, and he didn't talk very loudly, so we could barely hear him. Sadly, after about the second stop, we left the group and explored the city ourselves.

We just wandered around for a while, admiring the architecture and old churches and all the naked statues. Then we went in search of some food. Brit and I found a bunch of small shops on a street corner that had sandwiches for around 2 euros, so we stopped at one of those, and each got a tomato and mozzarella sandwich. They even toasted them for us, and I would have to say that it was a pretty damn good 2-euro sandwich. That is until I dropped it on the ground about halfway through eating it. The most depressing part of the day for sure, especially since I was so hungry. But life went on, and we decided to spend the rest of the day exploring Florence from the map of main attractions we had.

We were able to walk through the entire city from point to point, admiring the rich culture and renaissance architecture. One of my favorite views from the city was along the Arno river, where all the bridges cross; spectacular. There was one bridge in particular, that was very old and unique- The Ponte Vecchio.

This bridge had tiny houses and shops attached to the outer walls; very authentic and old-world looking. The bridge instantly drew us in, so we had to explore. Come to find out, almost every single shop on the bridge was a jewelry shop. Some had a few trinkets and knick-knacks, but mostly jewelry.

The Ponte Vecchio was built in 1345 and was said to be the "first segmental arch bridge in the West." The original shops on the bridge consisted of blacksmiths, butchers, and food shops. But obviously, modern-day consumerism culture has ruined that with all the jewelry shops. This magnificent bridge has most definitely stood the test of time. During World War II, the Ponte Vecchio was the only bridge in Florence that the Germans didn't destroy. Then, standing the test of time and nature once again, in the great flood of 1966, where the Arno river destroyed millions of Florence's priceless treasures and even killed over 100 locals, the Ponte Vecchio gave the middle finger to mother nature and stood firm. To this day, the Ponte Vecchio is one of the most famous bridges in the world.

Although I didn't get the shopping experience I had hoped for while crossing the bridge, taking in the majestic architecture and rich history was well worth it. After the bridge, we headed on to check out our last site of the day, a recreation of the statue of David done by Michelangelo at the top of the city. The original creation of the figure is safely nestled away in the Galleria dell' Accademia di Firenze. Michelangelo was only 26 years old when he started working on the statue of David in 1501 and completed it in 1504. Also, for those of you wondering who David is, the figure represents David from the biblical story of David and Goliath and David's victorious triumph over Goliath. This statue is unique because Michelangelo decided to portray David BEFORE his battle with Goliath instead of other artists representing David AFTER his victory. More so, the figure is carved from one single block of marble. Although it would have been amazing to witness in person one of the most famous statues in the world, we weren't really feeling another museum or gallery. So we opted for the outside hike to see the recreation of the figure.

Once there, the view was gorgeous from the top. You could see all the bridges scattered across the waterway and the city's main buildings. It was a perfect way to end the day in Florence. Florence was beautiful but again, just another city. I think I would have appreciated it more if I hadn't seen so many cities so far during this last month, but just like Venice, it didn't match up, and after a while, city after city just starts to look the same, and you find the same kinds of shops and things in each one. It was still a fantastic experience to be somewhere so rich in culture and history, but it would have been better as a one-stop week vacation.

Once we arrived back at the campsite for the night, we were starving again since we couldn't find another market during the day for dinner food, so we headed for the restaurant above us for dinner. We decided to order a large marinara pizza which was the cheapest thing on the menu for around 5 euros each. For future reference, when you order a marinara pizza in Italy, that is all that comes on the pizza- marinara sauce. We were all quite disappointed, but the pizza was still flavorful despite the lack of cheese. The rest of the evening ended with research for the next leg of our journey.

After many days of furiously writing, I am finally caught up with my journal! So incredibly happy to be living in the present with my writing and I hope to keep on track. So far, I don't have much exciting news to report for the day. Last night we booked a Tuscany wine tour and tasting in two days, so today we decided to stay at the camp village and just relax and save money since we were splurging quite a bit on the wine tour. So far, the day has consisted of journal writing in the morning coupled with a bit of web surfing because we splurged for the 5 euro internet connection, and an afternoon nap. We will probably head upstairs to the restaurant in search of another cheap dinner in a while. But for now, I will write about a few things that I have forgotten. This next one, I will call the toilet diaries.

The Toilet Diaries

One of my main concerns before this trip was planned was public restrooms. Online I read many horror stories about different restrooms that people have come across while traveling Europe. So, while I was over here, I figured I would take pictures and document the different bathroom experiences. Unfortunately, I haven't been keeping up with that, so I would just like to rewind and give a glance at the experiences I have had so far.

#1 I am pretty sure that there have been a few days where I have spent more money on bathroom fees than I have on food. From .30 euros to 2 euros, you must pay to use the toilet in most places we have come across so far.

#2 They don't always have toilet paper, which luckily, I always have a stash in my bag.

#3: Many places have a nice bathroom area but have no toilet lid for some reason.

Those are pretty much the overall summaries in short. Now to give a few distinct instances…

Interesting Experience #1- Only once have I come across a 100% complete "squat toilet." This "toilet" consisted of 2 spots on the floor to put your feet on and a small hole directly beneath you. I was not impressed, and although I have a decent amount of experience peeing in the woods, trying to aim for a tiny hole was a whole different task. This restroom was just off the beach in Cerbère, France, where we had a train layover.

Interesting Experience #2 -A café/McDonald's in a train station in Venice. For this bathroom, you had to walk upstairs into a room with sinks where one door was marked male and the other female. While I was waiting, I could see a kind of glowing light under the door, which was odd, and when it was my time to go in, I discovered that it was because the bathroom was solely lit by blacklight. My first disco bathroom experience.

Interesting Experience #3: While hiking in the Swiss mountains, we found a small shop where we stopped to get cheese and use the restroom. In the bathroom, there was a cross between a regular toilet and a port-o-potty, complete with a bucket of water in front of it and a pitcher attached with a string so that you could wash the toilet after you were done.

Those were the three experiences that have stood out in my mind so far. Other than that, I have run into many different toilets and flushing mechanisms, including a button on the floor, pull handle from the ceiling, motion sensor you ran your hand over, etc. But, oh! I almost forgot about 2 other ones! One was on the train from Venice to Florence, where a sign read, "do not use the facilities while pulled in or near a station." So, in translation, whatever went down the toilet went directly on the tracks. This also became very apparent as you sat down to use the toilet and could not only hear the train below you but feel the breeze of the tracks going by.

One of the best and most surprising bathrooms I have found was halfway up the Eiffel tower. To get to the restroom, you climbed a small spiral staircase to the top until you got into an opening with a few separate rooms. When I entered the room, I found a nice red-painted and decorated room that was extremely clean with a little chair in the corner and your own private sink and mirror. I didn't even have to wait in line. I was pleasantly surprised, thinking that I would find small dirty, and gross stalls with a long line due to the sheer traffic of people who climb the tower daily. But it was very nice to have a clean space and some time to wash my face after the sweaty climb up the stairs. But that is about it for now for my bathroom diaries. I look forward to the next time I update this with more experiences!

Wine Country and Roma

Finally made it to Rome; Well, on the outskirts of Rome at least. But, before I get to Rome, I need to write about our fabulous trip to Tuscany! We booked a tour to the Tuscany Countryside for our last day in Florence. On the morning of the tour, we woke up with the sun and took the bus into town to catch yet another bus out of the city. The tour seemed like it would be a good one right from the beginning. We were in an updated air-conditioned coach packed with other tourists, and the tour guide Eliza seemed very upbeat and friendly. Our first stop was the lovely town of Siena. This was a medieval town that was once a rival of Florence.

Once there, we had a guided tour of the town from a local. She was charming even though it was hard to understand her with her accent. She explained how Siena is separated into 17 separate districts, and each section got a chance to represent its district with a horse race in the main square twice a year. They did not compete for prizes or money but basically just bragging rights. Oh, and the race was also held in honor of the Virgin Mary (no connection in my mind). But the race was highly celebrated. It takes the whole year to prepare for but lasts shorter than one minute and only consists of three laps around the town square. Each year about 50,000 people pack into the tiny square to watch the race. The race's official name is Palio di Siena or Corse del Palio to the locals. We only had a few hours to spend in Siena, but we truly appreciated the tour and history lesson, as well as the gorgeous architecture.

After Siena, it was off to Chianti country! We visited the Chianti region and an organic farm where we indulged in lunch and wine tasting. The view was absolutely stunning from this farm. The rolling fields of vineyards lit up the countryside. Grapes and greenery everywhere. It was just how I had imagined Tuscany and wine country. We even got a small tour of the farm where we got a chance to see the winery, vineyard, olive grove, and cows. I also learned that extra virgin olive oil is produced when the olives are pressed the first time. Virgin olive oil is from the second press, and regular olive oil is from the third press. Basically, extra virgin olive oil is the purest form of olive oil that still has all its vitamins and minerals. In contrast, regular olive oil is often processed and lacks the vital nutrients-And now you know.

After the tour was the best part - lunch and wine tasting. I cannot begin to tell you how unbelievably excited I was about this. Not only had I worked at a winery for the last year learning about wines and dreaming of one day drinking wine in Tuscany, but pair that wine with homemade Italian food while I was overlooking the countryside where my olive oil and wine came from? I was in heaven.

We began lunch with bruschetta paired with a glass of white wine. The toasted bruschetta with garlic was so fresh and aromatic, and the white wine made a perfect pairing bringing out the flavors and spices of the bruschetta.

The meal and wine tasting set-up was a family-style table with one bottle of wine on the table every so often. About one bottle per 5 people. This essentially meant that we had the chance to pour our own wine-as much as we wanted. Granted, we still had to share the bottle with others as well. Someone pinch me. Typical wine tastings in the states are limited to 1-2 oz pours- Not in Italy!

The second course was homemade al dente pasta with Bolognese sauce and parmesan. This was paired with their Chianti wine. A perfect combination. It was different eating al dente pasta because typically, at home I cook my pasta past the point of no return and boil my noodles to death until you can gently just mash them in your mouth with the same consistency as mashed potatoes. Don't hate- everyone has their preferences. The Italians would probably have me jailed for this, but no one has to tell them.

But I did really enjoy the way the pasta was cooked this time, and it almost made the dish seem heartier and filling. The Chianti by the way, made from the Sangiovese grapes- Oh man, chefs kiss. The dry, almost bitterness with subtle fruit flavors hit your tongue perfectly. It was also the ideal match with the Bolognese sauce, the flavors dancing off the tomatoes and acidity.

The third course was a salad served with 2 kinds of cheese and 2 cured types of meat, one salami and one ibérico ham. This dish was paired with a Merlot. The cheeses were fantastic, and the salami was pretty good, but I just couldn't stomach the ibérico ham. I think the taste was all right, but the consistency was something that I have not experienced in meat before, and it was not pleasing to my palate, so I just gave my piece to Ron. But the Merlot and the cheese had me in heaven. Also, by this point, I think I had downed more than a bottle of wine to myself, thanks to Ron's heavy hand pouring and our table mates being very reserved about their wine consumption. I should also mention that this salad course was Ron's first vegetable consumed since we started traveling. He is less than a fan of vegetables, and Brit and I almost spit out our wine when we saw Ron take a bite of his salad. The moment was so unbelievable, we had to snap a picture of it. The last course was a dessert butterscotch port paired with almond biscotti. First off, the biscotti were absolutely phenomenal, and when you dipped them in the port wine? - OMG, food orgasm in my mouth.

First, the biscotti had a perfect shape and looked like it was crafted by bakers who had spent years of their lives perfecting this little miracle. Second, the biscotti had the perfect crunch when you bit into them, and then the flavor profiles hit you ever so slightly and perfectly, with the almond coming across as the star player. If you have never had it before, port wine has a much higher alcohol content and is typically a much sweeter and almost a bit thicker type of wine. When I took the first sip of wine, the strong alcohol flavor was the first that came across, and then my mouth was hit with a strong butterscotch flavor with another strong alcohol component that finished off my palette. The port was a bit strong by itself. However, I could have soaked a pound of that biscotti in the port wine and consumed it as a meal.

As a whole, the entire meal was "Bellissima," as they say here in Italy. This is how the Italians say "beautiful", but also meaning delicious while also rubbing their finger on their cheek. It was so refreshing eating hot homemade food that was completely fresh from only a few feet away. We also had more than enough wine to satisfy our souls. As we were leaving the table, I even rolled up as many biscotti in a napkin as I could to take back for a snack later! Then, after a few pictures of the picturesque countryside and getting a few wine corks for souvenirs, we headed to the next stop, San Gimignano.

San Gimignano was another lovely little medieval town complete with a "world's best choice of gelato shop!" So of course, Brit and I had to sample some! Ron wasn't the biggest fan of gelato even in Italy, but that just meant more for us! I tried raspberry-rosemary, Blackberry-lavender, and grapefruit sparkling wine gelato. Brit tried caramel, coffee, and coconut. The raspberry-rosemary was unlike any ice cream flavor I have ever tasted. The combination went together very well. It was so different but good. The blackberry-lavender was also very good, and the grapefruit was good but a bit too sour for me. Brit and I each tried each other's, and after all the sampling, it was very easy to see why they were voted the best gelato in the world for two years. My heart was happy. My tongue was happy. And my stomach was packed full of gelato.

Fun facts about San Gimignano that don't have to do with gelato. The town was filled with medieval towers that shot up toward the sky. Many more towers than in Siena. This was because the buildings were a sign of wealth and power. Out of the original 72 towers constructed, only about 14 stand today. The historic center of San Gimignano is a UNESCO world heritage site. It was a relatively affluent city until 1348, when the black plague killed many locals and caused others to leave. It's estimated that a little less than 8,000 people reside in San Gimignano today. Exploring this medieval playground with its massive towers was wonderful, but it was back to the bus to continue onward to Pisa before we knew it.

It didn't take very long to get to Pisa, but we were very rushed once we were there. As we hopped off our bus and into the city, we explained to our tour guide that we would not be taking the tour bus back because we had to catch an earlier train back to make it back to our campground on the last bus from the city center. I'm glad we planned ahead because if we had taken the tour bus back to Florence, we would have been stuck there for the night because it would have been too late to get another city bus back to our campground.

After getting everything in order, we were let loose to explore! Although we didn't get very much time in Pisa, it was just enough to see the leaning tower and take a few pictures with it. Just like the rest of the trip, it was remarkable to visit places that I have read about and seen in movies all my life.

Walking up to The Leaning Tower of Pisa, I was surprised it was not leaning as much as I thought, or as much as it seemed in the movies. Apparently, the tower was not leaning as much anymore because a few years ago, architects had to re-stabilize the monument to prevent it from falling over; therefore, the building was not leaning as much as it once was. It's an interesting concept that to preserve a site, you must interfere with its integrity. But then again, most of the places we have seen would probably be in ruins by now if they hadn't been preserved. It was still really cool to see The Leaning Tower in real life because I had seen it in pictures so many times before.

Also, a brief history lesson on The Leaning Tower of Pisa, because we didn't get to spend much time there learning about it, so we had to do our research later on! In Italy, the tower is officially called the Torre Pendente di Pisa and is located in the Piazza del Duomo, which is the city's main square - and the only area we were able to visit in the city. Construction on the tower began in 1173 and was initially built to be a bell tower. After five years, the building started to lean once the third floor was complete. The foundation was built only 3 meters deep, and the clay soil could not take the tower's weight. Construction was then halted for the next 100 years as Pisa focused on its war with Genoa. Finally, after 100 years, an engineer came in and continued building, attempting to correct this mistake to only make it worse. Time after time again during construction, each correction only made the tower lean more. Miraculously, the building survived the bombings of World War II, and then in 1990, the tower was closed to the public and reopened again in 2001 with a little less lean.

Even though the lean wasn't as severe as it used to be, we spent a decent amount of time trying to get one of the famous "hold the learning tower up with your hands" obligatory picture for all tourists. After the whirlwind of pictures, we rushed to catch the connecting trains and buses it took to finally get us back to our campground.

The hefty price tag of 85 euros per person for the tour was hard to stomach at first but ended up being more than worth the price of hard budgeting a couple of days before to be able to afford it.

The following day we woke up and began packing our bags for Rome when one of the housekeepers came into our room. She spoke Italian, and we had no clue what she was saying but eventually figured out that we think she was trying to ask us when we were leaving. Always an interesting experience trying to communicate with others in another language. But from there, we hit the bus station and figured out our route to Roma!

We took the slow train and not the high-speed train because we didn't have to pay for the slow-speed train. But in exchange, it was much longer to get to Rome, and we had to change trains a few times. Once we finally got to our stop, we thought we would have to walk to where we were staying, but we were more than happy to find a free shuttle to take us there!

Checking in was a game of hiding a person again because technically, we only paid for two people to stay because adding a third person to your hut would cost more. So this time Brit went to go hide in the bar nearby. At first, the woman couldn't even find our reservation, but thankfully, they still gave us accommodations. The camping village was a pretty big area whose surroundings reminded me of the Dominican Republic. The whole space was lush and green and filled with flowers and beauty. The little cabin we had was just a tiny area, about 8x7 feet, and just big enough to fit two twin beds with a little space in between them to walk.

After getting settled in, we took a trek to the market down the road and we were so happy to find our first "real" market in Italy, where we bought way more food than needed. But on the upside, for dinner, we dined like royalty-like backpacking royalty at least! I spent a whole 5 euros and 11 cents at the store and bought iced tea, yogurt, an apple, 2 bananas, sliced chicken, bread, munchies, and a pretzel snack pack. So much food! Of course, we all shared our food and were able to save some for the next day as well. Other than that, we just explored the area and found some wild animals in a little farm area at the end of the campground. We stayed out playing with the animals until the mosquitos got too bad to stand, and it brought us back to our cabin, where we are sitting now and where we are informally getting a chance to meet our neighbors through the paper-thin walls.

I should have mentioned that the tiny cabins we are staying in are all connected in small groups of 4 and have only about one wooded panel in between each room. So Ron was watching his comedy show, I was writing, and Brit was reading, just relaxing and minding our own business, and our neighbors showed up and barged in the room like a pack of wild hyenas. Cackling and laughing, or crying, we couldn't even tell, so hard that the whole campground could probably hear them. Not only that, but they are constantly throwing themselves against the wall, doing God knows what, which makes the entire cabin shake. Do I sound like a grumpy old lady?

Maybe, but I just wanted to rest and relax. And I shouldn't be complaining at only 6 euros a night for accommodations. But, this should be an interesting night. Stay tuned for tomorrow's update on the night's activities.

The night ended up being not as bad as we first thought. Everyone quieted down after a while, and we were able to sleep. That is, everyone except me. I woke up around 4:30 am and couldn't go back to sleep, so I read until about a little after 6:00 am, and then I dozed off before we woke up to get ready for the morning. I think we are starting to miss sleeping in because, especially in Italy, we haven't been waking up as early as we usually would around 6 or 7am, but yet sleeping in until 8 or 9 or even 10 am on some days.

Our commute into Rome was also pretty long, so we didn't even get into the city center until around noon. When we got dropped off by the train, a bazaar or flea market was going on in the street. We couldn't resist stopping and looking, and my shopping instinct took over when I found an adorable pair of tree earrings that I had to have. (I do miss shopping and buying things!) The bazaar was such a great experience though, and full and bustling with life! There were little tents all over the place that included anything and everything for sale, from clothes and jewelry to handmade goods and old antiques.

Once we had our fill of the bazaar, we continued into the city to see the Colosseum. We bought a 12-euro pass to get into the Roman Forum and the Colosseum. But before we started exploring, we sat down and ate lunch. It was a simple lunch of peanut butter and jelly sandwiches, but the fact that we ate lunch with the Colosseum as our backdrop was priceless. Yet another world-wonder that I had seen all my life in movies and pictures, and now here I was, eating lunch on a grassy knoll just marveling at its beauty.

It was a relief to take a break from walking because I wore flip-flops, which was a horrible decision considering the blisters and dirt covering my feet. All I wanted was to give my toes a chance to see the sun, but that backfired.

Back to Rome. The Colosseum was draped in a mysterious and ancient beauty. Exhibiting unwavering strength and knowledge from all the events in the ancient world. It was so different witnessing the colossal giant in real life. Like most things, the movies made the Colosseum appear much bigger than it is, but even so, it is still a massive work of stone art.

After soaking up the views of the outside of the Colosseum, we decided to first visit the Roman Forum and the surrounding area. It still amazes me how much deep-rooted history was in the very place we were standing. It always makes me think: who was here before I was? What are all the events that have taken place here that were never recorded? Just the sheer magnitude of trying to simply absorb all the history is enough to knock you off your feet.

A little backstory on the Roman Forum, this was basically the epicenter of activity in Rome. This area consisted of many government buildings, religious buildings, and social events. It's estimated that the Roman Forum dates back to 735 B.C. This area was first used as a local marketplace but evolved into the heart of Rome around 500 B.C. Many original structures in the forum were built to honor Gods, Goddesses, and men. Over time, most of the Roman Forum was destroyed and turned into pastureland until it was rediscovered again in 1803. Excavation of the land took over 100 years to get the structures and sites tourists visit today.

We could have opted for the headphone guides while we walked around the forum, but it was extra money, and for me, sometimes I just appreciated the silence while walking around and soaking it all in. We soaked in the sun. We soaked in all the dirt and dust on our feet and legs. And we soaked in the rich history all around us.

After the Roman Forum, we headed over to the Colosseum. Since we had purchased tickets for the Roman Forum and Colosseum together, we skipped the long line of people that had now formed to buy tickets and went right in. Stepping into the Colosseum, I had mixed feelings. Although it was magnificent inside, I was again confused about how much smaller it was from what I was expecting. Don't get me wrong, I still had goosebumps and that "Oh my God" realization that I was INSIDE the Colosseum, but it's just different experiencing something in real life for the first time versus just seeing it on tv or reading about it.

This grand amphitheater was initially commissioned by Emperor Vespasian as a gift to the Roman people around 70 A.D.-72 A.D. and then opened to the public around 80 A.D. by Vespasian's son. The first opening of the Colosseum included "100 days of games", with animal fights and gladiatorial combats. The inside of the Colosseum could house around 50,000 spectators, making it "the largest amphitheater in the Roman World." Compare that to a modern-day football stadium, which on average can hold about 60,000 spectators. This was a massive undertaking to build this kind of structure in ancient Rome. The gladiators who fought inside the Colosseum were often criminals, prisoners, slaves, and even an occasional woman who would compete. Years of hardship, weather, and natural disasters have destroyed a good portion of the Colosseum, but restoration efforts have kept this ancient marvel standing over the years.

Walking around the Colosseum, you could see intricate passageways and tunnels under the arena, but unfortunately, that area was roped off from the public. We decided to sit down in a corner overlooking the stadium and snack on some fruit as we let our imaginations run wild, fabricating these intricate fighting scenes that may have taken place in the very place we were sitting long, long ago. So far, this has been one of my favorite things to do in the places we have visited. To just sit in silence and take a minute to appreciate everything around me. To take a few minutes and let my mind run wild, imagining what this very spot looked like thousands of years ago. Sometimes as a tourist, you may just hop on a guided tour of somewhere and try to soak up as much information as you can and take thousands of pictures without taking the time out to appreciate where you are and live in the moment. Never let that moment pass you by, to just appreciate the sheer magnitude of where you are. We spent a decent amount of time just soaking it all in before we realized that we still had a long commute to get back to our campsite for the night.

Once we began our commute back, we ran into some unfortunate luck of it being Sunday, so not all trains were running, and we had to wait for quite a long time for a train to take us back. On the train, Ron and I sat next to a nice older gentleman who began talking to us in Italian and then realized we spoke English, so he switched to a mix of broken English, Italian, and some Spanish for some reason. It was hard to understand him, but from the conversation we had, I believe he was talking about the weather and how bad it was and how it was raining in July but never any other time. He also went on and on, telling us about different places in Florida and Islands we should visit and how beautiful they are. From what Ron gathered, the gentleman was a former sailor. Even with the language barrier, Ron and I just smiled during the conversation when we weren't sure what the man was saying. Friendliness translates in all languages.

I think he was just happy to be talking to others, and we were more than happy to listen. When we got back to the city where our campground was, the bus going to the campground was no longer running, so we hiked it back instead. It wasn't the most pleasant thing to do in sandals after a long day already, but it's not like we had a choice.

Vatican City and Backtracking

Three days later, the writing and catching up continues. Backtracking to the last day in Rome, we woke up pretty early to visit the Vatican, and even though we were "churched out," a trip to Vatican City was essential. Which, by the way, if you didn't know, Vatican City is not only a church, but its own independent country. It is the smallest country in the world, to be exact, about 2 miles in size. However, unlike other countries, no customs or passport stamps were needed to enter Vatican City. You wouldn't even know when you crossed the border between Italy and Vatican City most of the time.

When we arrived in the courtyard center, the line to enter St. Peter's Basilica and The Sistine Chapel wrapped around the entire square. Ron was more than exhausted from seeing one too many churches, so he sat down against a wall in the shade, and Brit and I joined the herd of people waiting to get inside. We were happy to discover that the line moved quickly, and although we were in line for hours, compared to the length of the line, we were glad to get inside before dark.

Although, at this point, we were utterly exhausted, we still tried to soak up all the beautiful artwork that covered the inside. The Renaissance artwork was stunning, and the sheer magnitude of the space took your breath away. We wandered around, marveling at the gorgeous artwork and masterpieces around every corner. Although it was a once-in-a-lifetime opportunity to be here, we did skip out on learning more about the history behind Vatican City, St Peter's Basilica, and the Sistine Chapel because, honestly, it wasn't one of our priorities. We knew we wanted to visit, but there was no need to fully immerse ourselves in Vatican City's culture.

That is one thing people will always criticize you on when you travel. People will gasp at the fact that you didn't visit a specific museum, statue, or restaurant while in a particular city, but you have to prioritize your own wants and needs. Vatican City was gorgeous, but once we had explored it briefly, it was a check off our bucket list, and we were moving on! That was of course, after we rejoined Ron outside and enjoyed a snack under one of the archways.

Before we left Rome, there was one other big site on our bucket lists: The Trevi Fountain. However, once we made our way there, my heart was crushed to see that the whole fountain was under construction and there was not a drop of water in sight. Instead of crystal-clear waters flowing from this masterpiece, it was covered in construction cloths and boards.

Hot tip, if you ever travel somewhere specifically to see a particular museum, statue, monument, etc. Do your research ahead of time to make sure it is open and not under construction!

If you have ever watched any kind of movie that takes place in Italy, chances are there was a scene with the Trevi Fountain in it. Not only is the fountain the largest in the city, but it is by far the most beautiful. There is also a myth behind the Trevi Fountain and why so many people throw coins in.

If you throw one coin in, you will come back to Rome.

If you throw two coins in, you will come back and fall in love.

If you throw three coins in, You will marry the love you found when you return.

Every year, millions of people flock to the Trevi Fountain to kiss a coin and toss it in the water to try their luck at finding true love.

Even though there was no water to toss a coin into, there was a bridge than spanned the length of the fountain over the empty construction mess. Even without water, we still had to walk across the bridge and throw a coin in the dry fountain. With a sour kiss on a coin, I tossed my wish to return to Rome backward into the fountain, where it hit bottom with a clunk instead of a splash. With shattered dreams, we spent the remainder of the day wandering the city and getting some gelato one more time before going back to camp early and heading for Naples the next day.

Misfortune in Napoli

The train ride to Naples was short and uneventful. When we arrived, we headed right for our campsite in Pozzuoli. Pozzuoli was a beautiful little Italian town on the water with mountains all around, just over 8 miles outside of Naples. We booked a campsite here because it was cheaper than staying inside Naples. We took a train to the outskirt of Pozzuoli and walked the rest of the way to our accommodations while overlooking the ocean and mountains.

Once we got there, the staff was extremely friendly, but we were right next to Volcano Solfatara, which, just as it sounds, emitted a horrible sulfur smell. But, smell aside, how many people can say they have camped right next to a Volcano?! I could have lived without the smell, but it was just a part of the whole experience. Unfortunately, the campground was also a breeding ground for mosquitos, so it was a constant battle with the little bloodsuckers. But for around 11 euros each a night it was a bargain. We spent the rest of the evening exploring the volcano and the surrounding area before settling in for a good night's rest.

The next day, we woke up early to explore Naples but sad to say that we didn't find much but a dirty city packed with streetcars and people selling things when we got there. So rather than wasting our time in another town, we decided to hop on a train to Pompeii. I was so giddy to see this ancient city buried by volcanic ash, but life had other plans. We weren't there even 20 minutes before the excruciating pain started.

To backtrack, a few days ago, I started having mild pain, which I knew right away was a UTI because I am used to getting them every so often. So, just like I would at home, I bought cranberry juice and drank water like a camel getting ready to cross the desert. Usually, this is all I need to take care of this problem, and the pain goes away in a few days. No doctor trip needed. Unfortunately, I couldn't keep up my consumption of fluids because I didn't always have access to water, cranberry juice, or a bathroom to relieve myself. I was still convinced it would go away on its own, but after battling pain on and off for the last few days, I guess my body had enough, and the pain quickly intensified.

As we started walking around Pompeii, each step I took was excruciating, and although it was hot out, I could tell the sweat rolling down my face wasn't from the heat, but pain. I desperately didn't want to take away from Ron and Brit's experience, but I was dizzy with pain and decided I needed to see a doctor as soon as possible.

I have honestly never been in that much pain in my entire life, and with every second of time that passed, the pain just intensified. The pain was so bad that I couldn't think, I had a hard time walking, and I would have done anything at that point to make the pain go away. So after only getting a precious glimpse inside this ancient city that I had waited my whole life to see, I was retreating back.

While we were waiting for a train to take us back to the central station in Naples, the pain was so unbearable that at one point, I honestly thought I wasn't going to make it back to Naples, let alone make it back to the US to ever see my family again.

Every minute seemed like an hour, and I thought the train would never come. I tried sitting down, but that made the pain 10 times worse, so I just stood there, hunched over in pain with a death grip on my own hands, squeezing them as tight as possible to try to take my mind off the pain in my abdomen.

At this point, my anxiety had taken complete hold of me, and I was baffled at what this pain could possibly be, and if I misdiagnosed my original pain as a UTI, but it was something much worse that I had now been ignoring for days. My mind was racing, and my body felt like it was dying. I had never in my life experienced this kind of pain.

It seemed like hours before we got back into Naples and figured out how to get to a hospital. I can't tell you how many locals we asked in our best Italian accents, "dov'è l'ospedale" - "where is a hospital," before we were finally pointed in the right direction. We walked for a few blocks before arriving at a tiny place with a red cross.

By this time, the pain had subsided to a manageable level where I no longer thought I might keel over and die. Somewhere on the train ride back to Naples, I had another sharp burst of pain, and little by little, the pain had started to subside.

When we walked inside the "emergency room," it was a small space with only a few chairs and a small front window. When I went to the front window to check in, not one person spoke English; not one. Preparing myself mentally, I grabbed out my little Italian translation book and translated the phrase "I have a UTI and need a doctor." Funny enough, the book had that exact sentence translated. I took a few minutes and scribbled down a few other choice phrases on a piece of paper and proceeded to the check-in counter.

With my very broken Italian, I told the man at the front what I was checking in for. He then brought me back behind the counter and handed me off to another woman. I again asked if she spoke English, and the reply was "no." I think she asked for my papers from what she was gesturing and saying in Italian, so I gave her everything I had, including my insurance information and passport. She kept asking me one question over and over in Italian, and after a while of trying to understand each other, I think she just gave up and then gestured for me to sit down.

Once I sat down, my mind was racing with concern, wondering what the doctor would be like or how on earth we were going to get by with the language barrier. I was so nervous that my original pain was now at the back of my mind.

When I finally got called back, one of the nurses took me down a long hallway where at the end, there was what looked like a triage room. The nurse walked me in, literally stood me in one of the corners, and motioned for me to stay. As I looked around, there were about 6 different beds with patients in them and two doctors rotating around each bed. I felt so uncomfortable and out of place.

A few times the doctors had to get behind me to get supplies, so I would just nicely move out of the way every time until one doctor finally approached me directly. He asked me something in Italian, to which I asked back, "Parli Inglese?" "Do you speak English?" Again, the answer was "no." From there, in my best Italian accent, I spoke a few phrases of the pain I was experiencing and what I needed. The doctor then nodded and pushed me outside of the room, and with a few awkward hand gestures and a minute of struggling, he told me to "wait," the first English word I had heard besides "no."

As I was awkwardly waiting just outside the triage room, chaos ensued inside. The two doctors were running back and forth between patients trying to take care of all of them at once. While the doctors were busily working inside, a man on a gurney was wheeled into the hallway. I'm not sure what nationality the man was, but he spoke English to whoever he was on the phone with. He was explaining to the person on the other line that the doctors were going to fix his foot and give him an operation. Strangely, I wondered how in the world he knew this information because no one here spoke English, and he most certainly was not speaking Italian to the nurses that were coming around to check on him. I'm not sure if he was just assuming they were going to save his foot or if he found someone who could translate into English for him, but I never got the chance to ask him. All I can say is that his foot was unlike anything I have ever seen before. Just imagine the most grotesque scene from Grey's Anatomy that you have ever seen, and then intensify it 100 times. From my observation, but also zero medical experience, his foot looked mangled and rotten beyond repair. I'm not sure if he could see the horrified look on my face, but my fear was that this guy would go under surgery tonight, thinking he would wake up with a working foot again, just to wake up instead, missing a limb. I could barely comprehend the horrific scene of this poor man's foot and the chaos all around me before they wheeled him out into the unknown.

I turned my attention back to the triage room, and at the far end of the room I saw a doctor struggling to communicate with another man on a gurney. It was clear there was a communication issue because hands were flying in the air, and the man on the gurney kept shaking his head and waving his hands in the air looking for answers.

After a few moments of struggling, one of the doctors motioned for me to join them and come into the room. I walked over to the doctors and the man on the gurney. One of the doctors started saying, "Parli Italiano Parli Inglese, Parli Italiano Parli Inglese," while waving his hands back and forth from the patient to the other doctors. Roughly translated, this phrase means, "speak Italian, speak English," meaning, the doctors wanted me to roughly translate from Italian to English.

Being in mild shock that I was called into the room to be a translator, I started waving my arms no and saying, "no, no Parli Italiano, no Parli Italiano," meaning I DO NOT speak Italian. The man on the bed then looked at me and said in English, "So do you speak Italian?". To which I explained to him that I knew a few phrases, but I most certainly did NOT speak Italian, and he told me neither did he. I told him he was more than welcome to take my phrasebook and try to figure out what the doctors were saying, but I didn't have a clue. He turned down the offer in defeat, also realizing that we were past the point of any help that a small phrasebook would have offered.

After my conversation with the man on the bed, the doctor again shouted, "Tu! Tu Parli Italiano. Tu Parli Inglese!" meaning "You speak Italian. You speak English." Again, I replied to the doctors, "no, no no no no no, no Parli Italiano" while waving my arms furiously. The only thing I could think was that because earlier I had spoken three sentences of roughly translated Italian from my translation book, the doctors thought I would be able to fully translate from Italian to English for this patient. But they were dead wrong.

This charade went on for at least a solid 5 minutes while a bigger crowd of doctors and nurses gathered around us. During this time, the doctors and nurses all began screaming and yelling at each other while making big gestures with their arms. This was literally like an old Italian soap opera with all the doctors and nurses standing around yelling and screaming. At the same time, I argue with a doctor trying to tell him that I do not speak Italian. Finally, one of the doctors must have just gotten so frustrated with me and given up because he violently shoved me back out into the hallway and again told me to "wait." I felt so sorry for the man on the bed, not knowing what was going on, but there was nothing I could do. Frustrated and confused, all I could do was stand outside the room again and "wait." I wasn't quite sure what I was waiting for, but I was waiting.

After a while, another gentleman showed up and just silently stood next to me. After looking at me a few times awkwardly and not saying anything, I finally asked him, "Parli Inglese?" Much to my surprise, his answer was "yes I do" in broken English! I was so elated to finally have someone to talk to in this hospital that somewhat spoke English and wasn't currently in a trauma situation! The man explained that his wife was in the hospital, and he was just waiting on her. We attempted to have a conversation in broken English and Italian, and I wanted to tell him that the doctors wanted a translator, but the man on the gurney was gone by then.

After a few minutes, the man walked into the room to visit his wife, and I was left alone once again. It wasn't long this time until the doctor came out and grabbed me to bring me back into the room. He then handed me a printed piece of paper, said something in Italian, and then said, "You take," and started motioning with his arms. His right arm started vertical and then moved down until it was lying horizontally on top of his opposite arm. The doctor just went on repeatedly saying, "you take" and making the arm motion. Clearly seeing that I was getting frustrated, the man I spoke to earlier came over and began slightly translating for the other doctor. Between the three of us, we eventually figured out that the doctor had given me a prescription to take to the "chemist," meaning pharmacy. We determined that I was supposed to take the medicine in the morning and at night with food. I guess the doctor was trying to motion sunset and sunrise with his arms when he told me to take the medicine.

No tests, no other questions, nothing. I was just handed a piece of paper and escorted out. By this time, my pain was all but non-existent, probably from the sheer magnitude of adrenaline running through my system. With my slip of paper and a new understanding of Italian hospital culture, I walked out of the room and back to Ron, who was waiting for me. At this point, Brit had left to go back to the campsite. I then proceeded to tell Ron about my whole experience with the Italian doctors on our walk to the "Chemist." Once we got to the pharmacy, I again asked the pharmacist if he spoke English which, surprise, surprise, he did not. I was silently handed my prescription, and we headed back to the campsite.

When we got back, I opened my prescription to take the first dose, and it definitely was not what I was expecting. I thought it would be a packet of pills like in the US when you have a UTI, but instead, it was a packet of white powder. With some help from Google, I tried translating the package and found out I think I was supposed to mix the packet with water and drink it. So that's what I did. Probably the equivalent of buying drugs off a stranger from the street and ingesting them, but it's not like I had a choice at this point.

Like I said earlier, I was at my wit's end from pain, and I was willing to do anything to make it go away, or at this point, do anything to make sure the pain didn't come back. My body had been through significant trauma. Physical trauma from the pain, and emotional and mental trauma from the Italian hospital. I just wanted to drink my unknown powder mixture and relax, but that wasn't the end of my suffering.

Sometimes when it rains, it pours fucking cats and dogs, and my pain and hospital experience was not the only bad thing to happen to me that night. After I took my white powder packet, I laid down in the tent to relax and write about my hospital experience while it was fresh in my mind. I was lying on my stomach writing when I felt a sharp pain on my chest. I jumped up and checked things out, but nothing was there, and I thought maybe it was just the way I was lying or maybe my bra had pinched me. So I laid back down and continued writing. A few moments later, I felt 2 more sharp pains in my chest, almost like a bite. And of course, me being the frantic person that I am about bugs, I jumped up again in sheer panic, looking down and searching in my shirt, trying to find what was biting me. As I looked down, I found a small red ant crawling around in my bra, and of course, right away, the screeching started, and I flung off my shirt and bra quicker than I ever have in my life. I just wanted it off me. That's when I looked down and found that there were three large bites on my boob where the ant had bitten me. Of course, it burned like crazy because it was, in fact, a fire ant that had bitten me. That is when the waterworks started.

I started sobbing uncontrollably, yelling, and screaming about how miserable I was. I was sad, mad, in pain, miserable, and just couldn't take it anymore. Not only was my day filled with excruciating pain, but when I came back to relax in our temporary home, I was attacked. Thankfully, Ron was in the tent with me, and while I was wailing in pain, he searched for the ant and found and killed it before it attacked again.

I cried and complained for the next few hours and got all my negativity out while Ron held me. I screamed how I just wanted to go home and didn't want to be there anymore. I also swore that I would never get in a tent for the rest of the trip because I was so tired of getting attacked by bugs. And to be honest, at that point in the night, I really did want to go home. I was exhausted, scared, and just overwhelmed. But, of course, it wasn't like we could just pack up that night and catch a plane home, so on top of my white powder drink, I downed some Benadryl and tried to get some rest. I woke up the next morning still feeling beaten down but with less of a negative attitude.

We didn't end up going anywhere because I was still trying to recover, and I needed to be close to a good water source and bathroom at all times.

It was nice to have a break again from doing all the touristy things. It gave my body a chance to rest and rehydrate, and I just transitioned from walking around the campground and lying in the tent reading and writing. I had also come to terms with the fact that I did not want to go home, and although I was miserable, I knew it would pass, and I wanted to continue with our journey, so I started researching for our next few stops.

That last night at the campground, we had a nice dinner that included different pastas, wine, and gelato for only 6 euros. The food was good, and the authentic Italian pasta and gelato nourished my soul back to life. It was our last night sleeping at a campsite outside of Naples next to Volcano Solfatara. To be honest, I was happy to get out of there. The people were extremely friendly, but the mosquitos were horrible, and at night, the sulfur smell would overwhelm you, and you would hear the weirdest dinosaur-like sounds coming from outside. I swear, in my dreamlike state of drifting in and out of consciousness, I imagined dinosaurs emerging out of the volcano and trampling toward the campsite, ending our existence in one furious stomp. I was both disturbed and intrigued by my wild dreams that night. Also, I might have been mildly hallucinating from the white powder drink mixed with Benadryl. But it's so long for now, as I hopefully close this chapter on my miserable experience, and off to the Port of Bari to set sail for Greece in the morning!

Before I start talking about our next adventure to Greece, there are a few things I wanted to mention.

#1 I was charged nothing at the hospital in Italy. Zero. I'm not sure if it was because of the language barrier or if it was a free hospital, or if everyone just felt bad for me, but I didn't pay a dime.

#2 To this day, I still have no idea what was wrong with me and causing me so much pain in Pompeii. Looking back on it now, I am incredibly lucky that I didn't die that day because although I didn't want to admit it, there was something majorly wrong with my body that I should have taken care of more promptly. Without a doubt, I know that what I experienced was not a UTI but some kind of major medical emergency that I was never able to get proper care for. Yet by some leap of faith, my body somehow magically navigated the means to self-soothe and heal itself in my absence to get the proper medical care.

Even after my bad experience at the Italian hospital, I should have sought out another hospital where I could find a translator and have a doctor truly examine me. I know that I made some poor choices that day, and I equate it to being naive and scared as my first time abroad experiencing a medical emergency. I now know that being my own advocate for a health emergency is of the utmost importance no matter where in the world I am. I wanted to make a disclaimer to anyone else wanting to travel abroad that this was a horrible first hospital experience, and my experience does not represent the good experiences that others have had in hospitals abroad.

If you do travel abroad, no matter where you are, you should always be aware of nearby hospitals or know how to contact a consulate nearby or your travel insurance rep in case of an emergency.

Greece

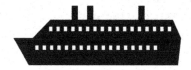

Although the official language in Greece is Greek,
English is widely known and practiced. But to be friendly
and polite you can always greet people
With Yassas- the formal Hello, or Yiasoo informally

After a horrendous experience in Naples and Pompeii, I was ready to move on to another country and start fresh, so we packed up our things and headed toward Bari, Italy, where we would hopefully catch a ferry over to Greece.

When we finally got into Bari, we approached the ticket window, hoping to get a last-minute ticket. We had looked online ahead of time but were unable to buy tickets so we just had to risk it trying to get tickets in person. Unfortunately, the woman at the window counter told us there were no more spots on the ferry, but we would be able to put our names on a last-minute waiting list. We didn't want to miss our chance at seats on the ferry, so we made base camp in the lobby for the day.

Like a regular travel day where we had time to kill, we researched things that we wanted to do in our next country, played games on the lobby floor, read, and relaxed while making a few friends with people around us. Finally, after about 8 hours, the ferry started to board, and slowly, the lobby started clearing out. As every new person walked up to the counter to check-in and walked out the doors, our hopes of getting tickets became smaller and smaller. By the end of the day, only a few handfuls of people were left in the large waiting area.

At this point, we started researching places we would be able to stay overnight in Bari because we were sure that we weren't getting a seat. Only a few minutes before the scheduled departure time, we heard "RON TRANDELL" called over the loudspeaker to report to the front desk. We ran up to the desk and were told that a few people did not check-in, so they had extra room on the ferry! We fumbled around to get to our passports as quickly as possible and pay for our ferry ticket. Yet another time, the clerk we had just purchased our tickets from looked at us and said that spine tingling word, "RUN." There were 2 other groups next to us also fumbling and rushing to get all their information together to get tickets before the ferry left port.

As soon as we had our tickets in hand, we started sprinting down the dock toward the ferry, full speed ahead. If you have ever tried running full speed with a fully packed hiking bag strapped to your back, it isn't the easiest thing in the world. I probably looked like a newborn baby deer wobbling down the dock, and I was sure at any minute that my backpack would sway too far to one side and take me down.

We approached the passenger terminal just as the ticket collector exclaimed "JUST IN TIME" as he rolled his eyes at our disheveled group. There was no greater feeling than turning around and slapping a high five with a kid from another group running alongside us to celebrate that we had all gotten tickets and made it to the ferry in time. We didn't care how ridiculous we looked; we had made it.

As we boarded the ship we were escorted to the outside deck. We thought this happened when everyone boarded but apparently, when you have a ticket that reads "deck passenger," that really does mean that you are confined to the deck, and that is where you must stay for the entire journey. No wonder the tickets were only 29 euros.

Deckhands were guarding every entrance inside the ferry like it was high security lock down at the royal castle, just to ensure the deck passengers did not come inside for some absurd reason. The only area we were allowed to visit inside were the restrooms, which were still only accessible from the deck. Even on the deck, there weren't really any seats except in the cafe area, which was being cleaned at the time. We reluctantly accepted our fate and decided to find a space on the deck that was at least out of the wind. The best spot we could find was facing the ship's rear with a big wall behind us to help block the wind. But we weren't the only ones sleeping under the stars. All around us, passengers were settling in on the deck floor with their sleeping bags and mats rolled out to claim their space.

I grew up camping all over Michigan in different campgrounds and parks and even venturing into the wilderness, but this was my first time sleeping outside with no tent and on the deck of a ship, for that matter. It was still beautiful being on the open ocean as the sun illuminated the shimmering water as she descended below the horizon. The cool ocean breeze was nice at first, especially since there were no bugs, but after a few hours of trying to sleep, the floor got harder, and the cool breeze turned into a viciously cold whipping wind.

Around 4:00 am, Brit and I decided to move inside to find somewhere warm to sleep. We were able to sneak inside, and we found a movie theatre that was relatively dark and quiet. We sprawled across a few seats to make a nice warm and comfy bed. We were both able to get a few hours of good warm sleep before we sailed into Greek waters. Of course, Ron faired just fine staying outside on the hard deck floor, exposed to all the elements. He was right at home considering he had grown up climbing pine trees and falling asleep nestled up 20 feet off the ground among the branches.

As we got closer to the mainland, Brit and I found a nice balcony on the ship's side, and we each had a pastry and some orange juice for breakfast as we enjoyed the ocean. The views of the islands while pulling into Patras, Greece, were spectacular. Clearwater and mountainous islands as far as you could see. There were also a few sailboats out on the water, and when they would sail in front of an island, it would create the most picture-perfect image. I did try to take a picture of it, but of course, you can never fully capture the beauty of reality in the moment through a camera lens.

After departing the ferry, we took a bus from Patras to Athens, and then we were on the hunt for our hotel! I would have to say that my first impression of Athens wasn't the greatest. At first, I just saw it as another city with foul smells coming from the side streets, but thankfully first impressions aren't the final impression. Oh, I almost forgot, there was also a bus ride and then a train commute between the Patras port and Athens. Thankfully both connections went smoothly, and both rides were free, thanks to our Eurail pass. Plus one for Greece! But back to Athens.

Once we found our hotel, it honestly wasn't bad for 14 euros per person. It had 3 twin beds, a small wardrobe, and a bathroom. However, when we first walked into the bathroom, we inhaled the most putrid smell ever. I instantly gagged. The smell subsided once we closed the windows and sprayed some Febreze over everything.

After the hotel experience, next came the search for food. We found a little Greek place just a few blocks away from us. Of course, the whole menu was Greek, and the gentleman behind the counter only spoke a few words of English, but we ordered by just pointing to pictures on the menu. Brit and I each pointed to what we thought were chicken gyros, but when the man rang up our order, it was only 3 euros total. We thought that couldn't possibly be right, and wondered what kind of food we would get, but sure enough, he brought us 2 chicken gyros at 1.50 euros apiece! They were delicious! I have had gyros in the U.S. before, but nothing compared to this! The gyro was complete with juicy chicken, tomatoes, onions, french fries, and 2 kinds of sauce and seasonings. Ron also ordered after us and was served some sort of lamb gyro. If you have never eaten a gyro with a healthy portion of french fries stuffed inside, smothered in tzatziki sauce, you are truly missing out. Never would I have thought to put french fries INSIDE a gyro, but damn was it good!

While we were in Athens, I think we ingested around 4 gyros each day. But that's jumping ahead.

After dinner, it was back to the hotel to have a peaceful night before hitting the ruins in the morning. When we woke up in the morning, we headed downstairs for our complimentary breakfast, which I expected to be cold cereal and toast like every other place, but I was pleasantly surprised to find a hot breakfast. The spread included mini hot dogs, scrambled eggs, fruit, cookies, melon, cereal, toast, tea, coffee, and an orange drink that tasted suspiciously like tang for those of you that remember that drink. Needless to say, we loaded our plates full and got our money's worth.

Next, we headed off to Lycabettus Hill to climb to the highest point in Athens. Lycabettus Hill stands 277 meters tall and looks out over all of Athens. At the top is the church of Agios Georgios, which dates back to the 1870s, along with a small restaurant. There is a small road up to the top of the hill, so we could have called a cab to get there, but we wanted to reach the top the "authentic" way and save a little money, so we hiked it. The hike was exhausting, but it was fun tramping through the woods and finding random sets of staircases, that had stood the test of time. We were all pretty sweaty by the time we got to the top, but the 360- degree views of the city were jaw-dropping. We could even see all the way out to the ocean. The cherry on top though, was getting a sneak preview of all the ancient ruins we would explore later. Right in plain view were the Acropolis, Ancient Agora, Panathenaic Stadium, and The Temple of Zeus.

I was awe-struck by all the ancient wonders right in front of me, and my soul was ready to explore. But before we could explore other old-world wonders, we realized that right where we were standing, on top of Lycabettus hill, was quite the oddity itself. You will notice Lycabettus Hill right away if you ever visit Athens because it seems so out of place. Just this huge hill dropped in the middle of the city. It's much higher than any other ruin sites, and it seems like it's a puzzle piece that doesn't fit. But there is a story behind this. The legend says that when the Goddess Athena was carrying limestone to build the Acropolis, she angrily threw a piece of limestone from her hands when she received bad news from a raven. That limestone piece thrown from Athena's hand is known today as Lycabettus Hill. I don't know if you like ancient legends as much as I do, but that seems like a more fun story rather than learning the history of geological anomalies like this. We spent some time at the top of the hill exploring outside the church, getting some pictures, and even getting an ice cream cone. The ice cream was the perfect momentary escape from the unbearable heat before we began our climb back down.

From Lycabettus Hill, we explored the city before heading to more ruin sites. We wandered around and found ourselves in the middle of some very crowded streets filled with various merchants selling goods and food. Out of all the shopping areas we have been to so far, this one was the most tempting. There were so many gorgeous handmade and colorful goods. The clothes, the jewelry, the purses, the knick-knacks, and the sweet, sweet smell of delicious food. Thank God I didn't have much room in my travel backpack because I could have stuffed it full from shopping in Athens. I did, however, pick up a gorgeous pair of handmade earrings that I couldn't resist, and Ron splurged on a travel chess board complete with handmade chess pieces.

We continued to get lost in the city streets for a little while and ingested our body weight in gyros before we stumbled upon Athens's Natural Gardens. The garden was created sometime around 1840, and over 500 plant species from around the world resided in the park. Originally the royal family were the only ones allowed to walk through the gardens until it was opened to the public in 1975.

It was like a miniature tropical paradise right in the middle of the city. Everything was lush, green, and gorgeous. There were even a few peacocks, ducks, and other animals running around. For a moment, we were transported to another world, far away from Athens' hot and sticky streets. It was the perfect pick-me-up before hitting the concrete again and tackling the Acropolis.

By the way, the Acropolis is another limestone hill in the city center of Athens that was once a religious center and a home for gods and kings alike. Although it isn't the highest limestone structure in the city, the name "Acropolis" literally means "High City" in Greek.

By the time we had made our way from Lycabettus Hill to the Acropolis, the sun had fully baked our skin, and we were drenched with sweat. Although the climb to the top of the Acropolis wasn't nearly as bad as the hike to Lycabettus Hill, by the time we made it to the top, it was like the sun god himself had descended upon us to lightly kiss each of our cheeks. When in reality, this light kiss made it feel like our skin was slowly melting off our bones from the sheer heat. Clearly, we had not prepared for this venture ahead of time or read all the warnings to tackle sightseeing the Acropolis in the early morning before the sun was at the highest point in the sky. But hey, at least we had worked off all those gyros we ate earlier!

However, our exhaustion was short-lived as soon as the ancient temples came into view, and we were only steps away from the Parthenon. It was magnificent. The white marble columns shot toward the sky, reaching toward the heavens and the Goddess Athena that the temple was built to honor.

Although the Acropolis was once home to many temples and monuments that have fallen over time, the star of the Acropolis is still and always has been the Parthenon. The Parthenon was constructed between 447-432 B.C. Since then, this remarkable structure has survived numerous natural and human disasters, including wars. I guess it's only fitting that a structure built to honor the Goddess of war and wisdom herself would withstand all the war and destruction around it over the years. This massive structure is over 23,000 square feet large and consists of "46 outer columns and 19 inner columns." The outside is adorned with various carvings of mythical battles between God and man, while the inside was said to once house a statue of Athena herself that stood at around 30-some feet high.

It was breathtaking just being in the presence of this ancient temple that was once a flawless piece of art. I can't even imagine witnessing the Parthenon when she was in her prime. After snapping a few photos, we walked around the grounds in silent awe, feeling like we were among the gods ourselves for a brief moment.

We wandered around all the ancient ruins on top of this limestone mountain for as long as we could stand before heat exhaustion took over. The other structures built on the Acropolis were various smaller temples and monuments also dedicated to either Athena or other gods and heroes. But again, nothing compared to the Parthenon.

Before we began our descent back down to the city, away from the gods and back toward the commoners, we made a quick pit stop in the newest addition to the Acropolis; a modern-day bathroom. I think I must have used more than 10 paper towels dabbing away about a pound of sweat from every square inch of my body. I splashed my rosy cheeks with cool water and tried to clean myself up as much as possible, even though it was a losing battle. But the damage we had done to our bodies by being out in the sun all day, walking countless miles, and climbing many, many stairs, was well worth a full day of getting to explore this amazing city.

The following day, we woke up to enjoy one more hot breakfast provided by the hotel before we began our journey to Crete, one of the largest of the Greek islands. We left earlier in the morning because although we had already pre-purchased our ferry tickets, we had no idea what to expect at the port, so we wanted to be prepared. We hopped on a bus that took us just a few miles outside of town to the port of Piraeus. We checked in with someone at the post office and gave them all our documents, and just like that, we were all set for disembarkation at 6:00pm that night.

If we had known how easy this process was, we would have spent more time exploring Athens before heading toward the port. But as a rule of travel, it's

run, run, run,

wait, wait, wait,

run, run, run,

wait, wait, wait,

and now we had time to kill.

Of course, we could have taken another bus back to the city to explore more and use our time wisely, but we didn't want to risk it. That is one thing that you will learn with travel: everyone has a different pace and different priorities. Some people will spend every second they can optimizing their time and exploring and then sprinting to their next plane, train, or bus at the very last second, risking not getting a seat. For our group, we liked to be to places early when we could because we were still novice travelers, and you never know if something might go wrong with purchasing a ticket or getting bus tickets back to a ferry port on time. But also keep in mind that I am the person who will religiously show up at the airport 3 hours early for a flight every single time- just in case. It's a trade-off, but we were right where we needed to be to continue onto our next leg of this adventure. So we just killed some time relaxing in a park nearby, playing some games, and reading until it was time to board the ship.

At 6:00pm sharp we boarded the ship and were escorted by a gentleman who told us we could put our belongings in the theatre and then proceed to the deck. Do you know where this going? Even with our previous experience of sleeping on the deck of a ship, we again bought "deck tickets" because they were much cheaper than buying a seat inside the ship, and after all, we are budget travelers. Again, the deckhand reminded us that we were not even allowed inside the ship's common areas, but we had to stay on the deck for the remainder of the voyage.

After one night of sleeping on a ship deck, we were pros at this by now. We found some space on the deck's side and rolled out our sleeping bags to make our beds for the night. Thankfully the night air between Athens and Crete was much warmer than when we crossed over from Italy to Greece. Although I didn't feel like I was freezing to death during the night, there was a strong wind tunnel that had formed inside my sleeping bag somehow. I have no idea how, but every time a strong gust of wind came bellowing down the ship's side, it would work its way into the small opening on top of my sleeping bag and create a cyclone of wind right at my feet.

The only way to prevent the wind tunnel was to completely seal myself inside the sleeping bag, which I did at various times throughout the night. But sooner than later, I would always have to come up for some fresh air, and the wind cyclone would start again. It was an interesting night for sure.

What first woke me in the morning was the loud clamor of footsteps from people walking around me and a gentle mist on my face as waves crashed against the ship's side. I sat up and realized we were pulling into port. This journey was shorter than the last, but it was still a restless night's sleep aboard a ship.

Another Goodbye

After departing the ship, we headed to the nearby bus station and bought our first bus ticket to Rethymno, Crete. It was a bittersweet bus trip because as happy as we were to be in Crete, we knew that we would be saying good-bye to Brit when we got to Rethymno.

I know I haven't even mentioned any of this yet, and it may seem out of the blue, but I think this moment has been coming for a while now. Brit wanted to go to another hostel on the opposite side of the island, and she wanted to go island hopping for a few days. Ron and I had different plans, and since we were halfway through our backpacking trip, we just wanted to plant ourselves in one place for a while and take a break.

To be completely honest, I am amazed that the three of us lasted this long traveling together without any significant breaking points. That is besides the one night that Ron and I had in Switzerland. But for three people to travel together, right at each other's sides for a month and a half? That's a lot. I know that we didn't all see eye to eye on everything we did, everywhere we went, or even how we chose to spend our money. Because let's be honest, when you travel in a group of three, if one person wants to go out and spend money, chances are the other two are going as well. But even so, we got along brilliantly, and even with the few tiny arguments we had while traveling so far, it was the best time of my life.

Up to this point, I know that Brit had different ideas about what she wanted to see and do, and I feel like our schedule was holding her back from being able to be free and really explore on her own. We knew we wouldn't be saying goodbye for good because we all had the same return ticket back home, but we kind of just left it opened ended that if we run back into one another or if things fall in line, we can meet back up, but if not, we would see her in Dublin a month and a half from now!

Once we arrived in Rethymno, we hugged and said our goodbyes, and I desperately tried to hold back a few tears. Again, it was so incredibly bittersweet because I feel like the three of us had experienced so much life together this last month and a half. More life experiences than some people get the pleasure of having throughout an entire lifetime. But at the same time, I was anxious and excited to travel with Ron, just the two of us, to see how it would work out with Brit not there to be the buffer in stressful situations. We knew we were good traveling as a group, but take away a group member, and now it's just a couple who has only known each other for a year and a half, still figuring out each other's triggers and annoyances, and now how to navigate the world together. This was going to be a whole different ball game. Thankfully we were starting off strong with a few days off from travel as we relaxed in a seaside village on a beautiful Greek Island.

Plakias, Crete

Once we had finished our goodbyes with Brit, we caught a second bus to Plakias and found our hostel quickly, thanks to all the directions on the website. We also made a few new friends along the way. We met a girl named Jessica from British Columbia and a girl named Danni from Australia, who were both also staying at our hostel.

From the moment we arrived at our hostel, it seemed like we had hit the jackpot at only 10 euros a night. We were instantly greeted by some of the people staying at the hostel outside before the owner came out to greet us. The atmosphere was so warm and welcoming, and the owner told us that "everything at the hostel runs on the honor system and trust." What a perfect place. He pointed us in the direction of a wine and beer fridge that we were more than welcome to help ourselves to and just sign the book to add the cost to our tab.

The hostel grounds included a few small separate buildings with 8-10 bunks each, colorful hammocks all around the property, and a beautiful outdoor patio. It was kind of funny to me because my books of choice lately have been the Divergent Series, and the hostel reminded me of one of the factions in the series called amity. Basically, the people in the faction are happy, loving, and laid back, which is precisely the vibe of this hostel.

After we got settled into the hostel, we took a stroll into town to swim at the beach which was only about a 5-minute walk from the hostel. The beach was beautiful, the water was warm and inviting, and it felt great to swim in the ocean again. After a little dip, Ron and I stopped at a small restaurant and had a Plakias version of a hamburger and shared some fries for dinner. Sadly, the meal was not good at all. The hamburger was cold, and it was more of a pre-cooked soy patty than anything. It filled up our growling stomachs but left our souls sad. But I guess that's what we get for ordering American food in Greece instead of sticking to our regular gyro meal. After the long few days of travel, we headed back to the hostel for the night to meet the rest of the hostel crew staying there and just get some rest.

When I woke up, it was hard to ignore the pain and pressure I was still having from my hospital experience in Italy. Finally, after a long battle inside my head and talking to a friend I had met at the hostel, I decided it would be best to see a doctor again before it got worse. So Ron and I headed into town and went to the local clinic, which consisted of a small office with one doctor inside. Thankfully the man spoke broken English, so now I at least had a doctor that I could understand.

He tested my urine for a UTI because that is what we both suspected, but everything came back clean. I gave him a picture I had taken of the prescription they had given me in Italy, and I told him the whole story of what had happened there. He took it and searched the internet for a while before he came back to tell me that what they gave me most certainly wasn't any kind of antibiotic, and just told me "I have no idea what they gave you."- Very reassuring. Since this doctor couldn't figure out what was wrong with me, he thought it might be some type of infection, so he gave me antibiotics and told me to come back the next day. So still no answers on my mystery pain, but I finally had some antibiotics.

After the doctor gave me my new antibiotic, he also delivered the painful news that I could not go swimming or have alcohol for at least two weeks because it might worsen the infection. My heart was instantly crushed. Here we were in paradise, and I wouldn't be able to enjoy the water or just sit and sip a glass of Greek wine. Talk about disappointment.

Last night, a group of us had already planned to go cliff diving today, and now I couldn't go. I knew that being by the water without going in would kill me, so I decided to stay at the hostel while the others went. That is until at the last minute, I decided that going for a walk to get to the cliffs was at least a better option than moping around the hostel all day. And off we went! A new group of vagabond friends in search of the infamous "One Rock Beach."

One Rock was a beach that the hostel owner Uli had told us about the night before and said we couldn't miss it while we were here. Our options for getting to the beach were either hitchhiking the long road or taking a shortcut through a series of hiking trails. Uli said once we arrived at the beach, it was surrounded by cliffs, and we would either have to climb down the rocks to get to the secluded beach, or we would have to swim out into the open ocean around the seaside cliffs to get to the beach.

There were 5 of us in the group, and we all decided we would rather see the countryside and find the hiking trails. Unfortunately, after wandering around forever in a grove of olive trees, we couldn't find where the hiking path picked up and we got pretty lost. After navigating ourselves back to where we started, we just decided to go down to the beach in town.

So while everyone went swimming, I sadly sat on the beach and watched everyone splash around. It absolutely killed me seeing everyone else in the water, but I knew better. Even though I couldn't go in the water, I still relaxed on the beach and soaked up the sun. We all grabbed some dinner at a restaurant on our way back to the hostel at the end of the day and finished up the night relaxing and meeting some more amazing people from all around the world.

The following day, we were determined to find One Rock Beach. So we got some better directions and also picked up another person for our adventure group- Hannah from Ohio. Three of the girls set off to hitchhike to One Rock while Ron, Hannah, and I took off hiking.

After not too long, we finally found the right hiking trail hidden behind a clump of Olive Trees. Unfortunately, we still got lost a few times. At one point, Ron ran ahead to see if we were on the right path and after about 15 minutes, emerged again from the top of a hill covered in dirt and blood brushing himself off and saying, "don't go that way". Apparently, he had climbed up a rocky hill to get higher to see where we were going. As he was climbing the jagged boulders along with the sheep next to him, he hopped a fence to get closer to the top. Once he got further up, he realized that it was a farmer's private property that he had crossed into and instantly turned to run back down as quickly as possible. Unfortunately, when he jumped over the fence again, running down, he landed on a group of rocks that gave away and sent him tumbling into a pit of cacti. Thankfully, Ron has monkey-like reflexes, and his injuries could have been a lot worse than what they were, but he got away with only a few scrapes, cuts, and cactus needles embedded in his skin.

We eventually found our way again, and after what seemed like forever, we finally made it to ONE ROCK! Not surprisingly, our other friends who hitchhiked made it to the beach first. They said quite a few vehicles passed them by before a friendly driver pulled over to offer a lift, but all in all it was safe, and much quicker than hiking.

We all peered down over the cliffs to the secluded beach and saw that the waves were way too big to swim. The way the beach and rocks were situated, the water was almost funneled right into this little area, and the waves were crashing against the rocks so hard that we didn't want to risk it. Instead, we went down to a nearby beach to swim and hopefully let the waves calm down at One Rock. After a couple hours, we went back to the beach and decided to scale the rocks down even though the waves were still monstrous.

The climb down the cliffs was actually pretty fun, being able to practice my hand strength and rock-climbing skills with little risk since there were small ledges the whole way down. Once we got down to the beach, it was even more gorgeous up close in person. White sand surrounded by high rock formations and bright blue clear water with one single rock right in the middle of the water surrounded by jagged cliffs on either side. Hence the name One Rock. Now at this point, after sitting on the last beach watching everyone swim and have fun, I know I still wasn't supposed to swim for a few more days, but I just couldn't take it any longer. The water was seductively calling my name like a siren to lost sailors. Plus, you only live once, right? I mean, I might die in a few days from an unknown infection in my body and lack of proper health care, so I might as well live it up and swim while I have the chance right?

By the way, do what I say, not as I do. It probably wasn't the most brilliant idea to jump in the water, but I didn't want to miss out on life happening right before my eyes without jumping in- literally.

The waves were still huge, so you had to be strategic about timing getting into the water. You had to either dive underneath the waves until you got past the breaking point, or you had to time the tides just right so you could swim out right after a big wave hit. If you didn't do either of these things, the waves were so strong they would sweep you up and drag you along the sandy bottom, washing you right back up on the beach where you started. After a few failed attempts from all of us getting battered by the waves, we finally made it past the breaking point and just swam around in the open water for a while, carefree and happy.

The waves started to die down after a while. And by die down, I mean they were more like 4-foot waves instead of 5-foot waves. Ron and I absolutely LOVE playing in the ocean waves, so the whole group decided to swim closer to shore so that we could play in the crashing waves. If you timed it right, you could position yourself right at the breaking point of a big wave and just let yourself go as the wave-tossed and tumbled you in the water. Although right after you came up for a breath of fresh air, there would be another wave right behind you, and inevitably sometimes you would be caught off guard by a string of waves and tossed and tumbled until you hit shore again. It was so much fun and the perfect adrenaline rush.

At one point, my adrenaline got the best of me, and I got stuck being rolled by the wave after wave and unable to break free. The harsh waves kept crashing me against the coarse sand on the bottom of the ocean and slowly sweeping me sideways where I almost crashed into the rock face on the right side. Thankfully one of our friends, Sheri, was paying attention and saw me struggling and was able to grab me just in time before I hit the rocks and helped me back to shore. A little bit of a death-defining moment, but friends and good fortune were on my side. As Sheri dragged my water-logged ass back on shore one of our friends was on the beach yelling at Ron "Holly Shit, did you SEE that?!" I don't think Ron even realized what was happening until he saw me gasping for air, trying to catch my breath with Sheri by my side making sure I was okay. I was okay, but my pride was a little hurt and my body felt like I had road rash from being drug across the coarse sand at the bottom of the ocean so many times.

Needless to say, that was enough adrenaline for the day. So I retired to the beach for the afternoon and enjoyed the beautiful scenery instead of defying death in the killer waves. That night, we all had a chance to explore the little town of Plakias and ended our day with games, laughs, and stories among new friends.

I should also mention that this day was a huge personal victory for me. A victory of overcoming my own insecurities about myself and just being present in the moment rather than worrying what I looked like. Let me start by saying that I have had body issues my whole life, and I have always felt insecure about the way I looked in a swimsuit, especially a two-piece suit because I was very insecure about my stomach. My weight has fluctuated a lot over the years, but for some reason I have never felt comfortable in my own skin. But Crete was different.

Maybe there was something magical in the glistening blue waters, or the fresh Mediterranean air, but before I got in the water earlier, I decided that I was going to forgo my full coverage tankini top and just proudly wear my sports bra with my swimsuit bottoms. Suddenly, I just felt like I wanted to be free, and I didn't want to hide or cover my body any longer worrying about my tank top riding up and exposing my belly. No, F-that. I just wanted to be free and swim in the ocean without a care, letting the sea touch and love my body like it deserved. Somewhere on the beach that day all my inhibitions and insecurities had just melted away. And I had never felt more free.

Wow, it's been almost 7 days, and I haven't even opened my journal, and now, this is our last night on this truly spectacular island. So much to catch up on, but first, I wanted to start writing because I wanted to capture my emotions at this very moment because right now, I have ALL the feels...

I will genuinely and whole-heartedly miss Crete and all the wonderful people I have met here. If someone were to ask me where my favorite place on earth was, I would reply, "A little youth hostel in the town of Plakias, Crete." Why? Because being here simply makes me feel alive with simplistic happiness. All the experiences I have had here, the people I have met, and the joy I have felt have made this last week a week that I will never forget. Ron and I came to Crete intending to go on a "vacation" from traveling and recuperate for a week, but we got way more than what we bargained for with all the incredible people we have met here. Just simply being in this hostel, even doing nothing, I am constantly surrounded by happy and loving people, warm conversation, gentle breezes, the sounds of nature, and a calming vibe. At night, sometimes there is music playing or someone singing or strumming the guitar, which you can just hear over the sound of the cricket or the saccades, and it is just the perfect ambiance.

This being my last night in this hostel, I am pretty emotional because, in all reality, a little piece of me never really wants to leave this place. Coming here was not only a break from jumping from place to place, but it was an adventure in itself, and being here has taught me a more than few life lessons to take home. That is, besides how to make a few Greek dishes!

Being here made me realize that I am not leaving my happiness behind me but taking it with me wherever I go. Happiness doesn't just magically manifest itself when you go on vacation or have an adventure.

You make your own happiness. You make your own happiness by the people you surround yourself with, the thoughts in your own head, and your reactions to all the things, good and bad, that happen to you every day. All the things that make me unbelievably happy here are also things that make me happy back home. Yes, being on a Greek island in the warm summer air with a beach just footsteps away enhances my happiness, but happiness is a state of being that you must create yourself. No one else is responsible for your own happiness but you, and if you surround yourself with the right people, that happiness will follow you wherever you may go. So although physical location can most definitely play a part in your mindset, it's just that- a mindset.

The problem is when we are at home, or get stuck in a routine, day in and day out, going to work, coming home, doing chores, cooking dinner, and washing dishes, just to wake up the next morning and do it all over again, we get stuck in a rut. In a pattern. Sometimes we get stuck in our safety net, and we don't realize how much life we are missing out on. Maybe take a drive one day to a beach that is 3 hours away just to splash in some waves and drive back home that night. Go to a rock-climbing gym, push yourself past your comfort zone, and scale that wall. Or even just come home at night, lock yourself in a bathroom, turn the shower on high to make your own personal steam room, and sit quietly on the floor for 20 minutes just meditating and relaxing.

In our short time here, I realized that happiness is not something you can travel the world searching for, but it's something you find inside. Happiness is not a physical place- it is a state of mind.

What I have also realized while here is that there are still good people in the world. Being at this hostel has completely renewed my faith in humanity. They say like-minded people attract like-minded people, and I have never found a place more deserving of that statement. Plakias Youth Hostel is like a black hole for exceptional people. Just sucking each and every one in, making it hard to ever leave. Once we had traveled to Switzerland, I never thought I would find a place that I would fall more in love with, but I think Switzerland met a close match with Crete.

Reminiscing

Yet again, it's been a few days since I picked up a pen, and I have found myself just relaxing and trying to soak in all the amazing moments that we had in Crete. Unfortunately, I let time get away from me again with writing, but that's okay. Sometimes it's more important to live in the moment rather than recoding every detail of each moment. Currently, we are on a train headed to Hungary, but before I get to our current predicament, I want to record all the little moments from Plakias before the precious memories slip my mind. All I can tell you is that the random hostel we found in a small town on the Southside of Crete that we had never heard of before turned out to be pure magic.

To start off, we were initially only going to spend six nights in this hostel, but we came to love it so much that we stayed ten nights. The first few days I wrote about were terrific, but our time in Crete only became more magical. There was just something so calming and warm about the hostel. When you are there, you feel completely at peace and rejuvenated. Even the people that visit and stay at the hostel are different. Everyone that stays is so kind and open and trustworthy. Just being there is like completely removing yourself from the outside world and the rest of society. I could have honestly stayed at the hostel for the rest of the trip, and it did cross my mind a few times. The days all started blending together, and the rest of the time at the hostel consisted of warm ocean water, beautiful beaches, adventures, great food, starry skies, and a whole new outlook on life.

One day, the hostel owner had organized a river walk for his guests; I think there were probably about 20 people that ended up going. Now I have been walking before and hiking before, but this "walk" was definitely more of a hike than a walk. Actually, more of a "swim" than even a hike at times! At first, we just took a few trails through the woods to get to a small stream. Then the group started walking through the stream, jumping from small rocks to small rocks to avoid the water. Slowly, the stream got deeper and deeper until we were transitioning from walking along banks and high rocks to jumping in waist-deep water to make our way to the next boulder. I don't know what I was expecting with this walk, but I got so much more than what I bargained for. To be honest, I was pretty nervous at times jumping into murky waters because I was never quite sure what was under me, but I got through it just fine.

In the beginning, the whole group stayed together but eventually, everyone split up depending on how fast they were traversing the river obstacles. Of course, Ron was at the front of the pack because he is a monkey in human skin and completely in his element. I was somewhere near the end of the group, and at one point, I was completely by myself for a while. I was a little scared at one point, wondering if the people behind me had turned back, but at the same time, it was very peaceful and exhilarating hiking up the river by myself. I'm not sure how long it took me to hike up the whole stream until I got to the small waterfall at the end, but it seemed like forever. Eventually, I caught up with the rest of the group at the waterfall, and we were able to jump into a small pool at the end and go for a short swim. By the time I made it to the waterfall, Ron had already explored the entire area jumping from rock to rock and just having a ball.

Once everyone caught up with the group, we continued on a small trail away from the river that led us to the top of the mountain. At the top, you could see all of the little houses scattered down the hillside, the rolling hills in the background, and the distant shimmering water. A few people broke off from the group to eat dinner at a restaurant on the way down, and the rest of us continued back toward our hostel home. The walk down was refreshing after climbing up the stream all afternoon, and if I wasn't so exhausted, we would have joined the others at dinner. But we opted for a quick gyro to go on the way back instead. That night, I slept like a rock. I remember how well I slept because before I went to bed, the last thing I remember was counting all my scrapes and bruises that had already formed from the river walk, and then the next thing I knew, I was waking up with the sun glistening in through my window.

One other big event that happened while we were at the hostel was a huge family dinner one night. Apparently, the hostel owner Uli puts together family dinners you can sign up to participate in every once in a while for a few euros. With the money, the owner goes to town, buys groceries, and then brings them back to the hostel where everyone gets together and helps make dinner.

Since I love to cook, I was more than willing to participate. Part of my job was cutting up the vegetables and making the stuffed peppers. Once the food was put together, the grill was fired up, and the food started cooking. I wish I could remember everything that we ate that night, but I can tell you that it was a great family feast. I do remember that we had peppers and mushrooms stuffed with Greek yogurt, feta, and garlic, cucumber, and tomato salad, chicken and meat kabobs, bread, guacamole, fruit, and a few other Greek delicacies. Everything was mouthwatering. The vegetables were so fresh, and I believe some of them even came from Uli's garden! I ate way more than my stomach could hold that night, but it was worth it. The family atmosphere at dinner was so incredible. Everyone from all different walks of life were all helping each other, cooking together, and eating together. We were just hanging out and having a good time like we had all known each other for years. It was just fantastic.

Some of the other highlights of that beautiful little hostel in Plakias were the homemade breakfasts, the fresh food in general, starry night skies, and the breeze blowing off the ocean while you relaxed in a hammock. Every morning, the hostel offered homemade breakfast options for only a few euros. Most mornings, I would get a fried egg with a piece of toast or sometimes yogurt and honey with museli, which is similar to granola. Both options were fantastic and a great way to start off the mornings. Also, the gyros in town were pretty damn good. Ron and I had them a few times as a quick meal, and although they weren't as good as the ones we had in Athens, they came in a close second.

We also went out to eat with some friends from the hostel a few times. One time we went to a Greek buffet, and the other time a seaside restaurant. Both meals were so satisfying and full of new and wonderful foods. At the end of one of the meals, we were given complimentary watermelon and a shot of alcohol to complete the meal. I was almost thankful that I still wasn't drinking at this point because of my antibiotics because the shots smelled like gasoline. Ron's face and our friends' faces confirmed that the shots tasted like pure gasoline as well as they gagged down the complementary drink. Even so, Ron wasn't one to refuse free alcohol, so with one good deep breath he also grabbed the shot in front of me and slammed it back with a little look of regret on his face.

Apparently, it is customary for many Greek restaurants to serve free dessert and even a shot at the end of dinner. The shots were either the traditional Greek drink called Ouzo or tsipouro, which are distilled liqueurs, but we never found out exactly what was in the shots.

There was also one little smoothie stand in town where Ron and I would stop and get a waffle with Nutella and bananas or strawberries. I'm not ashamed to say that this dessert was a substitute for lunch or breakfast quite a few times. The waffles were always crispy and warm, and you can never go wrong with Nutella.

Speaking of treats, not on the food spectrum, one of my favorite things to do while we were at the hostel, was to just relax and read or nap in one of the hammocks outside. It was a treat because it was an extra escape from reality and a little cocoon of happiness. My favorite hammock, for some reason, was a bright orange one right in the middle of the others.

I could easily curl up in the hammock and just close my eyes and feel the cool breeze while drifting off into a state of pure bliss.

Another blissful spot on the property was on the top of the roof. On the outside of our dorm building was a small set of spiral stairs that went up to the roof. The roof was a wide-open space with a few lounge chairs at the top. This was a perfect spot at nighttime to just sit and gaze at the stars. From the roof, you could see all the way up the mountains, and all the little villages and houses lit up against the hillside. At the same time, it was so dark that you could see millions and millions of stars while also just barely hearing the ocean crashing against the shore at night. Again, this was the perfect place to just relax at the end of a long day.

Besides the highlights that I mentioned, most days in Crete included little adventures, treks to different beaches, or meeting new friends at the hostel. But each day we spent there was long and sunny and filled with memories to last a lifetime. I should also mention again some of the amazing people we met while we were there. Although everyone we ran across at the hostel was warm and welcoming, there were a few girls that I met with whom I spent most of my time at the hostel with. This included Jessica from British Columbia, Sheri from Canada, and Danni and Hannah from Australia. I spent many beach days and exploring days with these fellow travelers, and they were all fantastic. It was so hard to part with these beautiful humans, but I would love to stay in touch with these women or maybe even meet up again one day during another travel adventure. During one of my last days there, Sheri even gave me a beautifully written postcard and a new Greek journal because she knew I had almost filled this first paperback journal. It was such a sweet gesture, and these ladies are some fantastic people that I will never forget. Overall, like I have said many times, this place in Greece was just a little slice of heaven on earth.

Oh my gosh, I almost forgot about the two nights when Ron and I each woke up in our beds, and we weren't alone! The first night was when Ron woke up with another woman in his bed. So let me start from the beginning...

There were 8 beds in our hostel room, and Ron and I were each sleeping on the top bunk of separate bunk beds. By a few days in, we had gotten to know everyone else in our room and had at least some kind of small adventure with everyone. One night I was sleeping, and I heard Ron kind of gasp and yell, "what the fuck" and I woke up to look over and see Ron sitting up in bed with one of our girlfriends sitting up in his bed wearing just a white t-shirt and underwear, about a foot from his face. I was so exhausted from the day, and when I saw this, I just thought, "huh- that's weird- Ron will probably tell me what happened in the morning," and I just went back to sleep. Just goes to show you how much trust I had in Ron to see another woman in his bed and for me just to go back to sleep!

But anyway, I woke up in the morning and asked Ron what had happened. He said he felt someone rattle his bed, and he woke up to one of our friends just sitting on his bed in front of him. Apparently, when Ron woke up, this also startled her, and she "woke up" from sleepwalking, apologized, and climbed down from his bed. Likely story, right? Either way, all of us had a good laugh the next day. I will never know for sure if another woman was trying to seriously get in bed with Ron right in front of me, or if it was all just an innocent sleepwalking accident where another woman ended up in bed with Ron. All I know is that it takes a significant level of trust to wake up and see your partner in bed with someone else and just go back to bed yourself. I don't know many couples with that level of trust, but let me tell you, that genuine, mutual trust in a relationship makes all the difference!

Now let me tell you about the night that I woke up not alone in my bed. However, I had a little harder time getting my guest to leave. When I woke up one morning, I was face to face with another pair of beady little eyes that belonged to one of the biggest grasshoppers I have ever seen.

It was so warm every night that we would sleep with our doors and windows wide open, so the little guy must have snuck in one night! Of course, I let out a small scream from surprise and jumped off my top bunk right away. I slowly coaxed the little guy back outside, but he jumped right back in the window when I laid back down. Either I was still half asleep, or my inner Disney princess took over because I decided to have a little heart-to-heart with Jiminy before setting him gently outside one more time. He must have gotten the hint because I didn't see him again. Not the same as having a half-naked person climb into my bed, but what I can say is that we never had a boring night at the hostel!

The morning we left the hostel was just as hard as I thought. Ron and I woke up early to pack everything and have breakfast, and we were joined for a morning chat by Uli. He talked about his guests and his love for picture taking and film. I really do wish the best for him, and he has made that hostel such a wonderful place that I hope he receives as much happiness as he has given to others. After breakfast, we said our goodbyes and headed to the bus station.

Thankfully the time we spent in Plakias, gave us both a chance to balance out our budget and get back on track. In this tiny town in Crete, we lived the simple life. Enjoying the free nature around us and spending less than 20 euros total some days between accommodations and food.

Thessaloniki

For this leg of our journey, we were headed to Hungary! But the journey to Hungary was very long and filled with many different forms of transportation. The two bus rides that took us back to port in Heraklion were long and bumpy. We were both happy to get off them. Once in Heraklion, we killed some time until we booked the ferry around 7:00 pm and left port at 9:00 pm. This time we had purchased actual seats on the ferry since they were the same price as the deck seats, and it was nice to have seats inside for once. As it got later in the night, Ron and I sprawled out on the floor between two rows of seats in the movie theatre since it was nice and dark in there. On the one hand, we had a warm place to sleep, but it wasn't very comfortable on the other hand.

We pulled into Piraeus on the mainland around 6:00 am and then had to wait around some more for the next train to Athens. Once we finally got to Athens, we bought tickets to Thessaloniki, Greece, to continue onward up Greece to our final destination of Budapest, Hungary.

The train ride from Athens to Thessaloniki was only supposed to take 5 hours but took around 8 because our train broke down. Suddenly, the train came to a halt, and the engine, lights, and air all turned off. We saw one of the train attendants running back and forth, and you could clearly tell that something was wrong, but everyone only spoke Greek, so we weren't sure what was going on. All we could do was wait. Eventually, we found someone who translated to us that another train had to come behind us and had to "push us" the rest of the way to our destination because our train had broken down. Apparently, everything had quit working on our train because we no longer had air circulating, and the train car became extremely hot and muggy very quickly. For some reason, with another train pushing us, our train car seemed to sway back and forth much more violently and hit some very anxiety-inducing bumps along the tracks. Once we arrived in Thessaloniki, we were more than happy to get off the train. Our next train connection wouldn't be leaving until the following day, so we booked a hostel for the night in Thessaloniki. We caught a taxi at the train station to take us to the hostel since it was too far to walk. The drive started off pretty typical, with the taxi driver asking us where we were from.

Hot Tip- Unfortunately, if you are from the States and traveling, some people in other countries really do not like Americans, so when someone asks where you are from, you always have to test the waters a little before you say you are from the U.S. And if you are traveling and you don't feel safe disclosing that you are from the U.S. it is always safer to say you are from Canada. Especially if you have more of a northern accent like us!

We decided to tell the driver we were from the U.S., and then he asked us a follow-up question that we couldn't understand because he had such a thick accent. After repeating himself several times, and then using his fingers as a make-shift gun, we found out that he was asking, "where is your piece." Meaning, "where is our gun" because according to him, "All Americans carry guns." Instantly the conversation had turned, and we were very uncomfortable. We tried to make jokes and tell him that we didn't need one for Europe and didn't have a gun on us. As the conversation went on, he warned us that "he needs a gun here" and the area where we were going to in Thessaloniki, we should have a gun. A very reassuring conversation to have with your taxi driver...

After that lovely conversation, he dropped us off in a shady neighborhood and told us to "walk quickly up the hill to get to the hostel." So we got out of the cab as fast as possible and started booking it up the hill, constantly keeping watch now that we were on high alert.

Later on, once we met our bunkmate, our cab driver's thoughts of heightened security were reassured when she said that her taxi driver had also warned her that we were not in a good area of town. At this point, though, there was nothing we could do about it.

In general, the welcome we had when we arrived was very friendly, but our stay was not the best. The hostel receptionist greeted us with iced tea and let us put our bags down, but once the gentleman showed us our room, we found that the bathroom was dirty, the kitchenette was unusable, and the room was infested with mosquitoes. So it wasn't the best conditions, but at least we were only there for one night to catch our train tomorrow.

While there, we also met a lovely couple, Anni and Adam, to whom we highly recommended the Plakias hostel because they were planning to travel to Crete. The bunkmate that we met was also very nice. I believe her name was Shawna. I can't remember where she was from, but she was 33 and had been traveling the world for a while. After a friendly chat, Ron and I went to bed early to catch up on sleep but unfortunately had an all-night battle with heat and mosquitos. The next day we took off as soon as possible and waited at the train station until around 3:00 pm when our train was scheduled to leave.

An Unexpected Stop in Serbia

Since we weren't expecting to spend time in Serbia, we were completely clueless about the language. Serbian is the official language, but thankfully English is widely used.

Again, time has gotten away from me, and I never thought I would fall this behind with journaling! On the one hand, I am getting more and more exhausted from traveling and daily activities to keep up with writing at night. On the other hand, I am experiencing so many amazing things and people that it is massively overwhelming to keep track of everything. This is the point where I have to realize that this simply is not possible. Although I will still record most of my memories and experiences, some things will just be kept to myself. Memories simply tucked away in a distant part of my brain until something happens one day that will spark a rare memory of my time traveling. But for now, I will keep track of what I can. So far, I am about a week behind writing and have gotten so lazy/involved in traveling that I have stopped entirely and now need to catch up!

**Also, as a side note, we have talked to Brit a few times since we split up, and she has been having a ball! She ended up missing her ferry over to Santorini, not once but twice! She felt severely defeated, but it all worked out for the best because she met some fantastic friends at her hostel in Crete who she traveled to Croatia with for a few days. By the way, I am incredibly jealous because Brit said she saw some absolutely amazing waterfalls in Croatia. Ron and I didn't have Croatia on our travel list this time because our Eurail passes were not covered in Croatia. As far as we could tell, it would have been very expensive to travel there, so we settled on seeing it another time. However, after hearing Brit's stories, we wish we would have gone! But we had our own unplanned adventures as well...

So to backtrack, after a miserable night in Thessaloniki, Ron and I were more than happy to board our night train with a sleeping cart to Belgrade, Serbia, where we would arrive the following day and be able to catch the morning train into Budapest. Unfortunately, things do not always work out like you plan them. Since we had stayed in a sleeper train car before, we expected there to be six beds where we could lay down and sleep our way through the rest of the day and night to pass the time. However, when we boarded the train, we found that the room consisted of two benches for people to sit on. Apparently, we could not convert the benches into beds until the conductor came around later and converted the beds himself. This was a HUGE letdown, now realizing that we had to sit up and just hang out for 8 hours before we could lie down, even though we had paid extra to lie down. After not sleeping at all the night before, we were exhausted. But sometimes, you just have to suck it up and deal with it.

A little while after we boarded the train, a lovely Serbian couple joined us in our cabin. Later, we found out that the woman was a Ballerina, and her husband was a dancer who did theatre. Once the train started moving again, about 15 minutes down the track, it halted and didn't move for two solid hours. For us, this meant a lot of uncertainty and a sweltering and sticky cabin since the ac had quit and there was no breeze. Come to find out, the train stopped due to a fire on the tracks, which actually happens quite often in Greece due to the heat. Who knew? After a few hours of clearing the way, we started moving, and we could feel the cool breeze rush through the hot cabin again.

A few more hours of travel had passed, and we had another exciting event on the train ride; A crazy passenger. As Ron and I were outside the cabin getting some air, we saw one of the train attendants fighting with a passenger. The pair got louder and louder until I was almost sure some-one was going to throw a punch. Everyone outside their cabin immediately moved back in and shut their doors to avoid the controversy, so we fol-lowed suit. As we ducked back inside, the Serbian woman also closed our curtains and locked us in the room so the crazy man would not be able to come in. We tried peeking out the curtain to see what was going on. We saw the man run past our cart a few times, with the attendant always not far behind, trying to prevent him from going anywhere. While this was happening, our friends were clearly terrified, so we asked them to translate what was going on. From what they could tell, the passenger was drunk and wanted to get to the other side of the train, but the attendant would not let him. After this altercation, we found out that the man had a knife and had either cut himself or possibly cut the attendant trying to get by him. We will never know for sure, but we did not see the man again after that. Just your typical public transit altercation…

For the rest of the evening, we exchanged travel stories with the cou-ple, and we got to know each other a little better. Thankfully the couple helped us translate many times when a few of the attendants came in and told us that we needed to buy additional tickets because the countries we were passing through were not covered by our Eurail pass. So we shelled out a few Euros here and there to pay our way through each country. The rest of the night included a lot of restlessness of trying to sleep as we crossed borders. Every hour or so, people would come around to check our passports and collect money.

The next morning, we arrived in Serbia about 3 hours behind sched-ule. This meant that we had missed our morning train to Budapest that we were supposed to be on. The next train to Budapest did not leave until 9:45 pm that night, leaving us to either explore Belgrade, Serbia or sit at the train station for the next 13 hours. When we first arrived, the couple knew our predicament, and they told us about a bus company that leaves every half hour that would be able to take us sooner. We trekked through the city to find the office only to discover that their next bus wasn't available until 9:00 pm that night either, so train it was!

To make my anxiety even worse, while we tried to find the bus office, we walked past several buildings with huge holes in the side and rubble below. These buildings looked like no kind of construction we had seen before but more like what a building on the news looks like after being bombed.

Unfortunately, Ron and I were not educated about Serbia because we were not planning to spend time in this country. We were very uneasy walking around at first, not knowing where we were, so we decided to go back to the train station to kill some time.

We just hung out at the train station, moping around for a little while. What pushed us to our brink to finally go out in the city and explore was when I got utterly swindled just trying to use the bathrooms at the station. Just like the rest of Europe, to use the bathroom at the train station, you had to pay. The attendant was only accepting Serbia Dinar, so we had to get some cash from the ATM. When I used the restroom, I gave the gentleman 1000 Dinar, which is close to $10 American. He only gave me back one bill and a few coins, and I didn't even think to look at them right away. I used the restroom, which was a simple hole in the ground accompanied by zero toilet paper, and I went back to where Ron was sitting. I pulled the extra money out of my pocket and saw that the gentleman only gave me less than 100 Dinar back. I went back to the man, hoping he would realize his mistake, but between the language barrier and his unwillingness to believe me, he essentially charged me $9 to use the hole in the ground bathroom. I was so angry because, especially with being on a budget, $9 could have been my food for the entire day. That was just enough to push us out of the train station.

We headed out into the town to get some food and found ourselves at McDonald's because it was cheap and offered free Wi-Fi and bathrooms.

So there we were, halfway around the world, adventure at our fingertips, and we settled at a McDonald's. Sometimes, when you feel so out of place, you just try to find something familiar and comfortable. At McDonald's, we played chess at a table outside and looked out over the world below to pass the time. At one point, I saw a flyer on one of the outside tables I decided to go grab. Come to find out, the flyer was advertising a Beer Festival in Belgrade that same day! And just like that, our whole demeanor changed. Now we were on a mission to find the beer fest!

We were able to ask a few people for directions, and we took off to trek through the city with our big backpacks in tote. Walking countless miles with a heavy backpack wasn't my favorite thing to do by now, but the beer would hopefully be worth it! Besides, I think we only walked a couple of miles before we started seeing the signs for Beerfest!

When we arrived, there weren't many people there yet and we were definitely the odd people out because we were walking around with full backpacks and small bags on our chests as well. We approached the festival gates, and we weren't sure if the security guards would let us in with our packs on. I politely asked them about it, and they said as long as they could search our bags, we would be fine. We dropped our bags and started unzipping all the locked compartments. For some reason, I suddenly became very nervous and aware that multiple armed guards were standing right above me, guns in hand, breathing down my neck, and waiting for me to open my bag. At this point, Ron was also struggling with the lock on one of his bags but eventually managed to get it open. Meanwhile, I was sweating bullets and fumbling to remember my combination locks to open my bag. Either the guards felt sorry for me, or the security wasn't as tight as it looked because one of the guards tapped me on my shoulder and just said "it's okay you can go in". Another guard simply rummaged through my smaller bag, and then we were waved inside. In hindsight, not the best security ever, but it worked in our favor.

We walked into the festival grounds, and it looked like things were just getting started because there weren't many people, and there were no lines at the beer booths! So all we had to do was visit one of the booths to buy tickets for the beer, and we were good to go! We wandered around, tried a few beers, and listened to good live music for a few hours. I have not a single clue who the bands were that we saw perform. However, one of the bands must have been a tribute band to the Red Hot Chili Peppers because we recognized all of their songs. We had a blast meeting some people, dancing to the music, and double-fisting beers while wearing silly goggles, beer crowns, and huge hiking packs. All previous fear of this unknown country had melted away with each sip of beer.

The festival was the perfect pick-me-up after a few long days of travel, but it was short-lived. We contemplated staying at Beer Fest and finding somewhere in Belgrade for the night to crash, but we decided against it because we had already purchased our train tickets to Hungary, so we didn't want to waste our money. However, going against my own advice, we stayed at Beer Fest for as long as possible, chugging one last beer before taking off full speed back toward the train station.

As we were running down the street, we ran past a group of people walking toward the festival, and one of them yelled out, "Hey! Are you American?!" Usually something you don't want to hear since Americans do not have the best reputation in Europe, but for some reason, this question stopped us dead in our tracks. Maybe it was because the guy who yelled it out sounded suspiciously like an American himself. So we slowly turned around and said, "Yes, why do you ask?". He asked where we were from in the states, and we replied, "Michigan," He got really excited and said he was from Michigan also and lived near Oakland College. Ron and I looked at each other in absolute shock because before we left to travel, we had lived right down the street from that College! Come to find out, this guy we were randomly talking to only lived 3 streets away from us and the apartment we had just moved out of. What an incredibly small world! Here we were, thousands of miles from home, randomly stuck in Serbia for the day, running to catch a train, and we ran into someone who was literally our neighbor.

We had a very rushed conversation with the group of people, but we could only spare a few minutes before continuing to the train station.

Sadly, we didn't even get a chance to exchange information, and I don't even remember the guy's name. But the few minutes we stopped to chat almost cost us our seats on the train. I never knew my little legs could run that fast. We alternated between sprinting and walking for a few minutes to catch our breaths before sprinting again. I don't know how long we ran, but I was ready to collapse by the time we made it to the train station. But thankfully, we made it just in time.

I did look up the distance between the train station and the Beer Fest when we got home- and it was 2.3 miles. 2.3 miles that we ran draped in our heavy-ass travel bags. I couldn't run 2.3 miles on a good day, just carrying my own weight. I guess it just shows what adrenaline can do.

Thankfully, we booked another sleeper car with beds. Although the train ride was hot and uncomfortable, we still managed to get a few hours of sleep before arriving in Budapest the next morning.

Hungary- My House in Budapest

Hungarian is the official language in Hungary,
but English is the second most common language spoken.

Hello- Helló
Thank You-Köszönöm
Please- Kérem
Yes- Igen.
Sorry- Sajnálom.
Do you speak English- Beszélszl angolul

We arrived in Budapest tired, hungry, and a little hungover. It's all a little blurry, but somehow we eventually navigated our way to the hostel we had booked. Unfortunately, at this point, after a few days of travel and countless hours on buses, taxis, boats, and trains, I think my brain had turned to mush because I was not prepared for the accommodations awaiting us in Budapest. When we arrived at our hostel, we were shown a shared locker space where we could store our belongings and then escorted to the backyard and to our "two-person hammock" that I had booked as our sleeping arrangements. Time stopped, and for a moment, I was waiting for someone-anyone to jump out and yell, "You've been punk'd!". But that didn't happen, and the woman who had shown us our accommodations told us to "enjoy our stay" and disappeared back inside the hostel.

That's when I vaguely remember booking the hostel a little tipsy at the beer fest and choosing a hammock as our sleeping arrangements- sealing our own fate. Now I do remember not being able to find many beds or hostels available, and I remember seeing the low prices of the hammocks and thinking, "Huh, these are pretty cheap, and hammocks in Crete were super comfortable, so this should be amazing!". Just an example that drunk ideas aren't always the best ideas. Ron and I looked at each other with a small glimmer of hope in our eyes that maybe this would be comfortable. That is until we sat down in the hammock and realized that it was anything but, and by no stretch of the imagination was this a two-person hammock. I desperately tried to reason with the woman at the front desk for a bed inside, but she reassured me they were completely full. Strike one against Budapest. Strike two against Budapest is quite more personal. So strap in and get ready for me to bare my soul. Anyone without a vagina, feel free to either skip this part or educate yourself and bravely dive into a vagina owner's mind for a minute.

After we started exploring the hostel, out of nowhere, one of my nightmares started unraveling in real-time. I had started my period early and didn't even realize that I had completely run out of tampons- in a foreign country. Before we left for the trip, I crammed as many tampons as possible in the space I had left in my bag because I was worried about what kind of tampons they would have in the different countries throughout Europe. Also, not to sound like a tampon snob, but there is one specific kind that I use and have become accustomed to. But anyway, I packed as many as I could and hadn't realized that I had run out. So there I was, hiding in a hostel bathroom, crying, exhausted from traveling and emotionally drained thinking about the night ahead, sleeping in an uncomfortable hammock. With no other option, I wadded up a handful of toilet paper to act as a pad and a temporary fix. I told Ron my predicament, and he stepped up to the plate and volunteered to go on the hunt for tampons. At this point, we had been together for about a year and a half, and this was the first time I had sent him out looking for my feminine products. After describing exactly what I was looking for and even finding a few pictures on the internet to help him out, he was on his way.

In the meantime, I thought maybe I could make some friends at the hostel and ask if anyone had any tampons or pads, but the hostel was like a ghost town. It was the middle of the day, so everyone was out exploring. So I made basecamp inside and curled up on the living room floor to do some research on Budapest while I waited for Ron. A few hours later, Ron called saying that he had been to every store that he could find, and not only did he not find the tampons I needed, but he did not find any tampons at all.

At this point, I resorted to the woman at the front desk to ask her where we could find tampons. She then delivered the soul-crushing news that I would have a tough time finding tampons in Hungary because the cultural belief is that using a tampon will take away your virginity, and most places throughout the country do not believe in using these products. Talk about culture shock. This was an emotional breaking point for me because I couldn't bear the thought of having to wear a pad for the next week while traveling, walking, and being active all day in the sweltering heat. I know it might sound ridiculous that I was this upset about having to wear pads, but everyone who has had to deal with a period for at least a few years knows that you develop your own routine and products that work for you. And once you find something that truly works for you, you stick to it. Some may prefer pads over tampons, but I was not one of them. Not only that, but if you have never worn a pad before, most of them are very frumpy and thick and make you feel like you are wearing a diaper for the world to see. Not to mention, a pad isn't the best option when you are very sweaty and active because well, without getting too graphic, personal hygiene comes into play. I just wanted to run and throw myself on a bed crying in the dramatic fashion of a Disney princess, but I didn't even have a bed to call my own.

When Ron finally returned, he was able to find one box of non-applicator tampons at a small drug store and brought me a box of pads as a backup. The only problem with non-applicator tampons is it's essentially like trying to shove a dry piece of cotton up into your vagina- strike that- that is exactly what it is like. I still attempted this but failed, curing my sensitive vagina for being so high class and needing a certain kind of tampon.

I felt utterly defeated, but I was not ready to give up. So I slapped on the pad for now, and we ventured out to town to continue the hunt for tampons and try to lighten our spirits. My saving grace was a few hours later in a small shopping mall at a drug store, where I was able to find one single box of tampons with a cardboard applicator that was almost hidden on the shelf. The universe must have been looking out for me because it was pure luck that we ran across the one store in all of Budapest that had tampons with an applicator.

By this time, both of us had felt defeated, and we just wanted a little comfort, so we decided to forego sightseeing in Budapest for the rest of the day and just hang out at the mall and have a date night. Our first stop was for frozen yogurt and coffee because I desperately needed something sweet to soothe my soul, and Ron desperately needed some caffeine after running around a foreign country all day searching for tampons. Our next stop was dinner. I was in no mood for any more disappointment today, and I did not want to risk trying foreign dishes, so we settled for a basic restaurant, and burgers and fries were our safety go-to meal. I was perfectly happy with this, and I know Ron didn't complain. We finished the night off at the theatre, watching Guardians of the Galaxy. When we bought our movie tickets, we weren't sure if the movie would be in English or not, especially since the previews were all in Hungarian. Thankfully, the movie started and was in English. Just another side thought about culture shock if you visit a foreign country- Don't automatically expect films to be shown in English. I think we lucked out on this one. Not only was it a great movie, but it was a perfect and relaxing night that we needed.

After the movie, we headed back to our hostel to make the best of our sleeping arrangements. We spent the first few hours squirming around in the hammock, trying to get comfortable and warm because it was freezing outside. I could only take it for so long before I bailed and told Ron I was going inside to sit in the kitchen and try to get warm. At first, I was the only one sitting in the kitchen writing and playing games on my phone, trying not to doze off, and then all the drunk kids came in. Usually, I would be all up for socializing and talking, but I was so tired, and everyone there was just very rude and very put offish that I was sober for some reason. I did however get the chance to talk to one kind woman who had told me that she and her boyfriend had a tent outside last night, but the zipper was broken, so the hostel staff assigned them a new tent that they could close. She told me that the broken tent was unoccupied until they could fix it, so we were more than welcome to crash in the tent where it would block us from the wind and where we might be more comfortable. I was so happy and ran back outside instantly to tell Ron. It was about 4 am at this point, and I didn't even hesitate to wake Ron up to tell him we could take the extra tent. We found the tent further back on the property, crawled in, and were happy to see that not only was there an air mattress in the tent, but also more blankets. Warmth at last! After another hard day, I could finally close my eyes and get a few hours of decent rest.

Good Luck, Bad Luck, Who Knows

Here I am again, on another train, headed for another country, and just taking this time to catch up on everything that happened while we were in Budapest. Overall, our time in Budapest started off as a complete train wreck, but by the end of our stay, there were fireworks-literally.

When I last left off, Ron and I finally got a good night's sleep at our not-so-great hostel. The next few days in Budapest were filled with culture and color, caves, and hot springs. After a while, all the days spent exploring seemed to blur together, but we squeezed a ton of adventures into the time we had.

What I can tell you is that the second night at our hammock hostel was just as miserable as the first. We didn't come back until quite late the second night, hoping we would be able to just pass right out in the hammock, but it was freezing cold again. We didn't want to be "those people" and crawl inside the tent again if someone else had reserved it. Just because we were having a rough time doesn't mean that we had to potentially ruin it for someone else and leave them out in the cold. However, this thought process only lasted until around 3 am, when we could no longer feel our extremities, and we figured if anyone had reserved the tent, they would be in there by now. So we crawled back inside the tent and were able to get some respite from the wind and cold.

Needless to say, we cut our stay short at that hostel and ended up booking a cheap hotel on the outskirts of the city. Although we were still trying to stick to our budget, we just had two sleepless nights out in the cold, and we felt like we deserved to have a nice private room with a real bed to lift our spirits for the next couple of nights. However, I guess saying that it was a "nice room" was a bit of a stretch because it was pretty dirty with a weird bathroom and no shower curtain, but hey, it beat sleeping outside. And this was also the first time in over two months we had a private room, just the two of us.

You can use your imagination for how we spent our alone time together, but let's get to the good part of exploring another country! When we were at the hotel outside the city, we had to buy a bus ticket to get into the center, and then we were able to hop on a trolley to get around town. Budapest is the capital of Hungary and quite a large city. If you want to get technical, it's two sections that were once separate cities- Buda and Pest. Buda and Pest are separated by the Danube River, and Buda lies to the Westside and Pest to the Eastside. Buda is hillier, quieter, and more romantic, while Pest is on the flatter side and known more for its city nightlife. These two cities merged in 1873 when the Széchenyi Chain Bridge was constructed as a permanent structure to connect the two cities. However, many locals still refer to Buda and Pest as two distinct cities. Also, fun fact- Budapest is actually pronounced "booda-pesht" because in the Hungarian language, "S" is pronounced like the "sh" sound. Just a little background information!

So back to my original thought, although we did a ton of walking around the city, we did hop on a trolley a few times to get to where we wanted quicker. Also as a side note, we think you are supposed to pay for the trolley, but if you sneak in the backdoor, no one ever really checks tickets. But one of the first places we stopped to visit was Gellért Hill on the Buda side. Gellért Hill was the site of a cave church built into the side of the limestone rock face, a natural waterfall, a Statue of Liberty, and a cave system. This was one of the first things we noticed when we arrived in the city, and we knew it had to be something we explored.

The marvelous architecture on the side of this hill was even more gorgeous in person. It was an entire structure that looked like it was magically emerging right from the hillside. You could even see a small waterfall cascading down the side of the hill, and since I am so mesmerized by waterfalls, we had to get closer to explore. We took a hiking trail through the woods up the hill, and the views of the city while climbing were fantastic. Finally, we made it to the waterfall, and I just sat there for a few minutes, watching the shimmering water against the rock and letting it wash away all of my stress from the last few days. The climb to the top was exhausting but being able to look out over the entire city was well worth the effort.

The next thing on our to-do list was exploring the city and checking out some authentic Hungarian food, wine, and beer. First, we explored an adorable outdoor patio restaurant where we had appetizers and wine and beer. Later on, we found another hole-in-the-wall place with seating outside that served different variations of hot dogs and hamburgers. We couldn't resist the amazing smells coming from inside and caved and got burgers and fries again with a side of beer. I'm still not sure what we ordered, but it tasted like a variation of a blue cheeseburger, and it was phenomenal. I think we hit the jackpot because the place started to fill up quickly with locals, and soon people were standing around eating their food on the side of the street because there was no more seating available. Either way, it was the perfect location to enjoy good food and good beer and get a show of everything happening on the streets. Such a good location in fact, that we visited this restaurant one more time while we were in Budapest.

The next day after our relaxing day of exploring the city, we decided to book a walking tour and a caving tour! We booked a caving tour because one of the girls I had become friends with in Plakias, had told me that she went caving in Budapest and loved it. I was feeling adventurous, and I adored cave exploring, so I splurged on our budget and booked a caving tour.

That morning, Ron and I went on an expedition to find the caving place. Just getting to the caving headquarters was an adventure in itself. We had directions and an address, but that didn't help. We hopped around on a few buses that we thought would bring us to the location, but apparently, the buses only took us so far. Once the bus dropped us off, we used Google maps to help us navigate, but it kept trying to guide us through side streets and bushes where there were no walking paths. We eventually just ended up kind of stalking a gentleman that was walking in an odd pattern in front of us whom we were really hoping was going to the same place. Thankfully we caught up to him, and we found out that we were both trying to find the caving entrance. After following few strategically placed signs, we finally found it. Once there, we went through the typical paperwork signing risk disclosures, and then we suited up! We suited up in these orange body jumpsuits made to protect us from the dirt and dust of the caves. We were also equipped with caving headgear, including a helmet and small head-lamp. While we were waiting for everyone to get ready, we got to know some of the people in our group then we took off!

We started by going through a small door on the side of a cliff. From there, we climbed down a steep ladder to the start of our adventure-and what an adventure it was. We climbed through jagged holes and scaled up rocky walls, taking in the magnificently carved caverns around us. We were told that the caves were carved by hot thermal waters that used to flow beneath the streets, and the tunnels we were crawling through were slowly formed from hundreds of years of the waters carving out the rock. There was one place we stopped in the caves that they called the amphitheater. This was a large opening in the caves, enough to fit probably 100 people if you squeezed in. The guides had both of our caving groups come in, sit down, and turn off our lamps until we were sitting in complete darkness.

I'm not going to lie; it was a little scary for me because I am not a fan of the dark, but it made it better to have Ron next to me and knowing it wasn't just us down there but many people. After a few minutes of sitting in the silent darkness, one of the leaders began to sing. I forgot what song she sang, but it was beautiful. The echoing in the caverns provided the perfect stage for her voice. After she was done, she invited us to all pick a song and sing it together to experience the proper range of the amphitheater's echoes. We all started shouting out songs to sing for a few moments, and by some miracle, someone shouted out "A whole new world," my Disney spirit song. Not only am I a huge Disney fan, but this was one of my all-time favorite songs. And much to my surprise, everyone agreed that this would be our song. So there we were, about 25 adults sitting in the dark, below the streets of Budapest, in a cave and singing "A whole new world"; This was my happiness. Talk about incredible. All our different voices echoed and bounced off the cave walls and made for a one-of-a-kind experience.

I don't know the next time I will ever be able to do something like this, let alone if I go caving again, it will be with a group of people that are all willing to sing a Disney song together. A core memory I will never forget. The rest of the caving trip included exploring the smallest paths we could make it down and trying to basically rock climb up some of the walls. There were more than a few walls we had to scale where I had Ron stand underneath me as my safety net if I fell. In particular, there was also one hole where our guide asked everyone if we wanted to attempt to fit through with some wiggling. Never have I been claustrophobic, but once I crawled in that hole and had to wiggle my butt and hips back and forth just to squeeze through, I got more than a little nervous. There I was, head in a hole and ass up to the world for the rest of our group to see, trying to wiggle my way through. At one point, I got so nervous that I wouldn't fit that I asked Ron to pull me back out by my legs. So he grabbed me by my ankles and pulled my ass out of that tiny hole. I proceeded to take an alternative route with the rest of the group instead of slithering through a hole barely big enough to fit my booty. The entire experience was unlike anything I had ever done before. By the time we explored to our heart's content and emerged back out into the daylight, we had made memories that would last a lifetime and bonded with a group of strangers deep underneath the streets of Budapest.

After caving and cleaning ourselves off a bit from all the dust and dirt, we started the long walk to the other side of the river to where our walking tour would begin. We wandered and stopped along the way, taking in the scenery. We had initially signed up for a guided tour of the city and a pass to get into one of the infamous bathhouses in Budapest, but when we arrived, we were shocked to find out that we were the only two people in the tour. The woman who was our guide was very pleasant but very soft-spoken, and it was awkward at times with only three of us there. Even so, we tried to make the best of it as she walked us around the Pest side of town. Our first stop was right outside the Hungarian Parliament. From the Buda side of the Danube River, we had an absolutely gorgeous view of this massive building, but we had no idea what it was. Come to find out, this neo-gothic style behemoth was the parliament building built in 1896. We didn't really have an interest in touring the inside, so we just passed it by. But the best part of this parliament building was when it lit up at night. From the Pest side, this building lit up the river, and all of it's lights glistened softly against the calm water and was just breathtaking.

But back to the current tour. Other sites for the day included The Great Synagogue, which is the second-largest Synagogue in the world, The Great Market Hall, where you could find anything and everything your heart desired food or goods wise, Vaci Street, a popular street for locals that extends for 15 blocks filled with cafes, bars, restaurants, and shops, and of course St. Stephen's Basilica which was just a pure work of art. I've mentioned before how "churched-out" I was from visiting various worship structures throughout Europe, but the eerie but beautiful gothic style of St. Stephen's Basilica just drew me in. It just looked like the type of building where at night, out of the corner of your eye, you would see a gargoyle swoop down and rest itself on one of the towers. However, while I was in the square just taking in the beauty of the architecture, I didn't see any gargoyles, but I did learn that St Stephen's Basilica was the third-largest church in Budapest and is dedicated to King István (Stephen), who was the first King of Budapest and brought Christianity to the country. Our guide also let us know that in just a couple of days was the National Holiday, St. Stephen's Day, to celebrate the founding of Hungary. Apparently, it was a huge festival day where all the locals celebrated and had music, food, and drinks in the streets, and then ended the night with fireworks over the Danube. Although we already had plans to leave the day before the festival, we decided that we could change our plans and stay in Hungary for one more day!

The second to last stop on our tour was Budapest's underground railway system which they claim to be the oldest electric underground railway in Europe- Only battling with London, whose underground railway is older but steam-powered. The exciting thing about this underground railway is that there is a massive bunker that has a direct route to and from the parliament building. It was supposedly built in the 1950s to prepare for a nuclear attack but has never really been used and is barely ever visited. That was an interesting piece of history I'm glad I was listening to, but to be completely honest, I was zoned out a little bit and kind of just existing in my own world during this tour. As we walked countless miles all around Budapest, I was soaking in all the gorgeous sites but wasn't absorbing a lot of the information. Maybe my brain just needed a break. I still enjoyed the tour, but I definitely didn't retain as much information as I wanted to. My body and mind were also ready to explore the sweet, sweet relaxation that awaited us in the bathhouse. As promised, we ended the tour at the Szechenyi Spa Baths, the first hot spring bathhouse on the Pest side and over 100 years old.

Budapest was built on a geographical fault line, and it's estimated that over 80% of Budapest has geothermal waters running underneath it, which supplies the bathhouses. This is another reason why Budapest has such an extensive cave system. The thermal waters have been slowly carving out intricate caving systems under the earth's surface for countless years. These hot springs often contain an abundance of minerals and can have healing effects on the body. There have been so many bathhouses established in Budapest over the years that it is now known as the "Spa Capital of the World." The Szechenyi Bath House is one of the largest and most famous houses in Budapest, housing over 18 different mineral pools. I couldn't wait to try them all.

When we first walked in, Ron and I parted ways to go to our locker rooms and get changed. I was given a wrist bracelet in my locker room, which would allow me to open one locker, lock it back up, and then access it at the end of the day. There were locker rooms all along the long hallway, but none of them had any privacy. At least from the locker room culture or etiquette I experienced back home, women tend to be more modest, covering up their bodies with a towel while changing and doing it quickly, but it was much different here. Young and old women alike were getting changed and walking around the huge locker room completely naked with as much confidence as walking around in the privacy of their own homes. Locker room culture is so much more conservative in the states. But then again, as I have talked about before, I think Americans have grown up with more of a body-shaming culture, while Europeans just seem to embrace their own bodies and practice a little more self-love. Something I think everyone could benefit from.

Once Ron and I were both changed, we headed toward the massive outdoor pool with jet stream arches of water in the middle. The pools outside were filled with people, either relaxing or playing games. It was pretty warm and sunny out, and after walking around the city all day, the pool felt great. The water was such a different experience since it was mineral-rich hot spring water instead of chlorine. So instead of having a potent chlorine smell, the water was fresh but a little off-color, and you could almost smell its minerality. There were little waterfall fountains strategically placed around the pool, and of course, we had to splash around in them for a minute and fully immerse our bodies in the healing waters. I could have just sat in the pool for a few hours and marveled at the gorgeous architecture of this ancient building. But we didn't stay outside very long because the sun had already been baking our skin all day long, so we ventured inside to check out the other pools and spas.

On the inside of the bathhouse was a maze of rooms, each unique but packed with people. Every pool was a different size and at least a slightly different temperature. There were also a few sauna rooms, including a dry sauna and a wet sauna. The walls inside the bathhouse were so beautiful, filled with colorful mosaic tiles and intricate patterns. We did a lap around the entire bathhouse before testing out the wet sauna. As soon as you opened the door, a hot, foggy mist seeped out and engulfed your whole body. It was so hot, and there was so much steam in the room I could barely see where I was walking. The room was very narrow, but I had no idea how far back it went because all I could see were pairs of feet on the ground poking out from a cloud of hidden bodies sitting on the benches. Finally, Ron and I found what we thought was an open spot and sat down for a bit to just breathe in the hot dense air and help clear our lungs.

The steam felt soothing and refreshing, but it got to be too much after a while, so we reverted to the dry sauna. The dry saunas here were pretty much like the dry saunas I've been to in the states. They were hot and dry and made with cedar planks. However, this sauna was a little too hot for me because I thought the flesh on my legs was going to peel off when I sat down on the boiling wood planks. We didn't stay long in that one. Instead, we decided to cool down from the heat and check out the coldest pool in the bathhouse. It was a small pool, about 6 feet in circumference. It was elevated compared to the rest of the pools, and you had to climb up a small ladder to get in. I don't remember reading the temperature gauge before we got in, but we knew it would be cold. Since this was the only pool we had to ourselves, we took the opportunity and jumped right in before our feet even had a chance to test the waters. As my body hit the icy waters, I instantly lost my breath. Both of us came up gasping for air. I'm sure the cold water wasn't that cold but it just felt like it, because we had just come from two extremely hot saunas. Either way, the pool cooled us down almost to the point of shivers, and it couldn't have been more than 5 minutes before we climbed back out. No wonder that was the only empty pool. It was torturous but refreshing at the same time if that makes any sense.

We wandered around some more and tried out every single one of the different temperature pools, including a lap pool. There was even one pool that was oddly discolored. Maybe the mineral content was higher, or perhaps it was the reflection from the mosaic tiles and paint on the inside, but either way, the water felt fine. After a few hours of pool hopping, I could already feel the mineral-rich water workings its magic on my skin.

Another discovery, later on, was a small trough-like sink with a tube coming down into it that dispensed ice. This was right next to the hot pools and sauna areas. After a few minutes of soaking in a tub and people watching, we saw a few people get out of the hot pools and grab chunks of ice to rub themselves down afterward. Monkey see, monkey do. So we jumped out and proceeded to rub ourselves down with ice as well. Like the cold plunge after the hot saunas, it was very refreshing.

For the rest of the day, we jumped around from the saunas to the pools and took a dip in the cold plunge occasionally. By the time we left, I still wasn't ready to go, but my hands and feet were completely waterlogged, so I figured I should give my body a chance to acclimate back to dry land. I wish I would have taken more pictures of the gorgeous architecture and art inside the bathhouse, but it wasn't really common practice to take cameras around a bathhouse and invade everyone's privacy, so we only snapped one quick picture of the pools outside and then put our camera away.

Even though it was getting dark already and we were miles away from the bus that would take us back to our hotel, we decided to hoof it back to the bus stop to see more of the city and catch a bite to eat. We stopped at a little to-go place, and each ordered a small bowl of Hungarian goulash that was to die for! We were getting closer to the bridge we would have to cross to get back to the Buda side when something caught our eye. Off to the side of the bridge, I saw a woman juggling and a crowd gathering around her. Without even hesitating, we headed below the bridge to check it out. As the woman was juggling, more and more performers started to assemble behind her, and it looked like they were getting ready to set up for something. There was also a group of a few people assembling instruments and a band stage in the back. Eventually, more and more people started gathering around, and it turned into an all-out street carnival. People who were just moving around freely turned into fire dancers, the jugglers multiplied, musicians started squeaking their instruments, and all kinds of other performers emerged. Just like in Scotland, we had randomly stumbled upon a street carnival. For the next few hours, we took a seat in the dirt with everyone else and just stared in amazement at all the talented performances and took in the sweet sounds of music.

Conveniently, there was also a beer cart nearby to indulge in while watching the performances. Eventually, one woman indulged too much and started seductively dancing in front of the performers. At one point, she even got close enough to a fire juggler to start touching his chest while he was literally playing with fire. She eventually backed away from the fire but kept drunkenly stumbling around and dancing while also performing a striptease for the audience; A sideshow to the already occurring performances. I'm not sure if the man she was trying to seduce actually wanted to impress her or what he was thinking, but he handed her one of his long juggling strings that was on fire; Probably not his brightest idea. Ron and I watched in horror as the drunk girl stumbled around swinging a string of fire.

Thankfully, one of the other performers chased her down and got the fire away from her just as she passed out half-naked in front of the audience on the sand. She must have had friends nearby because a few of them went to take care of her once she was face down in the sand. Not a clue why no one stepped in while she was stripping or handed a wand of fire. But this is exactly why you choose to walk the town when traveling sometimes- you never know what you will run into. After a while, the performers started to clear out, and we figured that we should head back to our hotel to make sure we got back while the buses were still running. As we walked back across the bridge, the city showed us her true beauty. The lights on the bridge lit up the night sky, and the water glistened under the moonlight. The town was stunning.

That next morning, we woke up to check out of our hotel and trek to a different hostel on the Pest side, right in the city center, so that we would be able to walk home from the St. Stephen festivities. I have to admit that going through three different accommodations while in the same city was a bit outrageous, but we've learned that if you don't like it somewhere, you move on! But also since we were staying one more night for the festival, sleeping in town made it easier to stay out later and catch our train out the following day.

So, we packed up our gear again and jumped on a bus that took us to a trolley that took us to the general area of our hostel, where we got lost wandering around a few streets before we found the entrance. The building was a huge old-world style building with creaky stairs that led to one of the middle floors, where a nice older woman answered the door and let us in.

She brought us into the kitchen and sat us down for about an hour to discuss everything at the hostel. She was so lovely and friendly and wanted to know everything about us, our travels, and our plans for the festival. So we sat there and chit-chatted with her for a while. Then she brought us to our room which was just 2 large bedrooms connected to one another with about 4 beds each. A few other travelers were bunked up and sleeping since it was still early in the morning. So we quietly set our stuff down and got ready to explore the festivities.

The extensive setup for the festival was back on the Buda side, just on the side street in front of the riverbank. We took our time wandering around Pest some more and indulging in the street art, shops, and some beautifully made gelato that resembled a flower. By the time we made it back down to the riverbank, most of the festival tents were just starting to set up and open for business. We wanted to give all the vendors time to get set up before we bombarded them, so we just strolled along the river while people finished setting up.

There were a few stages with bands on them, art, beer, and craft tents. But the best tents of all are the food tents. Even early in the day, the delicious smells of the homemade Hungarian cuisine filled the streets. People flocked to the street quickly, and before we knew it, we were among a sea of people all waiting in line for homemade beer, food, and sweets. In one tent, there was an older couple cooking Hungarian stew in clay pots on the ground next to open fire. It was mesmerizing just watching the cooking process, and this adorable couple sit on the ground and put all their love and energy into the authentic food they were making.

Throughout the day, we walked around exploring everything and stopping at each stage to watch the performances and even getting to know some of the locals. Our original plan was to save our money and just spend it on food, not the beer, but we caved eventually because a nice drink paired perfectly with the lively music and atmosphere all around us. Ron bought a local red beer, and I had some kind of fruit cherry beer. The drink was such a beautiful color of burgundy, and it tasted way better than any other cherry-flavored beer I have ever had in the states.

Once my hands were free, I wandered back over to the tent where the older couple was making goulash and bought my dinner for the night. The traditional Hungarian goulash was a mixture of meat, potatoes, peppers, and a few other mystery ingredients and some spice combinations that were out of this world. Ron also bought us an adorably decorated sugar heart cookie, but sadly it was decorated better than it tasted. It was pretty much inedible but still very cute.

As if the festival couldn't get any better, we got a surprise visit from Brit because we had connected, and she just arrived in Budapest the day before!

We found a place on the wall by the river and made base camp to catch up over a few beers and to secure a good spot for the fireworks later. It was so good to see her after a couple of weeks apart. Traveling solo suited her because she looked happy and upbeat and was even sporting a new headband and purse that she had purchased in Croatia. She told us all about her new friends she met in Greece, how she missed her ferry to go island hopping twice, and all about Croatia and the fantastic waterfall hikes she went on. She ended up meeting a group of fellow travelers and they all just clicked and continued to travel together in Croatia. Brit even met one of her best travel buddies in Crete that strangely enough had the exact same birthmark on her leg. I was so happy for her to see how much she was thriving exploring Europe either on her own or with newly found friends. At the same time, I felt a glint of sadness and jealously. Like I missed out on something special not traveling with my best friend or having the freedom to travel alone and know that you alone are responsible for your journey and decisions. But I know I was on my own journey with Ron, growing and exploring our relationship as we traveled. I'm sure one day I will take off on my own to see a part of the world on my bucket list, or even get another chance to explore and travel with Brit. But we continued to share travel stores and we told Brit all about our amazing hostel stay in Greece and the random day in Serbia, and then we recommended that she had to go caving while she was in Budapest. It was like we hadn't seen each other in forever but also as if no time had passed at all. The world of traveling and backpacking is strange like that. Even with the strangers you meet, you form such strong bonds so quickly, that you just know they will last for the rest of your life. No matter how often you see or talk to them. If you ever happen to run into someone you met before while traveling, you instantly connect again like no time has passed at all.

Finally, after the long-anticipated wait, the firework show over the Danube River began. I would have to say that next to the Christmas firework show at Disneyworld, this was the most incredible firework display that I have ever seen and probably will ever see. The main firework display took place over the river, with the lights and explosions reflecting on the calm water as far as you could see. But there were also multiple other firework displays going off on each of the bridges that crossed the river. The colors were vibrant, and the entire night sky lit up with fireworks and smoke. I also think this was one of the longest firework shows I have ever seen because it seemed to go on forever. Just as one grandiose explosion displayed stopped, another one just as grand would keep the show going. It was the perfect way to end our time in Budapest. The three of us sat on the banks of the Danube River in quiet amazement. I don't know if Ron and Brit felt the same way, but every so often we would glace at each other with a half-smile or wide-eyes and all I could think about is the remarkable adventure that we had been on together so far and how good it was to be together again, even for a short time. We had shared so much life together in such a short time, that sometimes it was still hard for me to grasp the reality of what we were doing.

After the show, we wandered around the streets for a little longer with Brit before we headed back to our hostel to catch our 5:30 am train to Prague, Czech Republic. We said our goodbyes to Brit again as I held back tears from yet another departure.

By the time we arrived back at the hostel, I think we had got an hour or two of sleep before we got up and wandered across town to find the train station again. Once on the train, we settled in for the ride just in time to realize that we were starving. We still had some Hungarian money left, so we decided to venture to the food cart. The food cart was very elegantly decorated with linen tablecloths and very fancy place settings. Ron ordered scrambled eggs, and I got a cheese and ham omelet. The food was surprisingly good as far as train food goes. But that could have also been because I was starving. But either way, we had a nice breakfast on the train as we watched the sunrise and waved goodbye to Hungary. And that is where I am currently as I write this sentence. I guess even if I don't keep up with my writing on a day-to-day basis anymore, at least have the long train rides to catch up on everything. Since we still have another 5 hours or so left on the train, it's naptime until we reach our destination in the Czech Republic.

At this point I have also given up on trying to keep track of every penny we are spending. I found that I let loose more in Budapest with spending habits because we could afford it. I have realized that it is okay to bob and weave on the budget instead of sticking to a strict daily plan. If our account starts to look too empty, we will just take a few zero spending days and relax. Should I still be writing everything down to at least kind of keep track? – Probably, but that's a problem for future Cally.

Czech Republic

*Most people in the Czech Republic understand
and speak English but Czech is the official language.*

Hello- ahoj
Thank You-Dekuji
Please- Prosím
Yes- Ano.
Sorry- Prominte
Do you speak English- Mluvíš anglicky

Pulling into Prague, we found ourselves utterly exhausted and just wanted some time to recuperate from the last few days. I know many people that we have met are also traveling for the long haul, and for some reason, they seem to be going out every night and living it up night after night. But for us, gas is running low. Although we are cramming as much sightseeing and life-living into every city that we visit, we have also been taking more downtime to just chill and hang out at our hostels, meeting other people and regenerating for the next few days. Even when we first started planning this trip, I thought it would be like college, and I would be fine staying up late every night, drinking and exploring. Just running off pure adrenaline and air.

The reality of the situation is that I am no longer in college, and even though 25 isn't very old, it definitely isn't the same as a wide-eyed 19-year-old who is discovering life outside of the watchful eyes of parents for the first time. Travelling does get to you, and constantly commuting on trains and busses and walking everywhere wears you down. Now I am finally starting to understand why some people at the hostels can sleep in until 3:00 in the afternoon or come back for multiple naps during the day. There were even a few people that as far as we could tell, slept through entire days in hostels because we never even saw them leave the beds. But now I know that's because constant travel is simply exhausting; therefore, this first day in the Czech Republic was our chill day.

When we pulled into Prague, the train station itself was overwhelming. Even the architecture at a public transportation building was stunning, and it made us that much more excited to see the city. We took a trolley downtown and wandered around before finding our hostel- Hostel Orange. Right outside, there was a huge stage and live music. We checked in, dropped our stuff off, and wandered around to check out the city. We found out the stage and band playing were part of some kind of festival, but this was their last day. We also found a little market of souvenirs that piqued our interest. There was everything from puppets and beer mugs to lighters and key chains and some specialty handmade items. After drifting around, we found a little bar to sit down for some traditional Czech food. The bar was empty, which is always a little nerve-wracking, but we were proved wrong.

To start things off, we each ordered a local Czech beer on tap, which tasted like tiny drops of heaven. Then we each ordered a traditional Czech goulash dish. I ordered a sweet dish, and Ron ordered a spicier dish. I was really fascinated with what kind of plate would be put in front of me because the Hungarian goulash was nothing like American goulash, so I was expecting the Czech goulash to also be completely different. But this goulash…was hands down, one of the best things that I have ever eaten in my life. I think my taste buds all had miniature orgasms, and I wouldn't be surprised if I had dreams about this dish. It was simply perfect.

The plating didn't really knock me off my socks at first because it looked like the typical plate of stew with meat and potatoes with these weird pieces of small white bread arranged on the plate and a red sauce off to the side. Come to find out, the bread was actually Czech bread dumplings that just melted in your mouth. The dumplings combined with the tender meat and vegetables and sweet yet savory sauce was a flavor explosion. The dish's flavors were good enough to stand alone, but the sauce on the side was some kind of cranberry and orange marmalade-ish type of thing that just enhanced the dish to the *out-of-this-world* category. If we weren't in a public place, I would have picked up my plate and licked it clean, but instead, I just used my spoon to scrape every single inch of mouthwatering goodness off the plate and into my mouth. I tried a bite of Ron's dish and although it was also good, it didn't hold a candle to my plate. The beer was also just the perfect drink to pair with the goulash and soothe our souls.

Right away, we found proper respect for Czech food and beer as we headed back to the hostel to chill for the night and recharge. So here we are now, hanging out on the balcony, listening to street music, and getting to know these two Canadian girls we met staying in the same hostel. A nice calm night to prepare us for the next few days of adventure in Prague is just what we needed.

Prague-ally Gonna come back

First of all- puns, I LOVE puns. Corny titles or tidbits of life that are either legitly good, or so bad you wonder what was wrong with the person who wrote the pun. Judge me if you want, but it's a good conversation piece either way. But back to Prague.

The city of Prague was a pleasant surprise, and it is definitely a place that we would come back to again. Also, I should mention that we are currently sitting on another train on the way to Germany now! But to backtrack to our time in Prague first- Prague is one of my favorites as far as cities go. Between the architecture, food, the gorgeous outskirts of the town, and the beer, this city life took these two vagabonds for a ride.

After our first chill night in Prague, we woke up the following day ready to explore. We walked around admiring the gothic architecture and taking in all the wondrous sights and smells. One of the town squares in Prague had quite a few street performers. There were a few people dressed in costumes, a unicycle rider, a man blowing bubbles, a girl with a minia-ture pig, etc. By the way, the pig didn't actually DO anything special. It was just a miniature pig that a woman was getting people to pay her to take pictures with. It was an eclectic mix of performers which sucked us into a trance.

That is, until we saw it; the bread cart. This bread cart wasn't just any bread cart; this cart was just like the ones that we saw in Budapest but had a line so far down the street that it would have taken days to get to the front. One in particular had a much shorter line, so we had to get in it. This delicacy that we were in line for was a roasted bread spiral cooked over an open flame and then doused in cinnamon and sugar, among other blissful spices. Now I know you think that this sounds an awful lot like the American carnival classic, the elephant ear, but not even close. The bread by itself was so savory that I could have eaten it without sugar, but the sugar on top and the way the bread was spiraled so you could tear off little piece by piece just made it so much better. I could have easily eaten three on the spot, but my logical side and wallet fought against it. This delicacy was apparently called Trdelnik and is common across a few countries in Central Europe. But that's another point- the bread throughout Europe is just different than American bread. Not just different-better. Like way better. All of the bread tastes so fresh and flavorful, and fragrant. I'm not even sure how to describe it, but hands down better than the bread in America.

After our second scrumptious food experience, we went on an adventure to visit Prague's famous Charles Bridge and search for the John Lennon wall. The Charles Bridge is the oldest bridge spanning across the Vltava River, and is the second oldest bridge throughout the Czech Republic. It is said that construction took over 40 years, and the bridge wasn't complete until 1402. That is probably why the locals refer to it as "the old bridge." However, what makes the bridge unique is the 30 statues that line the bridge. Each sculpture is either of a Saint or has a religious meaning. The oldest statue on the bridge was placed in 1683 and depicts St. John of Nepomuk. The figure of St. John was erected and placed on the bridge at the exact spot where the king threw John to his death from the bridge because he wouldn't tell the king what his wife said during confession. Many people actually travel to Prague every year to touch the statue for good luck. I have no idea what this story has to do with good luck, but to each their own.

When we got to the famous bridge, it was overloaded with people. Both tourists and people painting and selling goods. All the gothic statues lining the bridge were covered with spider webs. I'm not sure if they didn't take care of the bridge to keep its historical significance or purposefully make it look aged, but the statues looked like they hadn't been touched in years. I guess it did make the bridge look more authentic. But between the painters and handmade jewelry and old statues, the most exciting thing that we came across on the bridge was the man playing water glasses.

I'm sure most people have seen or even tried putting water in a glass and then rotating your finger around the edge to play squeaky music, but this was nothing like that. This man had an intricate cart of different sizes of water glasses with tiny sensors connected to each one to amplify the sound. Before he began his performance, the man also dabbled in some comedy with the crowd to get everyone's attention. After the comedy routine, he began playing the best thing that I have ever heard come out of water glasses. This man played Bach on water glasses. Just take that in for a minute. Bach on water glasses! He positioned his hands like he was playing the piano and proceeded to move his fingers in circular motions while moving back and forth through the wine glasses, making the notes come to life. Everyone was awestruck. Out of all the street performers that we have seen so far, some were just sad attempts to get money, while others had real talent, and this was one man with true natural talent. First off, for coming up with the idea to play water glasses at this complicated level, and secondly, for teaching himself how to play the glasses like this. Not only the time and precision it must have taken using different water glasses and water levels to get each note correct but taking the tedious time to master something of this magnitude. Bach compositions are hard enough to learn on the piano, let alone water glasses! This was one street performer that we did give money to at the end of his performance even though we were on a budget. He deserved it.

Side note, that in the Eastern/Central European countries, we could buy a lot more things than we could in Western Europe. For starters, food and beer were a lot cheaper in Eastern and Central Europe, and secondly, the conversion rate for money was much better, so we felt like high rollers here, eating and drinking to our heart's content.

Anyways, we left the water glass playing man with fewer coins in our pockets but more music in our hearts. Our venture across the bridge also included wandering around part of the city for hours, trying to find the famous John Lennon Wall. We were told by a few different travelers that this was a good stop with a lot of Beetles nostalgia and beautiful artwork.

Long story short, even with the help of others, we failed at finding the wall, but did find some other fun activities along the way. Down a little side street, we found an outdoor museum. This was a place where the street was filled with life-like staged props and cutouts that you could pose with. Of course, I took the opportunity and posed like I was part of a postcard and being dragged by a massive fish out to sea, as well as posing with Nessie the Loch Ness Monster. After our shenanigans, we ventured up to tour the Prague Castle.

This castle was situated at the top of a huge hill, so the leg muscles went to work again. Once we made it to the top, the castle was so big that we had a difficult time finding the entrance. Inside, the grounds and the architecture included beautiful Gothic columns, paintings, and statues. It all went perfectly with the atmosphere of the whole city. Surprisingly, the castle grounds were open to the public to tour daily for free. I was even more surprised to see the lack of guards or security at the castle. There were a few guards standing watch every so often, but I thought for sure there would be more considering the castle is where the president of the Czech Republic lives and where the Crown jewels are kept.

But the walls and architecture of the castle were so stunning and mysterious. It almost made me think about the castle from Beauty and the Beast and how I first pictured it in my mind when reading the book. Full of beauty, secrets, and sorrow. Fun fact- Prague Castle is actually the "Largest ancient castle in the world," according to the Guinness Book of

World Records. It measures in around 18 acres large and was constructed in the 9th century. We spent plenty of time admiring the castle and exploring the grounds before we headed back down the daunting hill.

At this point in the day, we figured we deserved a well-earned drink. On our walk down, we talked about this Ice Bar that we had heard about in Prague, and Ron told me how he had visited one while he was in Japan. Also, at this point in our trip, the whole ALS ice bucket challenge was blowing up on social media, and my old manager had challenged me to this feat.

First off, if you don't know what ALS is, it's more commonly known as Lou Gehrig's Disease, and it's a progressive disease that targets nerve cells and affects the control of muscles. To raise awareness and research funding for ALS, there was this social media challenge going around where you had to first dump a bucket of ice water over your head, nominate three other people, and then donate to the ALS community.

Weirdly enough, the day before we were searching the city for ice so we could complete this challenge, but I don't think there was an ice cube to be found. None of the grocery stores we visited sold ice, and even when we asked the hostel manager, he had no idea where you could get ice in the city. So, if we couldn't find any ice for the challenge, we figured for the challenge we would do the next best thing- visit an actual ice bar.

Basically, the ice bar was a completely enclosed room entirely made of ice, complete with an ice bar, ice sculptures, and ice drinks. No ice in the drinks though- just actually glass made of ice. Each group of people would enter the room and have about 45 minutes and access to one drink with options to buy more. Before you could go into the room, each person was given an oversized insulated poncho that covered you entirely for warmth. You also had the option of getting a pair of gloves and a hat. Once inside, the music was turned up, and the temperature turned down. Since I was always cold, even in 80-degree weather, I instantly froze even with the winter wear covering me. But we made our way up to the bar for our ice shots served in an ice cup and made our way around each of the ice sculptures playing around and taking pictures. Nearing the end of our time in the bar, we had to record a little video of me taking my gloves and poncho off to take an ice shot in an ice bar wearing a tank top and shorts. Not exactly a textbook ice bucket challenge but as close as I could get! Thankfully, not soon after that, the doors were opened to let us back into the main part so that we could all warm up. We wandered the streets and filled our stomachs before we retired for the night.

The next morning, we woke up early to start our walking tour of the city. Again, I can't tell you enough how great these walking tours are, and what a good chance it is to see the city and learn more about the culture and customs. On this tour, we walked around the old square and learned about the separation of Czechoslovakia into the Czech Republic and Slovakia. This happened in 1993, and I remember this happening when I was just little because in elementary school, I remember doing a report on Czechoslovakia, even after the country had separated. I didn't learn until years later about the separation, and I think the US took that much time to learn about or transition into the mindset of two separate countries as well.

It's crazy to think that the internet was not widely used back at that time, so I couldn't have just gone and Googled information on Czechoslovakia to do a school project. Just imagine, having to do a school project or presentation and flip through actual history books and go to the library to get your information instead of just doing a quick search on Google. This is probably another reason why the US didn't publish any new information about the separation of Czechoslovakia right away. Because it would be much harder to relay information rather than updating the Wikipedia page. Just mind-blowing. I'm not even that old, but I am aging myself, just saying that I was around before the internet was available to the public. But let me get back on track. Like most separations, the separation of The Czech Republic and Slovakia had political roots, but the split was very amicable. Besides the few speed bumps of splitting towns in half over the border, the two new countries split their fair share of goods and resources according to their populations. We also learned that a typical Czech household consists of only two children and that it is common for extended families to live together.

On the tour, we also got a chance to witness the striking of the famous astronomical clock, otherwise known as Orloj. Just as the name says, an astronomical clock is a clock that displays the time and astronomical information such as the position of the sun, moon, and zodiac information. This particular clock located in the heart of Prague was built in 1410, making it the oldest astronomical clock that is still operating today.

At the beginning of each hour, the 12 apostles would appear in windows right above the clock, the skeleton waves his lantern, and the clock strikes. I will have to admit that the clock tower itself and the intricate details were pretty impressive, but the hourly strike of the clock wasn't as grandiose as I expected it to be. I'm sure historians and the people who travel thousands of miles to come marvel at this medieval wonder would strike me down for saying that, but I just wanted to be honest. Don't get me wrong, it was still a great experience and something not to miss while you are in the city, but when something is hyped up so much, it's usually hard to live up to the expectations you may have. But still a great experience.

While at the clock, we also learned that instead of celebrating a birthday, the Czech Republic celebrates name days. Because each day of the year is associated with a particular name. Basically, when a child is born in the Czech Republic, their parents have to choose a name from a pre-approved list. If they do not want to select from the list, their child's name must be approved by a special office. The woman giving us the tour told us that depending on what part of the Czech Republic you live in, it is very common to still celebrate your name day over your birthday. It's crazy to think that you would have to name your child from a list of preselected names, but I do like the idea of celebrating a name day. Just something culturally unique.

One other unique stop I want to talk about on our tour was The Dancing House. The Dancing House stood out like a sore thumb out of all the old world and gothic-style architecture throughout Prague. First off, the building was newly designed in 1992, and it has a very unique architectural style and shape, with one side of the glass face bowing and caving inward and the other side with its 3-D style windows. The building is said to resemble the famous dancers Fred Astaire and Ginger Rogers. Strangely enough, it was probably the most unique architecture I have ever seen.

After the tour around the city was complete, Ron and I wanted to change pace, so we hopped on a trolley to the outskirts of the town to do some hiking in a gorge I heard about. Thankfully the gorge wasn't too far away, and we were able to jump on the trolley until the last stop and then walk from there. It dropped us off on a road next to a McDonald's, and right behind it was a little trail going into the woods that we followed. Before we jumped on the trail, we couldn't help but treat ourselves to a little snack.

Once on trail, the city scape gave way to jagged rock faces, and gorgeous greenery. It was just what we needed. The path led down to the bottom of the gorge, where there was a little walkway and a small stream. The whole walk, you could look up to the naturally carved stone walls above you. It really was a tranquil and beautiful walk to get away from the city and out into nature.

Once we followed the trail around the bottom of the gorge, we decided to take one of the trails heading up through the trees to the top. At the top, we found a few small rolling hills of grass and sharp cliff edges. Once you reached the edge of the hills, it was rockface all the way down to the bottom. When we got to the place where the grass ended, there were enough rock formations to climb down and do some minor rock scrambling. I absolutely love rock scrambling because it isn't as intense as professional rock climbing but is still a little more adventurous than just hiking, and it definitely gets my adrenaline pumping because I am afraid of heights. Especially being so short standing at only 5'1, I love being able to climb and scramble up rocks and try to figure out different ways to get my short little legs down or up to the next spot. The view over the rocks and gorge also painted a beautiful picture as a background. Naturally, Ron and I explored all around the rock faces before settling on one spot and just sitting on the edge and enjoying the scenery for a while.

Once we had our fill of fresh air and countryside scenery, we headed back down the gorge to take the bus back to the city. When we hopped back on the trolley, we got off a little early to try to find a beer garden on the other side of the river. We wandered around aimlessly, walking through a few parks and different areas, trying to find the beer garden. Eventually, we wandered close to what looked like a wedding. Naturally, we were curious, so we got closer to see the reception celebration taking place. Behind the reception was a large area with picnic tables and a few scattered people who were obviously not a part of the wedding party. There were also two canopies that looked like they were serving beer and food. We didn't want to crash the wedding party but still wanted to sample the spread.

One of the attendants told us that this section was not a part of the wedding but was the beer garden, and we were more than welcome to stay. We were so happy to finally make it to our destination and grabbed a beer from one tent and sausage from another. We picked a table right on the garden's edge that overlooked the beautiful city skyline. I will always love simple moments like that where an effortless lunch and good atmosphere whisk you away from reality for a while, and you can just relax and let all your cares drain away. Now don't get me wrong, traveling Europe is already an escape from reality in itself, but I can't say it enough that traveling day after day is also stressful and exhausting. But again, the beer and food did not disappoint.

On the walk back to town, we explored more of the sites above the city before settling back into the main strip. After stumbling down a few back alleys and talking to some locals, we decided on a cute outdoor restaurant for dinner and more beer. The waiter entertained us with witty joke after witty joke, which made the dining experience that much better. By his recommendation, we both sampled a local Czech beer, and I indulged in the ribs while Ron was captivated by another Czech goulash dish. Again, the food was phenomenal, and the beer was just as good. So good that without questioning our budget, we didn't stop at just one beer. We were satisfied yet again with another excellent dining experience and a little more insight into the Czech culture provided by our quirky waiter.

Our stomachs were full, but we wanted to take on one more adventure for the night, and that was to find the coveted green fairy beverage, absinthe. Now for those of you who have not heard of absinthe before, it is an alcoholic drink that, in the past, had tendencies to cause dramatic hallucinations. A few of the locals had informed us that certain bars in Prague still sold this type of absinthe, and it was quite the experience. While many bars carried the dulled-down version of the authentic absinthe, it was hard to find the old version with the strong wormwood. Prague is known for having a great nightlife and bar scene, so we had a great time wandering around the streets and checking out the bar scene.

I should also mention that Brit had joined us at this point since she had just arrived in Prague, and we all got the chance to catch up again, wandering the streets of Prague in search of the green fairy drink. At one point in the night, I got exhausted and a little too nervous about possibly tripping out on absinthe, and we decided to end our hunt. It was probably for the best anyway, maybe another time and another place. As the night got darker and the bars got louder, our eyelids got heavier, and we decided to retire to our hostel for the night so that we could catch the train the next morning to Berlin. Prague had treated us well, and although I'm not a huge fan of cities, this was one city that stole my heart.

Germany- A Drunken Haze in Berlin

German is the official language of Germany,
but around 50 % of the population know English.

Hello- Hallo
Thank You-Danke.
Please- Bitte

Yes- Ja.
Sorry- Verzeihung
Do you speak English- Sprechen sie englisch

Another country down, and we are already on our way out of Berlin as I catch up on everything that happened over these last few days. Before we even arrived in Berlin, let me backtrack to tell you about the amazing people we met on the train on our way out of the Czech Republic! On the way to Berlin, we had two different train connections that we had to catch. We didn't have assigned seats when we jumped on the first train, so we just picked a random cart to sit in since it was empty. Before the train took off, two gentlemen joined us in the cart. Now, whenever you share a closed compartment with people you don't know, it's a bit awkward at first, but soon the awkward small talk turned into an entire conversation which turned into them cracking open a few beers to share with us on the ride. I would have to say that out of all the random people we have met so far on public transportation, we haven't had the chance to bond with any of them over shared beers and good laughs like this. We learned that these two men were from Belfast, Ireland, and were going to Berlin from Poland because they were on holiday.

I don't know if I have mentioned this or not, but in many places in Europe, it is just called going on holiday when you go on vacation.

But as the first train ride came to an end, we all jumped off and realized that we were on the same connecting train directly into Berlin. The unfortunate part was that this time we were assigned compartments, and they were nowhere near one another. As we hugged and said our goodbyes, I got a little sad realizing that we wouldn't be spending any more time with our newfound friends. As Ron and I boarded our train and found our cart, I sat there thinking, "This is stupid, they are somewhere on the same train as us, and we are both going to the same city! Why don't I just ask them if they want to hang out?" Funny enough, the anxious feeling that came with this thought was probably the equivalent of a school kid asking someone if they want to be their friend and nervously waiting for a reply.

I wasn't sure if the train-cart-laughter was simply passing the time with good conversation or friendship material, but I figured "what the heck" and wrote down my Facebook to connect with us if they would like. I then took off venturing down the train and looking into every train cart like a complete creeper searching for our friends. Finally, after spying on about half the train, I came across their cart, and they said they would be happy to meet up with us in Berlin. Walking back to our own train car, I was like a giddy little kid who had just made new friends. Once the train stopped and we got off on what we thought was the closest stop to our hostel, we walked outside to realize that the connecting train to take us closer to our hostel was broken down. We stood on the overpass, looking over the city for a solid 20 minutes, trying to figure out how to get to our hostel with no map and no directions. Also good to note that you can't always depend on Google apps for directions when you arrive in a new country.

We tried talking to a few locals, and after some half-ass directions, we eventually walked around the city and found our way to the hostel. Unfortunately, we also may have made things harder on ourselves because by the time we found a map, I had decided that I wanted to take a stab at navigating again, which probably wasn't the best decision. Nevertheless, we made it there, and we were able to get settled in before meeting our new friends for some beers.

First of all, when we arrived at the hostel, I was overjoyed that Tommy and Adrian had messaged me on Facebook to get together later that night, so we picked a spot and met up. We went to a few different places through-out the night, including an outside bar and a club complete with a dance floor and strobe lights. Good conversation and good beers lingered into the night until it was official that a good friendship had formed. Full of beer and happiness, we made our way back to our room at the end of the night.

That next day we just wandered around near the hostel for a little while before our friends Wilhelm and Daniel arrived. This is part of a story where you realize the true potential of what social media should be all about. Wilhelm is a guy from Germany that I have known since I was little. When I was in elementary school, Wilhelm and his father came to Michigan on an exchange program, and my dad hosted them at his house. We had a great summer playing together and getting to know one another and spending time on the water in the warm sunshine. I still remember that when it was time for Wilhelm and his father to leave, Wilhelm gave me my first Britney Spears CD as a parting gift.

Can I just tell you how cool it is to meet someone from the other side of the world when you were young and then again meet up 18 years later with them and one of their friends? Without social media, I don't know if we would have ever reconnected, but being able to see each other again was just awesome! Wilhelm and Daniel even brought in a few bottles of wine to celebrate the reunion, and that's exactly where the rest of the night went:

to the wine. But we had a blast. We caught up and reminisced, listened to music, and drank our hearts out.

After a few drinks that night, we needed some food to soak up some alcohol, so Wilhelm and Daniel wanted to take us to a good burger place that they knew of that served beer. It was a cute small restaurant with barely any seats but some picnic tables outside where we settled. The burgers were mouthwatering, and the beer paired perfectly. Since we had beers with dinner, we didn't exactly sober up with the food, but we were okay with that. The sun had just set, and a nice cool breeze rolled in as we sat laughing, joking, and enjoying our food. The aroma of the cooking food inside also drifted out every once in a while, which just enhanced the experience. Not much of Berlin was explored that night, but the splendid company and good times made up for that.

The next morning, we still had to get up decently early to explore the town. We started with a walking tour of Berlin, where we got a chance to explore the city led by a great tour guide. Some of the sites we saw during the tour were very humbling, while others were more intriguing. There were so many incredible historically rich sights to see during the tour, and I don't want to give you a complete history lesson on Berlin, but I will touch on a few important sites of the day.

We started our tour at the Brandenburg Gate. Brandenburg Gate is probably the most famous landmark in Berlin. This massive structure was gorgeous and was the first example of neo-classical architecture in Berlin. The enormous columns of this structure were designed to form 5 different passageways separating East from West Germany. The horse and carriage sculpture on the very top is meant to symbolize peace and now stands as a national symbol of unity.

Another fantastic architectural spectacle was the Berlin Cathedral. Every time I see a new church in Europe, I think it is the most massive thing I have ever seen, but this actually was the largest protestant church in Germany. This enormous building was gorgeous from the outside and drew you in with its massive green domes shooting toward the sky. Its architectural influences were inspired by the Baroque and Renaissance style. From my perspective, it looked like the type of church where Quasimodo would hang out. The church was initially established in 1465, but remodeled many times over the years. Deep beneath the Cathedral is The Hohenzollern Crypt, the most important burial place in Germany for prominent rulers. Again, we didn't bother touring the inside of the cathedral, but we did stop for a few selfies of our group and a few pictures where we attempted to capture this grand masterpiece.

The most humbling site that left an impression on me was the holocaust memorial. The most interesting thing about this memorial, was that there was no explanation for it. No big plaque or sign describing what it was, what it symbolized, or how to experience it. The memorial consisted of large stone slabs of varying heights and sizes, all arranged in a large opening of the city. The slabs were evenly spread out, and there were walkways between them. As you walked into the memorial, the sidewalk sloped downward. As you walked further and further inward, the slabs overtook you until they were towering over you, blocking out most of the light and sounds from the outside world.

Walking through the memorial, I felt very alone and isolated from everything else as I got deeper. Inside it was very confusing and sad. As I walked along, I touched a few of the slabs, and they were cold and dark. While walking, I could only think of how much fear and sadness the people went through that had to endure this horrific event. I think the memorial was designed this way so that each person could interpret the experience in their own way. For me, the slabs represented the tombs of those that were lost. The sizes symbolized the people, young and old alike, all different and unique people. But yet the slabs were all the same color, because no matter who we are as people, we are all still the same. We are all still human. For me, experiencing this memorial was more eye-opening and more humbling than reading about something or seeing a statue. This memorial was an experience; An experience that I will not soon forget.

The other site that was amazing to experience was what was left of the Berlin wall. I can't imagine one day a wall being put in place that separated families, neighbors, and friends, leaving some people unable to cross the border, losing jobs, their freedom, and day-to-day life completely changing in the blink of an eye. I remember as a child studying about the Berlin wall and trying to picture what it was like. In my mind, I always thought, "Why would something as insignificant as a wall be able to stop people from crossing over to the other side of the city?" What they never told us in school, or I never paid attention to, was that this was so much more than just the wall. Besides the wall, there were also booby traps on each side to prevent people from jumping over. Everything from sandpits to barbwire, grenades, and attack dogs. But in all darkness, there is still a little bit of light. We learned a select few people were able to make it over to the other side of the wall. One man constructed a tight rope to walk across, and a few others did it with a zip line. Some people constructed fake passes or passports indeterminable from the real ones, and they were easily able to pass to the other side. The most creative story that stuck with me was from a hot air balloon that made it across. No matter what it was, some never lost hope. What was left of the wall wasn't much, but it was kept in place to serve as a memory and a memorial.

The whole experience of the walking tour was very informational, including some somber times, as well as an upside of jokes and laughter. Not only did we get to soak up all the history and historic sites and buildings, but the company and jokes from the German side of our group made the tour that much better. I also have to add that as per Daniel's idea, we had to take group selfies with almost all of the famous locations- only where appropriate, of course. By the end of the day, we had a wide variety of very cheesy and funny group photos. We were just being typical tourists, learning about the city and not caring what others thought. It was a day filled with fun and history, with a little more flare than what we are used to.

Although Wilhelm and Daniel had been raised from a young age to learn English, of course some words were still hard to translate back and forth. While on the tour, we had fun talking and using Google translate to figure out the meaning of some German words translated to English. After the tour, we came across a stand selling some street food, where we all grabbed lunch. Ron and I ordered a basket of fries covered in ketchup and mayo because the tradition here was to dip the French fries in mayonnaise.

Ron was not impressed as he hated mayo, but I thought the combination was delightful.

After spending the rest of the day exploring the city, we decided to indulge in some traditional German food at night. Daniel and Wilhelm spoke with some locals and found a good small hole-in-the-wall restaurant for us to eat at. Thank God Wilhelm, and Daniel were able to communicate with the waitress and read the menus, otherwise Ron and I would have gone hungry. Just as always, we started the meal off with some authentic German beer. My choice this time couldn't have made me happier. It was so delicious that I could have just substituted a few more glasses of beer over food, but authentic food was why we were there.

With a bit of help reading the menu, we each chose our dishes. When mine arrived, it was a dish complete with pork, sauerkraut, and spåtzle, a noodle dish made with eggs. This was probably my first official time eating sauerkraut because I have tried small bites before but never liked it, so I was a little nervous to dig in. To my surprise, it was excellent. I'm not sure how they cooked it, but it was sweet rather than sour and mixed well with the other food on the plate. It was a perfect meal.

When all our stomachs were full, we returned to the hostel early after making a quick alcohol run. We retired early and decided to have a pajama party in our room, drinking and getting to know our new roommates that moved in while we were gone. They were two girls from Scotland. It was so hard to communicate with these girls at first because their accents were so strong that I could barely understand them. Which only meant that Daniel and Wilhelm could barely understand them at all. So that night, I attempted to translate two groups of English speakers to each other. The German girls would say something in a thick accent, and I would try to translate what they said to Wilhelm and Daniel the best I could. Mix this with copious amount of alcohol, and it was a hilarious night. We all had our laughs and could barely understand the language and accent barrier, but we were able to break it enough to have some good conversation.

The next morning, we planned a full day, ready to explore all the less popular sites of the city. Before heading out, we grabbed some breakfast downstairs at the bar. Just a simple breakfast of bagels and yogurt as we overlooked a map for where we were headed. Our first stop was the Magicum Museum. We had found a small pamphlet with a discount on it and, let's be honest, we all love magic, so we decided to check it out. When we first walked in, there was a woman who showed us some brain puzzles and teasers in a small area where we could fiddle around with them for a while. As she started the tour, she gave us a quick palm reading and then took us to a big bowl of water where we had to see if we could make the water vibrate with our hands. Depending on how the water waves dispersed, this was supposed to be some type of future predictor, but I couldn't even vibrate the water, so I guess my future is unknown! From there, the tour was self-guided.

When we headed down to the basement, there were a few display cases of old witchcraft, goods, and pictures. As we kept walking, I was not sure what we expected, but we didn't find it. The museum was very anticlimactic, but with the group we were with, we could make anything enjoyable, so we did! Taking crazy pictures and attempting to jump off a ledge with a witches' broom to make it look like we were flying. The one interesting thing there was a corner of old torture devices. Creepy but cool at the same time. Once we came back up from the downstairs museum, we took some time to play with some of the mind twisters in the corner again. I've never been very good at those puzzles, but Ron whizzed through them, and the other guys did well also.

After the magic museum, we headed down to the Botanical Gardens. On the walk we got thirsty, so we stopped at a convenience store to get some drinks. While inside, Wilhelm and Daniel reminded us that you can walk on the streets with alcohol in Germany, so that is exactly what we did. We each popped open a can of beer with smiles on our faces as wide as can be and continued to stroll down the street, enjoying complete freedom. Once we got to the gardens, we weren't sure if we would be able to bring alcohol in or not, but the nice woman at the front told us that it wouldn't be a problem. Score two for Germany; open intox on the street, and alcohol allowed into a private garden.

For the rest of the day, we continued to walk around the gardens, viewing the beautiful plant life, different sites, and smells. In the garden, there were several different greenhouses filled from floor to ceiling with diverse flora and fauna. There were also outdoor spaces and gardens to walk around and a beautiful footpath all around the grounds. The greenhouses were gorgeous, complete with different species from all around the world. The air in the greenhouses was so fresh it was probably the freshest air that I have ever inhaled. There was even one greenhouse that had a small waterfall and koi fishpond, complete with stepping stones to walk across. On the other side of the grounds, we also found a huge willow tree with the limbs cascading to the ground to provide a beautiful shelter protected from all the elements. The boys had some fun climbing until we were disrupted by an elderly woman who began screaming at us in German. Daniel calmly tried talking to her, but she was screaming so much it seemed like we had just murdered someone.

After what seemed like a forever conversation between the woman and Daniel in a language where we had no idea what was going on, the woman finally walked off, talking to herself and shaking her head. Apparently, she was so angry because this "park was not a playground to use as a jungle gym and disrespect it." She had the idea that we were ruining the nature around us and making a bad example for the smaller children that might be walking by. For us, this has never been the case. First of all, climbing a tree does not harm the tree. No marks were being made in the tree, no carvings, and nothing was left behind. Second, that is what nature is there for, for people to enjoy it. Trees were made for climbing, and the grass was made for rolling around in, enjoying the outdoors, and taking it all in! But obviously, we had different opinions on this matter. The whole interaction was a bit of a downer, but we bounced back quickly.

Next on our list were a few other museums. We happened to find pamphlets and discount coupons for more random things, so we added them to our sightseeing list! The first museum was the car museum. Not as thrilling as some other things, but still cool to walk around looking at the old and new automobiles. The next space we went to was the sound and light museum. We didn't know it, but the tickets we had were exclusively for this particular part of the museum, so this was the only one we could explore, but we had so much fun! It was a completely hands-on and sensory experience. There were four floors, and each floor had a different theme. There were all kinds of setups to play with sound and light waves. I can't even remember everything we did in that museum, but it was awesome. It made me feel like a little kid again, exploring and having fun. Safe to say that we spent the rest of the day in that museum until they closed. After countless hours of acting like kids, we switched to adult mode again and grabbed some beers to head back to the hostel.

That night, fun ensued again, getting to know the others in the hostel and drinking and enjoying our time together. After a few too many beers, we had to show Wilhelm and Daniel how to play the bag game that we had played in Paris. Always a good time watching drunk people struggle to be flexible and pick a bag up off the ground. After many failed attempts at the bag game and more drinks, we decided to take a trip to get some donor kebabs. The German Donor is similar to the gyros we were living off in Greece. They were made with shaved meat on Turkish flatbread but with different toppings and spices.

Drunk Cally thought it was hilarious trying to get the correct German pronunciation of "doner" from listening to Wilhelm and Daniel. And this process/argument continued for the entire walk. As alcohol tends to do, I thought this was hilarious, while the others got annoyed after a while. There are quite a few words I managed to master in different languages with various inflections and tones, but the German language was not one of them.

Once we got to the food stand, I indulged in an amazingly flavorful doner. It might have been the alcohol, or maybe the food really was that good, but I was in heaven at that moment. The rest of the night was a blur. The next morning, we woke up with one of the few hangovers we had during this trip. However, the fun night was worth the suffering the next morning. With sad hearts, we said our goodbyes to Wilhelm and Daniel and packed up our gear to head onto Amsterdam. Overall, this hostel wasn't the cleanest or the nicest that we had stayed at so far, but the company more than made up for any shortcomings with our room and board.

It took us quite a while to shower, get ready, and pack up everything before we started walking back to the train station. Our train was leaving in the afternoon, so we were pretty hungry by the time we got there. Especially with having quite a harsh hangover, a pizza sounded so wonderfully good at this point that we had to hit up the pizza place in the train station. We ordered a large pepperoni and onion pizza but unfortunately waited for about an hour until it was ready. By the time our pizza was done, it was already time to board our train. So with large pizza in hand, we ran through all the people to get to our spot to board the train. Navigating our way through the train car carrying a huge pizza box and pizza fumes trailing after us through every cart was quite an awkward experience. We received some odd looks, but we were accustomed to that by this point in our journey. When we found our seats, we sat down, popped open the pizza lid, and enjoyed. Not an ounce of shame insight.

At this point in our trip, we had graduated from eating dried fruit and seeds on our train trips to now bringing on whole pizzas and the occasional beer. I think this can be our official stamp of graduation to the label of "experienced travelers." Even from the beginning of the trip, we were never worried about what others thought of us, how we traveled, or when we made fools of ourselves, but this became even more apparent as the trip progressed. I guess it's a good thing we have learned to travel comfortably. So here we sit now, lounged back, enjoying a cold slice of pizza every now and then before we arrive in Amsterdam.

Amsterdam- Venice of the North

Dutch is the official language of Amsterdam but depending on where you are in the country there are many distinct dialects.
Thankfully, almost the entire population also speak English.

Hello- Hallo
Thank You-Bedankt.
Please- Alsjeblieft
Yes- Ja.
Sorry- Mijn excuses
Do you speak English- Spreekt u Engels

The first glimpse of Amsterdam, Netherlands, was from the train station. Inside the station, it was clean and filled with the hustle and bustle of everyday life. Outside, the station had a beautiful facade towering above us and full of color. It was drizzling outside, but our first impression of the city was so beautiful that it didn't matter. We hopped on a trolley that took us into the middle of town. After admiring the Dam town square, (Literally, the name of the main square), we got our directions straight and headed toward our campsite. When we were booking accommodations for Amsterdam, most of the hostels in the city were pricey, so we opted for a campground on the outskirts of town.

We walked for a ways, and it seemed like we saw all of the random sites of the city, crossing a few big bridges and swamplands along the way. In one of the swamp areas, there were a few old houseboats that looked run-down but like they were still being lived in. It kind of reminded me of those shows you see down in the Louisiana bayou with everyone living on the river. It was an interesting little community, but nothing that I would ever want to live in, especially with all the mosquitos in the swamp. As the cool rain came down, we continued walking until we came upon a colorful campsite. At the reception desk, we were told our reservations were not there but at their sister site further down the road. The campsite seemed really lovely with a hangout and internet area and a cool gazebo outside where a few people were playing music. But the price tag for the campsite was much pricier, and we were told that the other campsite down the road was cheaper and catered more to the budget backpackers. So we hung out under the gazebo for a few minutes enjoying the live guitar music and some snacks before we continued walking to the other campsite.

When we finally made it to the right site, we were greeted by an extremely friendly man at the desk that explained everything to us. He then proceeded to ask us if we were English. Either we developed English accents along the way, or we were becoming better at blending in and not standing out like sore thumbs as Americans. Either way, the man got a map for us and started circling all the good areas to visit. The best marts for shopping, some good sites, the trolley station, and the best "coffee shop" in town, which I will explain later. The man showed us to the plot of open land where we could pitch our tent. Unfortunately, the land had flooded last weekend from all the rain, so our space was limited. We found a small patch of high ground and made base camp. There were only two handfuls of other tents at the camp because this was the last weekend that the camp would be open for the season. The campground was pretty basic, but we had everything we needed. The bathrooms at the site consisted of a kind of mobile home unit with men's stalls and showers on one side and women's on the other. There was also a small tent area with a few picnic tables.

After we made camp, we headed out to a nearby market to get some food for the night. We ended up with some fixings to make PB and J's, a few snacks, and enough water to last us the night. It was getting late by now, so we decided to go back to the camp and get settled in to get some rest. That night it was so cold in the tent that I barely got any sleep. The morning sun couldn't come soon enough because that meant things would warm up soon. As the sun was rising, I decided to go take a shower and get ready, but it was still freezing outside. The shower barely had any pressure, but at least it wasn't freezing cold. After the shower, I was making my way back to the tent, and it was so cold that I could see my breath. Thankfully after we got moving, my body started to warm up.

The hostel owner let us know there was a trolley station right outside the campground, so we could purchase tickets to get to and from town and wouldn't have to make the long walk back and forth again. We hopped on the trolley and made our way into Dam Square. This square was the heart of Amsterdam and seemed to be where every single person in the city was gathered because it was packed. The Dam Square got its name because the original Dam on the Amstel River stood in the center of town, bringing the name "Amsterdam" to life. Currently, more canals and waterways are running through the city of Amsterdam than Venice. This is where it gets its nickname, "Venice of the North." Even from the small amount of time we had been in the city so far, I liked Amsterdam much more than Venice. The water was clearer, the streets were cleaner, and the people were nicer.

In the main square, we tried to sign up for the free walking tour, but by the time we got there it was full, and we were turned away until the next day, so we just decided to do some exploring on our own. We came across a long line jutting out into the center of the street. We found a woman in line and asked her what she was in line for, and she told us it was to tour the Anne Frank House. This was one of the things on our list to see in Amsterdam, so we jumped in line. It was still pretty cold and windy out, so standing in the long line outside wasn't my first choice, but we had the time. It took us a good few hours of standing in the cold to get up to the front of the line, but the wait was well worth it.

As we approached the entrance, the outside of the house looked like a typical home. However, a few people pointed out how the part of the house that Anne hid in was blocked from view from the street and surrounding buildings. When we first walked in, we received a tour of the front of the house and the workspace until we came to the movable bookshelf that blocked the rest of the secret annex from view.

As you began walking through the house, you got this intense realization of where you were. All the memories of reading Anne Frank's Diary when I was younger came back to me. Chills instantly ran down my spine at the thought of all the sadness and turmoil in this building. As you walked through each room of the house, pictures and original documents were hanging up. Passages from Anne's diary were also displayed throughout the house, and in a few rooms, there were video recordings of people that knew Anne and the family.

The size of the space that Anne and her family were confined to actually seemed quite a bit bigger than what you imagine it to be in the book. Although the area did appear larger, all the windows had to be boarded up to not let any ounce of light in or out. And of course, being confined to that one dark space with quite a few people living there would be agonizing day in and day out, let alone always having to be quiet and living in fear that you would be discovered. The whole experience of walking through the house was very touching and emotional. I can't even begin to describe all the feelings that washed over me while in that house. I think we spent at least two hours in the house, and the whole thing was an experience that is hard to put into words.

We left the house feeling very somber and with a chill that ran deeper in our bones than what the mere cold of the weather could stir up. By the time we got back out on the street, it had warmed up a little, and Ron was ready for a pick-me-up, so we went in search of Amsterdam's best coffee shop that the hostel owner had pointed out on our map. However, it seemed like it wasn't open when we got to the storefront. We could see tables and chairs inside but no lights on. The door was still open, so we walked into the first room, which was a small hallway leading up to a window counter. Once we got closer to the window, we realized that instead of a coffee menu hanging on the wall, it was a weed menu. We approached the man at the counter and asked if they sold any coffee just like oblivious tourists. After enjoying a hearty laugh with himself, the man shook his head and told us that this was not a coffee shop but a weed dispensary.

Ron then asked him where he could get a real cup of coffee, and the man told us that to get a cup of coffee, we would have to go to a bar because all of the "coffee shops" in Amsterdam were actually weed shops. Imagine that, not a single coffee bean in the coffee shops. After having a good laugh ourselves, we realized how silly we must have looked to the campground host when he pointed out the best coffee shops on the map, and we told him that we could use a good cup of coffee. He must have figured that we would sort things out eventually. Long story short, we found a bar and a real cup of coffee.

After the caffeine pick-me-up, we headed back toward the Dam square to go on a Red-Light District tour that we had heard about. Now before we even came to Amsterdam, I had heard stories about the Red-Light District, and I knew that it was an area of Amsterdam filled with prostitution. Furthermore, I had heard that the Red-Light District was the most crime-ridden and filthy area of Amsterdam. I had even heard stories about the street being lined with needles and drugs and people not being able to go there after dark because of all the crime. In reality, these pre-conceived notions were due to nasty rumors and fabricated social media depictions of this place. Over the last day, however, we had heard so many good things about this area of town and even how good the guided tours of the area were that we decided we had to take a tour, and that would be the safest way to see the neighborhood.

Once we met up with our guide, a large group was going on the tour together, but our guide was loud and well-spoken with a good sense of humor. To be completely honest with you, I was still nervous about going at the beginning of this tour because of all the bad things we had heard, but common sense got the best of me, and I thought that if this was a guided tour that was given on the regular, then people wouldn't be attending if it wasn't safe.

So off we went on our official tour of the Red-Light District! We started walking down a small street, and our first stop was the Condemeria. The Condemeria was a small shop on the left side of the road filled with color in the front window. As we got closer, you could clearly see that all the colors hanging in the front window were assorted condoms as colorful as a rainbow. Condoms of all shapes and sizes and even different characters. Most condoms were more novelty items than useable items, but they were fun to look at and seemed like the business was booming.

As we kept walking, our tour guide explained the Red-Light District to us and how safe it was. He told us that the district was ridden with drugs and crime years ago, but now, it is the safest place that you can be in Amsterdam. The women who work in the district are STD tested every week to ensure their own safety and the safety of their customers. Years ago, the police started to patrol the neighborhood more often and cleaned up the streets. Now, the Red-Light District has a trendy, safe night scene where people can simply go out and enjoy themselves.

As we got further into the district, we finally came up to a few of the famous Amsterdam windows. If you haven't figured out by now, the Red-Light District in Amsterdam is the old area of the city where the majority of sex shops and prostitutes work. We walked up to the first few windows, which were pretty much full-size see-through doors where women with varying degrees of clothing were standing in each window, each illuminated by, you guessed it- red lights. There were stools or beds in some windows that the women sat on, and some windows were more intricately decorated than others. Before we got to this part of town, we were instructed not to stare at the woman. We were told that we could look at the woman as we passed by but not stare for too long otherwise, "they will get furious, and some of the women will walk outside and throw a cup of bodily fluids on you." True story according to our guide. Apparently, this is how the women deal with disrespectful men who visit their windows, and unfortunately it has been the best method to deter unwanted attention.

While we were walking, our guide explained that according to statistics, 60% of the women there were trying to support a habit, and 10% were still there due to sex trafficking. Policemen regularly patrol the windows and interview the women to ensure they are there on their own terms. The city also has programs to help women under drug addiction recover. The guide also explained the women's different services and various options. Everywhere you looked in this district, there were red windows with women. In some areas of town, there were other sections with women where people could pick and choose what type of woman they wanted. He also went over that there were men in the windows for a short time. Apparently, this was very popular but faded fast. Our guide also told us that these women were like any other workers in the community. They paid their taxes and helped contribute to the city. The wealth of information that this man had about the Red-Light District was amazing. We were in complete culture shock from the information we were absorbing.

It was so strange walking the streets and experiencing such a culture shock. Some women seemed more than happy to be there, and others were very casual. It was so unique to see a culture where prostitution was not only legal but accepted and a contribution to society. Part of me was so captivated by this information and this culture that it was cool and very progressive at first, but then reality hits, and you realize that some of these women are being forced into this. We walked past many sex shops, bars, and coffee shops as the tour continued.

We learned that technically, marijuana was not legalized in Amsterdam, but it was widely accepted and decriminalized. So much so that even the police officers would smoke out in public. This was so widely accepted because the dispensaries were positively contributing to society. It was explained that you had to have three things to run a business in Amsterdam.

#1 Plausible deniability

#2. You could not harm anyone

#3. You had to contribute to society (pay taxes)

To break this down, first, plausible deniability. This means that to sell marijuana, you could not advertise it as so but had to have a front, hence the "coffee shops." Everyone that lived anywhere in the area understood no coffee shops actually sold coffee, yet there was one on every corner. And no town wants marijuana dispensaries on every corner, so instead, they have coffee shops- plausible deniability. Second, these coffee shops were causing no harm to others. And third, they were paying their taxes; therefore, it was an acceptable part of a functioning society.

Keep in mind this was well before most states in the U.S. legalized marijuana like it is today.

Speaking of rules, there was one other rule that this city had to keep things in line. Alcohol and sex could not be sold in the same location. Therefore, a few bars you could visit for strictly alcohol, and a few other bars served, well, sex. However, one bar, in particular, found a loophole in this rule and decided to start selling their beer glasses instead and offering free beer from the taps once you bought a mug. So, this bar found out how to bypass this law and sell sex also because technically, they weren't breaking the rules. Loopholes.

The tour ended close to where it began with a few witty jokes and one more round of information from our guide. I would have to say that this one and the tour we had in Dublin were the two best tours we have taken so far. The tour was not only highly informative, but it was filled with wit and humor. Not only that, but this tour was unlike any other tour we have experienced before.

We explored around a little longer but decided against beer for the night since we were exhausted before heading back toward our campsite. The day before, we had seen a small restaurant on the way to our campsite advertising a Turkish pizza for pretty cheap, so we had to stop. We had no idea what a Turkish pizza was, but we were interested. Once inside, everything smelled so good, and the gyros on the menu were only 2 euros, so we each ordered a gyro and a Turkish pizza just to be safe.

The gyro was surprisingly good but still couldn't hold a feather to the first gyros we had in Athens. On the other hand, the Turkish pizzas were pure gold! And the fact that they only cost 1 euro was even better! The "pizza" looked kind of like a taquito rolled up, but with ground meat, peppers, and other spices inside that left an unbeatable flavor combination in my mouth. Overall, it was a great day in Amsterdam to explore the beautiful city and learn about the culture, and the fantastic food just topped off the perfect day.

Apparently, I didn't learn from the night before because the following day, I woke up just as tired because it was so cold at night that I had a hard time sleeping. However, I was determined to get a good night's sleep this time, so Ron and I ventured off to find a cheap store with a good blanket. We found a discount dollar store not too far away and picked up some things we needed and a small fleece blanket. It was just enough for me to have another layer for the night, but not too big that I couldn't pack it in my bag for the rest of the trip.

From there, we continued onto the square early enough this time to get signed up for a regular walking tour of the city. This time, the group we went with was at least double the size of the group we were with the day before. The guide was young, probably younger than me, and he was very nice but just didn't bring as much humor to the table as the gentleman from last night.

The tour was still beautiful and informational as we crossed back and forth through Amsterdam's many canals and bridges. Our guide explained that Amsterdam was a thriving cultural center because of many museums, theatres, and venues. Some of the more prominent museums included the Rijksmuseum, otherwise known as the National Museum, The Van Gogh Museum, which houses the most extensive collection of Van Gogh's work, Madame Tussauds Wax Museum, Rembrandt House Museum, and the Jewish Historical Museum. We wandered past the outsides of many museums on our tour, but Ron and I never returned to spend any time inside the museums. I honestly don't even regret not visiting these wonders while they were in the palm of our hands because I think the contents wouldn't have been as appreciated as they should have been. Strike that- I definitely regret at least not visiting the Van Gogh Museum! But, another time and another trip, maybe to dive into more of the cultural significance of Amsterdam.

We were, however, intrigued by the cheese museum that we passed. When we passed this window, it was hard not to notice the giant wheels of cheese on the shelves that were bigger than my own body. Amsterdam actually produces some of the world's most famous cheese, and this particular museum is said to house the most expensive cheese cutter in the world. We did say we were going to revisit this museum and come back in for a taste of some cheese, but we must have overlooked it somewhere along the way because the cheese was forgotten.

Oh, I almost forgot to talk about all of the bikes in Amsterdam, which we learned more about on tour! We barely saw any cars while we were in the city, but instead were constantly dodging bicycles. The town was filled with pedestrians either walking or biking around the city. Bikes obviously ruled the road, and bike racks were everywhere filled with large and small, pink, purple, blue-white, basket, and non-basket bikes. Pretty much any kind of bike you could imagine. We found out that driving is discouraged in the city because of the size and the citizens are more eco-friendly. Most opt for bicycles instead of motored vehicles. It was all very quaint and beautiful and made for a more enjoyable city experience.

On the tour, we also visited some prominent neighborhoods in the area. We noticed that some of the houses were slightly slanted to where the home's second story was leaning over the top of the first story. Our guide explained that this was due to the early construction of the homes. The staircases were often too narrow to haul furniture up, so the houses were built on an angle so large items could easily be pulled up to the second story from a rope. Ingenious idea if you ask me. Imagine walking down the street and seeing a bed hoisted up on a rope to a second-story window. I imagine it like the scenes you see in movies where they hoist up a grand piano by ropes to get it to the top of the building. I would have never thought that far in advance while building a home, but I guess that's why I'm not an architect. The rest of the tour was gorgeous, and we learned the ins and outs of all the streets. After the tour, we walked around a bit more, exploring on our own until we decided to go back and visit "The best coffee shop in town."

And with that comes my muffin story...

Before we even arrived in Amsterdam, I was trying to decide if I would indulge myself in the local greenery while I was there or not. At this point in the trip, I figured that this trip was already an adventure of a lifetime, and I didn't know if I would ever be back in Amsterdam again, so I might as well treat myself to one of the city's specialties. Back at home, I drank socially with my friends and loved my wine collection, but I am not a smoker of any substance. Don't get me wrong, I did do it on and off when I was a teenager, but nothing that I ever really got into. I figured that I might as well try while I'm here.

So, we went back to the best coffee shop in town, and I talked to the gentleman at the window about what to get. I knew that I didn't want to smoke anything, so he suggested a muffin. So I chose a blueberry muffin as my poison. We went back to the campsite so that I could get a sweater for nighttime, and while we were there, I sat down to eat my muffin. I wasn't sure how long it would take to kick in, so we figured that I could eat the muffin at the campsite and then head back into the Red-Light District for a night out.

We jumped back on another trolley to take us back into town. On the way in, I felt a little happier than usual but other than that, nothing really kicked in. I thought to myself, "that couldn't be it," but I didn't feel anything else. That is until we got to the casino. After walking around the Red-Light District for a while, I saw a small casino that I wanted to go into to check out the culture. We stepped inside, and the whole casino was probably about as big as a one-bedroom apartment. Near the back, there was an automated roulette table that we were drawn to because it's one game Ron and I both knew how to play; at least, we thought we did. As we stepped up to the table, the setup wasn't what we were used to, and we weren't sure what to do, so we just put a few bucks down and went for it. We weren't there for very long before it all hit me.

All of a sudden, in a blink of an eye, literally, my vision went from normal to complete tunnel vision. It almost felt like something hit me in the chest and knocked me backward. I calmly took my money off the table and told Ron that we needed to go outside. The 15 feet it took to get outside seemed like a lifetime. By the time we hit the street again, the muffin had taken full effect. My face got so heavy that I felt like my jaw was going to hit the floor. It felt like I was at the dentist and had just received a strong dose of laughing gas.

As I started walking, I felt like my brain was a solid 2 seconds behind what my body was doing. In my mind, I was watching myself walk as my body tilted backward to watch my legs extend out in front of me. Every few steps, my mind would catch up with my actions for a few steps before it would fall back behind, and I felt like I was leaning back, watching myself walk. Now, consider that all of this had happened within probably less than thirty seconds of stepping outside.

I was trying to desperately take in all the feelings I was going through when I looked up to see where I was going, and things got even more strange. For those of you that have seen the movie Inception, that is the best way to describe this experience. You know the scene where the street starts curling up all around them? That happened to me in real life, or at least in my head. As we were walking, the road in front of me began to curl up as the side street also started curling in. Of course, as anyone would do, I started to freak out, but I couldn't even verbalize what I was seeing. My face was so incredibly heavy that I tried uttering words for the first time since it hit me, but nothing came out.

I tried so hard to form just one sentence, but it felt like my jaw was wired shut. Eventually, I got out the phrase, "If you could see what I am seeing right now." However, according to Ron, this phrase came out one to two words at a time, with at least a few minutes in between each word. His response was so quick that my brain wouldn't even comprehend the words coming out of his mouth, "What? What are you seeing? Are you alright?

What's going on?" To which I just could not utter a reply. All I could do was grab his arm tighter to prevent myself from falling down and continue walking down the street.

Eventually, we found a bar that we went into and just sat up at the bar on the stools trying not to fall over. Ron got a drink, and I remember not wanting to drink alcohol, so somehow, I managed to get out the word

"W-A-T-E-R." As we sat at the bar, I attempted to drink my water, but it took every single ounce of concentration in my body to pick up my water cup. So I grabbed my water cup as firmly as possible with both hands and slowly tried bringing it to my lips. At the same time, my concentration was focused on not spilling the entire glass of water on myself. I felt like my hands were shaking, and it was so hard to hold the water glass steady. Once I set the water glass back down, I could concentrate on other things, such as trying not to fall off my bar stool.

The whole time we were at the bar, I just kept thinking about how much I wanted to tell Ron what was going on and how I felt, but there was no way I could get that many words out. I was freaking out because I was nervous that the muffin might have been laced with something else. I had never felt like this before, and I was so worried that something was wrong, but I couldn't get the words out to say this. These thoughts were flying through my brain at a mile a minute, and I just couldn't communicate any of them.

After being at the bar for a while, we started walking around outside, just exploring for hours. While we were walking, I remember walking through a few back alleys with people going crazy and partying. So many crazy and odd things happened while we were walking around that I couldn't even begin to explain it. I've never been on acid but navigating down the back alleys and having people with light bands and masks run at my face, made it feel like acid was melting my brain.

Eventually, I managed to get the words out to Ron, "I want to go home"; Again, one word at a time. We then turned back around and started heading back to camp. We were starving, and Ron wanted to stop at a store nearby to get some food and see if he could find some "coffee shop hot chocolate special" because he didn't know what was going on with my brain, but he wanted in. At this point, I felt like I just couldn't walk any further and had to sit down at the nearest bench I saw. As Ron sat me down, all I could think was how scared I was for him to walk away from me and go into the store. The reality was that the bench was no more than ten yards away from the store. But yet, I was so nervous that I had to tell him something, so I was trying to think of the one word that I could possibly get out of my mouth to say to him how nervous I was for him to leave. Those two words ended up being "30 Seconds". Now Ron is a very fast talker, so he rapidly fired his response to my two words much quicker than I could possibly process words in this mind state yet again. I think his response went something like this, "30 Seconds?!, You want me to be back in 30 seconds?! You need 30 seconds? What do you want? Do you need anything? I will try to be back quick!" I just simply sat there and stared.

As promised, Ron came running back to the bench, probably somewhere close to 30 seconds after leaving. By that time, I had completely forgotten about the deal anyways. Not soon after, we jumped on the trolley and arrived back at our campground, where we were greeted by our generous host. By this time, paranoia had completely consumed me, and I was still nervous that there was something wrong. My nerves got the best of me, and I pulled the campground owner aside and whispered to him, "I think... I'm really.... stoned", again with long pauses in between each word. He had a long chuckle before he escorted me over to a chair outside and told me not to worry and that he would be right back. Within a few minutes, he showed up with a glass and a gallon of chocolate milk. He told me to drink two glasses, and I would be fine. He then proceeded to tell me how all of us Americans come over here and try the local green, thinking they will be just fine, but it is a lot stronger than what we are used to. He also informed me that my current ensuing scenario happens at least once a week with a camper coming back to the site freaked out that something is wrong, but they are just entirely stoned. At least it made me feel better about the situation, but at the time, I didn't care very much at all. After a few glasses of chocolate milk, I still felt out of it, so I retired to the tent for the night, where I could finally fall asleep after my head stopped spinning.

By the time I woke up, I felt a strange mixture of being hungover and embarrassed. After I was able to drag myself out of the tent, I had to go talk to the owner with whom I had made a complete fool of myself the night before. As I approached him, a slight grin came across his face as I began apologizing. He just laughed it off and reassured me how often this really does happen. There was also another gentleman at the desk, and as I was explaining everything that happened to me last night, still sure that my muffin was laced with something else, the man just looked at me and stated, "Nope, that's just the regular stuff here, sometimes you have a good time and other times it goes a little wrong." I wasn't quite sure how to take that statement.

On the one hand, I was reassured that I didn't just get drugged, and it was a "normal" Amsterdam muffin. But, on the other hand, I was pretty upset that I got more of the wrong side of the experience. But when in Rome, I had my authentic Amsterdam experience. Even after last night, I still don't regret trying the muffin and having this as one of my life experiences.

Moving on from there, it was a very slow start to the morning, but once we got going, we explored around town yet again. One of the incredible sites we got to see for the day was the floating market. This consisted of many boats tied to the side of a canal, filled with tulips and small souvenirs. As you stepped off the dock onto the boats, sometimes you didn't even notice you were standing halfway inside a boat until a small wave would come along and start slowly rocking the boat. This UNESCO World heritage site market dates back to 1862, when gardeners would sail in to sell along the Amstel River. The market was a beautiful canvas of colors and smells that were overwhelming. Tulips and wooden shoes as far as the eye could see. I wanted to buy some beautiful flowers so bad, but it would have been pointless trying to cart them around.

While at the market, we started talking to some locals to find some authentic windmills that we could visit. We thought about taking a short trip outside the city to see the windmill fields, but at this point, we were so exhausted that we decided to settle for just seeing the local windmills. After talking to a few people, we found out that there was a local brewery that was housed inside of a windmill. We had to check it out. Once we got there, the windmill was beautiful, and it was definitely one of the coolest bars I have ever seen, but they were completely packed. We had the whole day though, so we didn't mind waiting. We got up to the counter, placed our order, and then tried to find a place to sit, which was a battle we lost. We walked outside to find a table, and there was a massive area around the bar sectioned off that you could stay within, but every possible table or even concrete slab where you could possibly plop down was taken. A few people randomly scattered over the grass, so we decided to take a seat on the ground and enjoy our beer. We found a comfy place and made base camp. Right where we were sitting, we were able to look straight up and see the windmill above us. The ground was a bit sticky, and there was broken glass all around us, but we were happy, so we stayed there for a while. I'm not sure how long we stayed at the windmill bar, enough to have a couple of beers, but we slowly sipped them, chatting and enjoying the moment.

After the windmill beers, we knew this was our last night in Amsterdam, so we just walked around appreciating the city as much as possible and then headed out to the bars for one last night. We finished the night off with one more beer from a little hole-in-the-wall bar that we found and then made our way back to our campsite on the trolley after grabbing one more Turkish pizza for dinner. I would have loved to stay in Amsterdam for longer, but the campsite we were staying at was closing for the year soon, so we would have had to move places again.

Moving on now, we are off to Brussels, Belgium, for two days to stay with a brew master himself! Here's to a short train ride over to our last new country on this incredible journey!

Brussels, Belgium

Dutch, French and German are all languages spoken in Belgium, with various dialects but English is commonly used as well.

As we arrived in Brussels, the city was hustling and bustling with people. We made our way through the city to explore the sites and the streets as we attempted to find our way to our accommodations for the night. While in Brussels, we are staying with a gentleman named Max, who we found on Air BnB. We eventually found our way to the apartment buildings where Max's house was, and we were met by a smiling bearded face. Max was very friendly and polite, welcoming us into his home. We put all our gear down, and he invited us out to the grocery store to get some things for the week. We were more than happy to go with him and find our way around the city to get some food.

As usual, I got utterly lost, but thankfully Ron was paying attention. During our walk, Max told us about himself and how he was a master brewer for a company in Brussels but recently started making his own beer. Once we got to the grocery store, Ron and I decided to pick up ingredients for spaghetti since that would be the easiest thing to make, and we had been spending all our money on beer lately. We shopped around and then headed back to the apartment, learning more about Max on the way.

Once we got back, Max invited us to sample some of his homemade brews. He told us there was a full fridge of beer and while we were his guests, to help ourselves to as much as we would like. Max handed us beer after beer from his own personal collection to try, and we did not object. All of them were fantastic. After a few beers, Max told us that he was going to his girlfriend's house for the night so we could have the place to ourselves. I was utterly blown away. Not only had this gentleman invited us into his house for the night and given us access to all the beer we wanted, but he was leaving and giving us the whole space for the night. I couldn't believe how trusting and kind this man was. I only wish that there was more trust among people and generosity like this where we lived. Don't get me wrong, we live in a great neighborhood, but if I told my friends that I was renting out one of my rooms to people and then giving them complete control over the house, some would think I was completely crazy for being that trusting. However, some other cultures are just filled with trust and mutual respect. Especially for those who travel frequently, it is like a completely open and trusting community of people who have walked in similar shoes before.

Just as Max was leaving, we started making our dinner for the night. We helped ourselves to a private kitchen for once and whipped up some spaghetti and garlic bread. It was a cheap, quick, and easy fix for our hunger. Once Max left, we had the entire place to ourselves, and we just sat there enjoying the food, beer, and the sweet, sweet sounds of relaxation and privacy. We spent the rest of the evening just planning out the last few travel stops of our European adventure and simply relaxing.

The following day, we woke up bright and early to explore Brussels. Although Ron and I didn't have an overwhelming urge to visit Belgium to see anything specific, we had the entire day to kill and had to at least try some Belgium chocolate and waffles. To be completely honest, now that a few more days have passed and I am trying to catch up on writing and remembering small adventures, there is no way I will be able to recall details from our day in Belgium. As this trip nears its end, more and more days have gotten cloudy while precious details of the trip have been stored deep away in my memory bank rather than all being precisely written down and recorded.

As we have gone through each country, I have also realized that the number of pictures we have taken has gone down tremendously. Either certain areas or towns are all starting to look the same, or we are just getting more accustomed to living in the moment rather than behind a camera lens. Either way, as the trip has progressed, the details and pictures have faded. What I can recall from our one day in Belgium was that although we had no crazy adventures, we spent a delightful day exploring the town. I remember walking around for hours and talking to a few locals, making sure that we at least saw the city's main sights.

The most important site of the city that we knew we had to see was the famous "peeing boy" statue, otherwise known as Manneken Pis. This small statue has been a part of Brussels history since 1618, and there are a few different stories about why it was erected and why it soared in popularity. Currently this statue is the most famous statue in Brussels and is even dressed up for various holidays throughout the year.

After wandering around for a few hours, waiting to see this famous statue and what all the fuss was about, we were almost disappointed when we came across a small corner of a street with a water fountain where the peeing boy was positioned. There was a good crowd around the boy taking pictures, but the statue did not live up to all the fuss. The figure was a mere 2 feet tall, peeing into a fountain, and if we didn't know what we were looking for, we would have walked right past it. Honestly, in every store window that we came across, there were all kinds of trinkets and souvenirs mimicking this statue. Anything from lighters to shot glasses to full-size lawn statues even bigger than the real thing! We never really got a complete answer to why this statue was so important to locals, but it will just be a mystery for now.

After the adventure of seeing the famous statue was fulfilled, our next task was Belgium waffles and chocolate. Since we were nearing the end of our trip and trying not to break the bank, we went for a two-in-one combo deal. We found a small hole in the wall place that was making Belgium waffles on the spot, and then you could top the waffles with whatever toppings we desired. In that instant, our hearts wanted chocolate. So in one foul swoop, we checked off both of our needs in the country of Belgium; the waffles and chocolate. Although we didn't sit down at a 5-star dining experience for a waffle or pay 10 euros for one bite of fine chocolate, we still enjoyed our side-cart treat of warm Belgium waffles and chocolate. Maybe another time, I would have thoroughly enjoyed sitting down at a breakfast restaurant with Belgium waffles or going to a sweet shop and gorging myself on Belgium chocolates, but not this trip. We were simply happy being simple. But back to the waffles and chocolate, they were perfect. The waffle had a slight crunch on the outside and was warm and fluffy on the inside. The chocolate was rich and smooth and made the ideal combination with the waffle. After walking off the waffles and chocolate and catching a few more glimpses of the city for the night, we retired back to Max's place.

Once we returned, I want to say that some sort of food was involved, but I'm really not sure. I am sure that we all sat down and shared a few beers for the rest of the night while getting to know Max more and his process of beer making. At the end of the night, Max asked us about the rest of our trip, and we told him our plans to go to Paris for a few more nights before we returned to Dublin to fly home. Without a second thought, Max went to the fridge and started stacking beers on the table. He told us that we were more than welcome to take as much beer as we wanted. He insisted that we fill our bags with beer. After grabbing two beers each, Max grabbed a few more and stuffed our backpacks full until they almost couldn't close. We were so happy that we had gotten more beers to try, and we fully planned to drink them under the sparkling Eiffel Tower. That night, we slept restful with our bags packed and ready to venture back to the romantic city of Paris the next day!

Paris Round Two

Here I am, back in Dublin, just trying to wrap my head around everything that has happened over the last 3 months. So many emotions and so many words swimming and thrashing around in my head, trying to find a clear path through. But what I can do is start by catching up on our time back in Paris.

The train ride into Paris was uneventful for the most part, just another train station, and another ride. Except for the part where we ran into a girl in the Brussels train station that we met while in Greece! While we were waiting for our train, I saw her a few times and thought she looked familiar, but I wasn't sure. After a while, she came over to us and asked us if we were in Greece. We had met this girl for one night and had a short conversation, but now we were both at the Brussels train station. Very small world in the travel community but so cool reconnecting.

When we finally made it back to Paris, I was even happier than the first time we arrived, which I didn't think was possible. We made our way through the winding streets to find our hostel right in the city center. It had views of the very top of the Eiffel Tower over the city buildings right outside the front door. When we first walked in, the hostel staff was friendly but a bit slow to respond. We were instructed that our room was not ready yet, so we sat and waited in the living room area. While there, we met a nice Brazilian man traveling for work, name Caesar. After visiting, we checked into our room, but sadly we were not impressed.

There were two rooms attached to one another, and it felt more like a cave than a hostel. In our specific room, there were four bunk beds totaling 8 sleeping spaces and zero windows. Strike that, there was one window that was permanently blocked off for some reason. There was also a permanently blocked door, probably for a good reason, so people couldn't sneak in and out of the hostel. Even so, it was smelly and dark and nothing what I expected in a hostel in the heart of Paris. Not to complain further, but the beds and mattresses were also horrible. The beds were very squeaky, and the mattresses were so thin that you could feel every single metal bar underneath you. When we checked out the bathroom situation, we found one toilet and one shower for roughly 20 plus people to share. Not to mention, electrical cords were hanging down from the ceiling everywhere. But what can you do? I mean, it was a budget accommodation in the heart of Paris. We were still happy to be in Paris again and have a roof over our heads.

Once we settled in, we headed out to explore the Louvre since that was high on my must-see list, but we didn't get to go in our first time in Paris. We had purchased tickets online and got there before our scheduled time, so we decided to pow-wow on the lawn and rest beforehand. There was a food stand right outside, so I grabbed a croissant before sitting down. Even though it was a simple croissant, it was so amazingly good. Each layer flaky and full of buttery goodness. Each bite was like a warm kiss for my soul. The top-notch croissant was followed by a couple of delicious beers courtesy of Max from Belgium. We enjoyed our time sitting on the lawn of the Louvre, sipping delicious beer and taking a break before doing some exploring.

The line to the entrance of the Louvre wasn't bad, so we didn't wait long to get inside. There was ample security, including metal detectors and armed guards. Once inside, it was spectacular. If you looked straight up, you were directly under the glass pyramid of the Louvre, which created a color prism that encompassed you. But then I snapped back to reality and realized I was surrounded by hordes of people being directed through passages like cattle. The Louvre is so big, and there are so many different sections that we just felt utterly lost trying to navigate our way through. We had to start somewhere, so we just picked an area and started walking.

Construction on the Louvre first began in 1546 with Francis I, building his residence on the grounds, but the idea to make it into a public museum did not come until the 18th century. Over the years, the Louvre has been expanded and renovated into the grand museum it is today at over 652,000 square feet and the largest museum in the world.

To be short and sweet, the magnificent and miraculous art and culture that we were able to see while touring the Louvre can't just be summarized in a book. I could tell you about all the antiques and artifacts that we saw that day, but there was so much to soak up that it can't be simply expressed in words. To even attempt to see as much of the largest museum in the world is a feat in and of itself. We desperately tried to soak in as much as we could with our time there, but unfortunately, my mind is not an automatic Rolodex, so I will never be able to recall all the spectacular art pieces we had the pleasure of experiencing in person.

There were, however, a few art pieces that we knew we had to experience while in Paris. The first was the famous Mona Lisa by Leonardo Da Vinci. By far, this was the most popular exhibit that we came across during the entire day. The Mona Lisa room was chockfull of tourists, wall to wall with cameras and phones and iPads, all trying to capture the perfect picture with the famous painting. Unfortunately, the crowd and crazy amount of technology completely took away from the experience. I would have loved a chance to quietly admire the artwork for a while without the pushing crowd, the chatter of noise, and the flash of technology, but the crowd was just crazy. Sadly, we also found ourselves sucked into this present-day fad of documenting every piece of our day and had to still attempt to get a picture with the painting. It sorely failed, and instead, I captured about

20 other tourists in the background of my photo, all taking the same exact selfie. The epitome of what travel pictures look like in real life. Again, if you are in Paris and going to the Louvre, the Mona Lisa is a must-see, but just be prepared to be disappointed.

The whole experience of making our way through The Louvre with the massive crowd of people was more than a little overwhelming. We bobbed and weaved our way through various staircases, corridors, doorways, and time periods. There were paintings and drawings, sculptures, Egyptian artifacts, and some pieces of artwork that looked more like they belonged in a kindergarten art class. But then again, take what I say with a grain of salt because I am clearly no art expert.

Ron and I walked around the Louvre for the rest of the day until our eyes were literally too tired to stay open any longer. I think we were in some part looking at Egyptian artifacts, and we looked at each other and just knew that neither of us had any steam left to continue. I would have loved to see more of the Louvre or explore it for a few days, but at this point, we were so exhausted that we were having a hard time putting one foot in front of the other. We spent almost the entire day in the Louvre, and we were ready for water, food, and rest.

On our way back to the hostel, we did stop by the Eiffel Tower for a few minutes just to sit down and rest our feet before finding a small market and some fresh baguettes and meats and cheese for dinner. It was just getting dark outside, but we had nothing left to give to the city, so we called it a night to get some rest on the prison mattresses.

Unfortunately, the night was filled with slamming doors and people coming in and out of our room all night long. Not to mention the squeaky beds every time someone rolled over and all the commotion from the street outside. But, regardless of the noise and the sleepless night, it still felt good to rest my eyes and my feet, especially because today was the day we were visiting the Palace of Versailles! Although now the Palace of Versailles is a grand museum, it was once a royal residence for Louis XIII. Although Ron and I didn't pay for the tickets to get inside the palace, we still really wanted to see the palace in person and at least get to explore the gardens.

The train ride outside of the city was relatively quick, and once we arrived, we were blown away by the sheer magnitude of the palace. However, it was most definitely a tourist attraction because the outside of the court was surrounded by guards and a vast array of souvenir stands. Thankfully, it was a beautiful day, and I was so excited that we would spend the day outside exploring the grounds rather than be kept inside. Once we got through security and went around to the back of the palace, the grounds were overwhelmingly huge, just like the front of the palace. There were lush greenery and garden sculptures as far as the eye could see. We knew that even if we spent the rest of the day here, we would never get to explore all the grounds, but we had to start somewhere.

We started in the flower garden, which was blooming with bursts of color that lit up the whole lawn. There were high bushes and green paths that led to different areas. Part of it was almost maze-like. We took one of the longest paths down to the right of the palace and ended up finding a huge fountain that was adorned with massive sculptures of different real and mythological sea creatures. Since it was the end of the season, the fountains were not currently running, but I could only imagine what they would have looked like while they were up and working.

On the exact opposite side of the grounds, there was a concrete walkway that overlooked a garden space. There were lots of people down there setting up for an event. It looked like it may have been a wedding reception, but who knows. Regardless of the event, this was a gorgeous location for it. Surrounded by greenery and perfectly manicured flowers. Directly behind the palace, was this massive metal arch you could stand under and look out as far as you could see to the full expansion of the grounds, greenery, water, and people. After getting our picture taken under the arch, we took a few minutes to sit on the steps to relax and marvel at the beauty. Then, after fully appreciating the beauty around us, we headed down to the water. I think technically, you could call it a pool, but it was the most massive pool I have ever seen. It was a little bit of a walk, and we were already exhausted from the day before, so once we got down to the water, we decided to make camp by the edge and enjoy some French bread and fruit that we had packed for lunch.

Down by the water, there was a small restaurant, a costly food stand, and a place where people could rent paddle boats to take out. While enjoying our lunch, we noticed a few families by the water's edge feeding these giant fish. They were tearing apart bread pieces and throwing them in the water where these massive fish would come up to the surface. We instantly reverted back to being children and gave up some precious bits of our own lunch for entertainment's sake. The same childhood bliss when your parents would take you to feed the ducks at the park instantly returned. Right away, we were little kids again, just playing around with the fish.

While we were so enthralled with feeding the fish, we hadn't noticed that a group of swans in the water had started coming closer and closer to us, wanting to get in on the action. I knew how territorial and nasty swans can be, so they scared me off at first. But they settled in among the fish and just wanted a little bread for themselves. So instead of being afraid, I slowly started to tear off some pieces of bread and throw some out to the swans. As I did this, one swan kept on getting closer to me inch by inch as my eyes grew wider with fear. As it got closer, I realized how massive these creatures actually were. I had never been face to face with a swan before, and at this point, he was only a few feet away from me. Thankfully he was more friendly and eventually grew bored with me.

After the magic of feeding the animals had worn off, Ron and I spent the rest of the time by the water with him telling me Greek mythology stories. I have always been interested in Greek mythology, and Ron read a lot about it while growing up, so I was more than happy to hear some of the mystical stories he had to tell. He told me the ancient stories about Narcissus and the nymph Echo, Arachne challenging Athena, and all about the titan wars.

There could not have been a more perfect backdrop to just sit by the water in the gardens of the Palace of Versailles and completely lose myself in Ron's captivating stories. This probably isn't how most people would spend their only one day at the Palace of Versailles, but it was perfect for us. It was a simple day, but whether it was the stories, the magic of the palace, or the beautiful scenery, it was so special and perfect. I don't know how long we spent down by the water just relaxing and telling stories, but I can tell you that we did spend the entire day at the palace.

By the time we got back into the city, it was already getting dark, so we decided to spend the rest of the night hanging out by the Eiffel Tower. Since this was now coined as a "regular hang-out," we were quick to find our way back to the tower and find a good spot to settle in. As the sun fell below the horizon, the infamous tower turned on its lights and began to sparkle just as we cracked open our first beer. Surprisingly, we still had beers left from the ones Max had given us in Belgium. We knew we wouldn't be able to take our beers on the plane that would connect us to Dublin in a couple of days, so we figured this would be the perfect opportunity to finish them off.

There seemed to be more people there than usual that night, and we think there was even some kind of fraternity doing an initiation cere- mony. Loud kids were running around everywhere and a few guys letting off small helicopter swirly things into the air, but that just added to the experience of it. Sitting in front of the Eiffel Tower, drinking Belgium Beer and having a wonderful night just enjoying each other. By the time we had demolished all the beers, we left and had a pretty good buzz as we stumbled through the streets of Paris before finding our way back to our hostel. The after-effect from the beers definitely helped us fall asleep faster that night and get some rest.

Now, our next adventure was off to Disneyland Paris! It took us a few days to decide if we should spend the money or not on Disneyland, but we only had a few days of our precious trip left, and Ron had never been to Disneyland or Disneyworld before, so it was a no-brainer in the end. Once we were ready, we headed out to the store to get our typical meal for the day of French bread and some oddities before catching the train to Disneyland.

When we boarded the train, there was no question that we were headed in the right direction because amongst the passengers traveling to work, or other tourists, there were also families filled with excited children all wearing Mickey Mouse ears. As a lifelong Disney lover, that made me even more excited that we had made the right choice on where to spend the money we had left.

Once we arrived at the front gates, I don't know why there was so much confusion, but it took us close to an hour and a half to even get in. Once we got closer, we found that some families were at the ticket counters asking questions for a straight 15-20 minutes. Typical. This was highly frustrating, but all we could do was wait. Finally, we made it to the front gate and through to the main attraction; We were finally at Paris Disney! We instantly ran to the first attraction we saw and then proceeded to jump in every line we could after that. I will have to say that Disneyland Paris was significantly smaller than Walt Disney World in Florida, but that much I expected.

Walt Disney World in Florida has the Cinderella castle as the main attraction, for starters. Disneyland Paris has Sleeping Beauty's castle as the main attraction, so just the sheer size difference between the two castles was more than noticeable. Next, there are more rides and attractions at Disneyworld Orlando than Disneyland Paris. Regardless of the size difference, we still had a fantastic day. We rode as many rides as we could multiple times, wandered around the different attractions, and took in all of the magic and wonder.

The first ride we went on was Space Mountain, which there was a long line for but totally worth it. I think we went on the Indiana Jones roller coaster over 5 times just because there was barely a line for it, and it was so much fun! The other attractions of the day included It's a Small World, Buzz Lightyear Laser Blast, La Cabane des Robinson, Sleping Beauty's Castle, Phantom Manor, Pirates Beach, and many, many more. At one point, we did come to the realization that we needed more food and would have to shell out copious amounts of money for park food. So we settled on a pizza place in the park and tried to order the cheapest thing on the menu, which was a pizza meal, complete with pizza, breadsticks, tiny salads, and fruit, for close to 25 euros. It filled our aching stomachs, but our wallets were not happy.

Speaking of not being happy, I also had a bizarre interaction at one of the bathrooms in the park. My odd interaction began when I was in the stall at the restroom, and the woman who was cleaning the bathrooms came around and started sweeping under my stall. She was so aggressive with her broom that she swept her entire arm underneath my stall and swept over the top of my feet. Clearly, she knew I was there, but it was so incredibly invasive and weird.

Unfortunately, not long after our expensive lunch, Ron came down with a horrible headache, which slowed down our exploring. He roughed it through a few more rides a little longer before the headache overtook him, and we decided to head back. However, the day was still magical and wonderful. Other than the few downfalls of the day, Disney was great and a perfect way to end our last day in Paris. On the way back to the hostel that night, we took one last stop in front of the Eiffel Tower to relax and enjoy each other's company in the city of love one more time before catching our bus at 4:00am the following day to the airport.

Lessons Learned

The streets of Paris in the early morning are eerily silent and dark, but walking them in beautiful silence, gave the city a whole new perspective. The cobblestone walkways glistened with the morning dew, and there were a few workers out meticulously sweeping the walkway in front of their shops, preparing for the morning rush. The scenery was straight out of a movie. When we arrived at the bus station, there was a huge crowd of people, mostly kids our age. We checked in and waited outside with the group for our bus time, but it was very chaotic and disorganized. Eventually our time got called, and we boarded the bus to the airport. We were expecting everything to go smoothly since we have flown so many times before, but it only went downhill from there.

We arrived at the airport early with plenty of time to spare. The gentleman at the counter asked us for our boarding passes. We handed him our passports and told him that is what we needed because we had never printed our boarding passes before we arrived at the airport. He then told us that for this airline, you had to print your boarding passes ahead of time, and we would have to get into another line at a different counter to have someone else print off our boarding passes now for 40 euros each.

My heart instantly dropped. There was no way it was 40 euros each just for someone at the airport to press a print button and hand us our boarding passes. But that is what it came down to.

Our options were to either leave the airport and find a place to print our own boarding passes, pay the 80 euros for the airport to print our passes, or forfeit our flight. We coughed up the 80-euro price tag to print two pieces of paper and reproached the check-in counter, but the bad news continued. Even though both of our bags were carry-ons, we were obligated to weigh the bags. Since this point in the trip, a lot of my extra belongings were stuffed tightly in Ron's bag, it was overweight. We were told that if we couldn't get rid of some of the weight from our belongings, we would have to pay an additional 50 euros as a heavy baggage fee. At this point, tears were streaming down my face from pure anger and exhaustion at this absolutely ridiculous airline.

We stepped out of line yet again and sat down on the floor to unzip both of our bags and see what we could do to cut the weight in Ron's bag. We threw out the few toiletries we had left, stuffed a few more items in my bag, and then layered up on clothes as much as possible. I felt utterly defeated while sitting on that airport floor with our personal belongings sprawled all over. I was crying through the whole process, angry at the absurd rules of this so-called budget airline. I've never understood the point of weighing a carry-on bag or luggage at all, for that matter. Whether our bag weighs 40 pounds or 30 pounds and the extra ten pounds are stuffed around our bodies to avoid the "heavy baggage fee," – the same amount of weight is still getting on the plane. All these rules do is rip off passengers and make a quick and easy few more dollars for the airline and the CEO's who probably use our extra money to wipe their asses. Seriously. I will never understand it, and to this day, some of these airline rules are the most infuriating things I have ever dealt with. But no matter how much I cried or argued, it still wasn't enough. At the end of the day, Ron's bag was still overweight, and yet again, we shelled out another 50 euros to get his bag on the plane. By now, we had paid more to print our boarding passes and for our luggage than we did for our actual tickets. Thanks, Ryanair-so much for a budget airline.

We tried as much as possible to just get past it and try to have a smooth last leg of this amazing journey, but still, the shit show just kept snowballing. First off, the organization of people boarding the plane was the worst thought-out process I had ever seen. Once our flight was called, everyone got in line to go to the gate, and it was a sea of people like always rather than a uniform line (no surprise there). From there, we were escorted directly onto the runway, where there were another two lines of people formed. We weren't given any instructions on what to do or what line to join, so we just picked one. Everyone was standing around confused, walking back and forth, just hanging out on the runway. As the flight attendants finally started looking at our passes, some people were instructed to go to the back of the plane entrance as others went to the front. Hence why there was supposed to be two clear lines, but no one was given any instructions. There was also the fact that between security and actually sitting down on the plane, our boarding passes had been looked at a total of 6 times now. A little overkill.

As soon as we found our seats and sat down, we hoped to relax, but the vultures swooped in right away. From the moment our butts hit the chair to the moment we stepped out of the airplane, flight attendants walked up and down the aisle selling things. This included anything from water (because there was no complimentary drink, let alone water on this flight) to magazines, timeshares, and lottery tickets. I have never been part of such a ridiculous scheme in my life. No wonder our plane tickets were so cheap. Not only did they gouge us with the boarding passes and luggage prices, but they were trying to sell us everything and anything under the sun. I'm surprised the flight attendants didn't come around and make us pay an oxygen fee just for breathing the circulated air of the plane.

Needless to say, the flight was not quiet or smooth at all because we were constantly being bombarded by advertisements and salespeople. Not a single flight attendant on this flight- only salespeople. But wait, there's more! We were seated in the last row during the flight, and there was water leaking from the bathroom that we only discovered at the end of the flight. Come to find out, it had been leaking all flight and just so happened to pool under our seats where our small bags were sitting. Just the cherry to top off this shit show Sundae of a flight. When we finally reached Dublin, not only were we ecstatic to be back in one of our most favorite countries, but so glad to be done and off that wretched airline. I was emotionally, mentally, and physically completely drained. Even sitting in my hostel bed in Dublin right now, I'm getting angry reliving our experience on this atrocious airline. Never again.

Travel Finale

Once we hit the ground in Dublin, we took a bus to our first hostel. We wanted to end our trip in the same hostel we first stayed at in Dublin because it was such a good experience, but they were booked up for the first two nights. So instead, we settled on a different hostel in a new part of the city for our first two nights back in Dublin. I was so emotional that night, realizing that we were back in the same city where we began this grand adventure three months ago. I'm sure all my emotions were heightened from the crazy flight, but I experienced an emotional roller coaster for the first two days in that hostel like I had never experienced in my life.

To put things simply, even after the huge turmoil we had just gone through, my soul was not ready to stop traveling. These last three months had ignited a fire deep inside me that I had no idea existed. I knew I always had a hunger for adventure and travel, but the thought of just going back home and settling back down into a "normal life," whatever that may look like, was terrifying.

I had fallen in love with the world. Fallen in love with the people of the world. Fallen in love with the daily unknown and adventure of it all. I didn't want to go back to the normal 9-5 and only living for the weekends and the occasional vacation. I was desperately trying to make sense in my own mind of how to avoid this and how I could continue to travel and mold my life into what I really wanted versus what others expected of me. I realized that I didn't really want to go home, but I wasn't sure what it meant if I were to stay or if that was even an option. I spent so much time just curled up on that hostel mattress crying to myself and dealing with all my thoughts and emotions and processing everything. Ron was so understanding and gave me alone time to deal with everything inside my head until I was ready to talk to him.

Before I even had things sorted out in my own brain, I broke down to Ron and essentially had verbal diarrhea of all the thoughts and feelings running through my head. Ron and I had obviously formed a very tight bond by now in our trip, but he was very honest with me that he did not feel the same way and he wanted to go back home. He already had a job lined up with the employer he had left before we started traveling, with the promise of a promotion and his own work truck. Ron absolutely loves what he does for work, so rightfully so, he was excited to go back. But my heart was shattered. In some distant corner of my mind, I had this fantasy that Ron would feel the same way I did, and we would make the impulsive decision on the spot to tear up our plane tickets home and just say, "fuck it- we will figure it out." But that didn't happen.

I felt like my heart was torn in two because I had truly fallen even deeper in love with this man over the course of these last few months, getting to know every corner of his soul. But I had also fallen head over heels for the long-term travel lifestyle, and I now had an insatiable hunger to discover the rest of the world. Plain and simple, I had to make a choice. I don't know if anyone else has ever loudly cried as long and as hard as I did for two straight days in a shared bedroom with countless other strangers, but I didn't care. I knew in my heart the choice I was going to make, but I was scared. I wanted to be with Ron more than anything in the world and spending every waking minute together for the last three months only solidified that thought. I was still scared to choose love over my own wants and needs, but I had hope that even though this one adventure was ending, there would be more for us down the road.

Before we transitioned to our last hostel in Dublin, I attempted to compose myself the best I possibly could. I didn't want to waste these last few precious days we had left crying, and I just wanted to soak it in as much as possible. Now enter the best couple in all of Ireland, who helped remind me of everything I had gained from this fantastic adventure and all that I still had to look forward to-Tommy and Adrian, who we had met on the train in Germany.

They knew we were spending our last few nights in Dublin before flying home. They were back in Belfast from their holiday and decided to take the train down for the day to spend one more precious day together. This was exactly what we needed. Tommy and Adrian arrived, and we spent the day bar hopping all around Dublin. We explored, laughed, drank, wore silly hats, took ridiculous pictures, and were reminded that traveling isn't necessarily about where you are, but who you are with. It is very hard to meet truly genuine and kind people in life, and after only knowing these two for such a short period of time, we knew that we had made friends for life. Before they departed on their train back to Northern Ireland, they gifted us a few small souvenirs to remember them by and our time in Ireland. My heart was overflowing. This is exactly what I needed.

If I wasn't enough of an emotional roller coaster already, we met up with Brit on our last night in Dublin, because we would all be flying home the next morning together. We cried and hugged and talked about everything we had missed with one another and how we were both feeling about returning to the real world. Then, we went out in style for our last night in Dublin, having a big dinner out with traditional Irish food and indulging in the live music at the bars. The night was bittersweet but the perfect end to our grand adventure.

Coming Home

The whole process of coming home was very surreal. I was still excited to get back to some of my creature comforts at home that were not available on the road, but a part of my soul was still crushed that the adventure had ended. The first few days home were very hazy and filled with mixed emotions. It's hard to express the feelings that come with transitioning back to a normal lifestyle after spending three months on the road traveling. It's like trying to transition a feral animal into a docile house pet. Well, not exactly, but that's what it felt like.

What I can say is that this adventure changed who I am as a person in the best way possible. This experience taught me patience, acceptance, flexibility, and opened my mind to a whole new world. This journey has pushed and tested me more than I thought possible. Traveling with my significant other has tested us both and allowed us to show our best and worst sides to each other, but I wouldn't have it any other way.

I am so unbelievably grateful to have had this experience, and it is something that I will cherish for the rest of my life. I'm not sure where my life will take me from here, but I am excited for the unknown and embrace it with open arms. What I do know, is that I will never look at life the same way again. Anything is possible, and you can always make your dreams come true. You just have to want it enough.

Epilogue

Eight years. Eight years is how much time it takes to publish a book- or procrastinate publishing a book. After reading over my final edit of this book however, I realized that it took me eight years for a reason. Every time I stepped away from my computer or got frustrated and didn't open my journal for months on end, each time, I grew as a writer. Over the years, I have only gotten stronger in my writing skills and learned how to show my own voice more efficiently and creatively. Every time I edited this journal, I added a new part of myself.

During my writing process, I also learned humility. I used to internally criticize other writers for simple editing or grammatical errors, but I realized how incredibly hard this whole process has been and even after editing something for the 40th time, how easy it is to miss little things. I spent so much time agonizing over the fact that every single sentence I wrote wasn't a masterpiece. I tore my own writing and mental health down to the bone time and time again, telling myself my writing wasn't good enough, that I wasn't good enough. But I slowly learned that wasn't true and started building myself back up to the final realization of being able to complete a life goal and publish a book. This was a much harder process than I ever realized, but I hope for those that come after me with the same goal in mind of sharing their words with the world, realize that you are good enough, and you have something amazing to offer the world, you just have to take that first leap.

It has been over 9 years since myself and 2 of my closest friends took off on this grand adventure. A lot has happened since then. Ron and I came back to Michigan and bought a house, thinking we were settling down. We discovered a few years in that the traditional "settling down" just wasn't in the cards for us, and we started planning our next adventure. All in one year, we celebrated our love and got married, traveled to Peru and hiked the Inca Trail to Machu Picchu, and then left for Asia with open-ended travel plans to explore. A little while later, we sold our home in Michigan, uprooted our entire lives again, and moved across the country to California to spend a year in the sun. In February of 2021, we took another giant leap of faith. We bought a school bus that we started converting into our tiny home so that we could travel the country and fill the wanderlust in our hearts. After that we threw another dart on the map and decided to move to North Carolina for a year.

We are still exploring and slowly achieving all the dreams that we set out for, as well as making new ones. The "conventional" lifestyle wasn't meant for everyone, and don't ever let anyone tell you how you should live your life. You, and only you, are responsible for your own happiness. We have found a great balance of pursuing our passions and molding our lives to ensure that we are always chasing our dreams. If we can do it, so can you.

Leaving Home

Guinness Beer Factory

Cliffs of Moher

Budget friendly accommodations
3 people crammed in a tent

Not the London Bridge

Scotland – Rub the nose
for good luck

Some Pretty Cool Rocks

Typical Night in Paris

Swiss cheese, Swiss Chocolate and Swiss Alps

Partying in Pamplona

Flying Above the Clouds

The First of many Gelatos

Ancient History

Ron's first
vegetable in weeks

Obligatory Photo Op

"Deck Passenger"
Boat Tickets

The Famous
One Rock Beach

Passing time
waiting on trains

Serbian Beer Fest

Caving under the streets
of Budapest